DISCARD

D0442197

BENEFIT-COST ANALYSIS
for PROGRAM EVALUATION

BENEFIT-COST
ANALYSIS
for
PROGRAM
EVALUATION

Mark S. Thompson

 SAGE PUBLICATIONS   Beverly Hills   London

For information address:

SAGE Publications, Inc.
275 South Beverly Drive
Beverly Hills, California 90212

SAGE Publications Ltd
28 Banner Street
London EC1Y 8QE, England

Printed in the United States of America

Library of Congress Cataloging in Publication Data

Thompson, Mark S.
    Benefit-cost analysis for program evaluation.

    Bibliography: p.
    1. Evaluation research (Social action programs)
2. Social policy—Cost effectiveness.   I. Title.
H62.T457   361.6'1'0681   80-13110
ISBN 0-8039-1483-0
ISBN 0-8039-1484-9 (pbk.)

FIRST PRINTING

CONTENTS

DEDICATION

To E., H., H., and J.

for many kinds of needed support; and in gratitude to Donald Cohodes, Eric Fortess, Alan Frohman, Marsha Gold, Stephen Hanly, David Hemenway, Emmett Keeler, Charles Smart, Cheryl Stone, Ernst Stromsdorfer, and Robert Wise for useful commentary on early drafts of the book;

to Linda Fasciano, Pat Fritz, Susan Kaufman, Penny Kefalas, and Leslie Stein for care, advice, and graphic skills as well as their typing;

and to the Commonwealth Fund and the Robert Wood Johnson Foundation for financial support through the Center for the Analysis of Health Practices at the Harvard School of Public Health.

Introduction

ROOTS OF BENEFIT-COST ANALYSIS

Sir William Petty found in London in 1667 that public health expenditures to combat the plague would achieve what we now would term a benefit-cost ratio of 84 to 1. In the United States, benefit-cost analysis (synonymous with "cost-benefit analysis") achieved statutorial authority with the passage of the River and Harbor Act of 1902 and the Flood Control Act of 1936. These pieces of legislation mandated that individual projects were to be justified by comparing their benefits ("to whomsoever they may accrue") with the costs.

Yet, to cite these initial efforts in benefit-cost analysis is misleading—inasmuch as the discipline as practiced only fifteen years ago barely resembles that of today. Until 1965, benefit-cost analysis was performed primarily for the Corps of Engineers in the prospective evaluation of water resource projects. In the mid-1960s, with the advent of Lyndon Johnson's Great Society programs and with a new stress on program accountability and assessment, dramatic change began. Heavy emphasis was placed on the Planning, Programming, Budgeting System (PPBS) and on quantitative program evaluation. Benefit-cost analysis began to be applied to social programs with startling results: for both the programs and the discipline.

Until fifteen years ago, benefit-cost analysis seldom consisted of more than (1) identifying main program effects, (2) somehow valuing them monetarily, (3) summing up costs, and (4) comparing the benefits and costs through division or subtraction. For social programs, it soon became clear that this was not enough: that diffuse secondary and tertiary effects might be as important as primary effects; that externality effects and subtle effects on market prices had to be taken into account; that discounting was a more sensitive and delicate art than had hitherto been believed; that effects on length and quality of human lives are extremely difficult to value. In response to these insights from applications in social programs, benefit-cost analysis has had to adapt itself to drastically new situations in order to survive.

In adapting, it has not just survived but has flourished. In contrast to the limited terrain of use fifteen years ago, benefit-cost analysis is now routinely applied in such program areas as criminal justice, education, the environment, foreign assistance, manpower, transportation, urban policy, and welfare—to name just a few. In the health field alone, hundreds of articles annually report benefit-cost investigations. Nor is the adaptation complete. Unanswered questions and pragmatic rough edges abound, forcing the continuing refinement of the discipline.

THE ROLES OF BENEFIT-COST ANALYSIS
AND PARTNERSHIP DISCIPLINES

Benefit-cost analysis has not, however, thrived in splendid isolation. Vital partnership disciplines have grown and developed in parallel—some providing the data acquisition and preliminary analysis necessary prior to benefit-cost methods; others aiding the interpretation and application of benefit-cost results.

Many tasks in evaluation lie outside the province of benefit-cost analysis. To determine the most appropriate focus for evaluation requires substantive understanding of programs and, often, the perspective of decision analysis. In getting most useful data, techniques of experimental design are important. Statistical methods are needed to estimate program effects from diverse available data.

Once these and other disciplines in evaluation have yielded best estimates of program effects, the stage is set for benefit-cost analysis. Increasingly, program evaluators are not satisfied to know that certain effects exist at specified levels of statistical significance. They also demand to know how various effects should be valued and how the different valued effects should be aggregated to facilitate program decisions. These decisions include (1) comparing all the good effects of programs (benefits) with all their bad effects (costs and disbenefits) to judge whether it is better to implement or not to implement a program; (2) determining which of alternative versions of programs are best; and (3) deciding what collection of programs or projects constitutes the best expenditure within a set, overall budget limit.

These tasks—valuing program effects and appropriately aggregating the values for decision-making—are the main roles of benefit-cost analysis. Yet, even in these roles, benefit-cost analysis requires the aid of other analytic disciplines. Techniques of operations research and systems analysis may be invoked to ensure that the benefit-cost analysis is covering the full range of relevant alternatives. Substantive program expertise enables complete identification of program effects—both good and bad—that are to be valued. The valuation itself often depends on contributory econometric analysis. Organizational analysis and political science also play vital roles: (1) helping to guide the appropriate assignment and aggregation of values for the benefit-cost analysis; and (2), when the benefit-cost analysis is completed, applying it suitably within complex organizational and political structures.

LEVEL

This book cannot comprehensively cover benefit-cost analysis: the range of applications is too broad and the number of variants of the techniques too large. It seeks instead to communicate the gist of the discipline at a level that the intelligent lay reader can understand. With the current ubiquity of benefit-cost analysis, no involved evaluator, analyst, or decisionmaker can escape it altogether. Although these persons need not have the sensitive understanding of the professional economist, they do need to know (1) when benefit-cost analysis is most useful; (2) what types of concerns it handles well and poorly; (3) what its pitfalls are and what types of errors are most frequently made; (4) what elements of the analysis have greatest impact on its results; and (5) how the findings of benefit-cost analysis should be heeded in decision-making.

The book is written for those who will inevitably come into contact with benefit-cost analysis in their professional careers. It does not seek to make of them highest-level practitioners of benefit-cost analysis, yet it does present guidelines indicating how benefit-cost analysis should be performed. The rationale is that understanding of how to interpret and use benefit-cost analysis will be improved if one can see the issues and problems involved from the perspective of the practitioner.

The arguments of the book are pursued via common-sense logic and simple examples rather than through complicated analytic methods. The rare sections that require of the reader a first course in economics or mathematics beyond the high school level are asterisked to enable the more casual reader to skim them or to pass them by. Despite the emphasis on simple presentation, some concepts will not seem evident at first glance. This is inevitable since benefit-cost analysis by its very nature includes a number of paradoxes and counterintuitive quirks. These are reasons why the discipline is fascinating and why it must be carefully presented and understood.

MYTHS

Failure to recognize the counterintuitive nature of many concepts in benefit-cost analysis has led frequently to the use of superficially appealing but fundamentally flawed techniques. Repeated adherence to convenient but unsound precepts has established many of them as accepted myths. These myths include: (1) the idea that a broad class of program effects (for example, reduced fear of crime or increased aircraft noise) are inherently unquantifiable and, hence, should be just mentioned but not included in benefit-cost analysis; (2) the belief that, of two alternative projects, the one with the higher benefit-cost ratio is necessarily better; (3) the contention that it is better to implement a project with a moderately favorable benefit-cost ratio of, for example, 1.05 than not to; (4) the attitude that a given project can logically have only one benefit-cost ratio (obtained by dividing the good effects by the bad effects); (5) the notion that the effects of limited projects on far-flung markets (such as the marginal raising of the interest rate) can generally be ignored; (6) the sense that units of money have invariant value and, hence, are ideal standards for comparison; (7) the idea—seen widely in the economic literature—that lives may be adequately valued as their economic product; (8) the belief that cost-effectiveness methods are exclusively or mainly useful when the issue is the best way to achieve a set objective; and (9) the assumption that the valuation of program effects need not explicitly reflect context. Some of these propositions are forthrightly argued for in the benefit-cost literature; others seem so broadly accepted that authors no longer bother to make cases for following them. *All are false*—as a number of recent theorists and practitioners have shown. This book will examine these and other myths, make cases against them, and will present alternative, more reliable, bases for analysis.

APPROACH

For the most part, this book presents benefit-cost analysis noncontroversially—being highly compatible, for instance, with the approaches of Mishan (1976) and Sugden and Williams (1978). The few departures that are made from prevailing notions in the literature are identified. At the close of each chapter, additional references are given—both to guide the interested reader in further study and to relate the material presented here to that in other works. Each chapter, in addition, has problem sets covering its contents.

PLAN

Chapter 1 takes a general look at problems of valuation that public decisionmakers face. Approaches to account for alternative aspects of interest are reviewed and are related to benefit-cost analysis. We examine in Chapter 2 a hypothetical business application of benefit-cost analysis—a context that avoids many of the murky conceptual problems faced in public benefit-cost analysis. These problems, however, must be faced up to in Chapter 3, which presents the fundamentals of a consistent and useful approach to benefit-cost analysis in the public sector. The application of this approach is pursued in Chapters 4 and 5: looking at how program effects should be identified, valued, and used in decision-making.

Chapters 6 and 7 present nuances and refinements of standard methodology and raise the pragmatic question, "Do the benefits of these refinements—in terms of improved accuracy and better decisions—exceed the costs they impose on the analysis?" One especially difficult topic in effect valuation—the appropriate value to place on human life extensions—is dealt with in Chapter 8. An important offshoot of benefit-cost analysis—cost-effectiveness analysis—is the focus of Chapter 9. Finally, in Chapter 10, attention is directed to the role played by context in valuing program effects.

1

Introduction to
Problems of Valuation

1.1 ILLUSTRATIVE PROBLEMS OF VALUATION

Program evaluation and other analysis for public decision-making must find ways to value a diverse range of concerns. We consider in this chapter nine illustrative problems of valuation, followed by eight methods that can be used to value alternative aspects of the problems. We compare, in summary, the different types of difficulty faced in the problems and the choice of analytic methods to deal with these difficulties.

The nine illustrative problems include one from the private sector and eight from the public.

Example 1: Plant Location

A company performs a prospective evaluation to decide where to locate a plant. Different proposed sites offer different advantages and disadvantages with respect to securing raw materials, marketing the finished product, and taxation. The company seeks to maximize its profits.

Example 2: Airport Planning

Transportation evaluators assess the merits of alternate airport plans. Site selection affects travel access, noise and air pollution, and property values. Design of the airport influences the type and volume of air traffic, margins of safety, and travel convenience. Subsequent management will affect many of the same variables: Regulations on the types and hours of air travel, for instance, will have impact on convenience, noise, and safety. The task of the evaluative planner is to foresee and to value all relevant dimensions of choice to arrive at an optimal plan.

Example 3: Road-Building

It is proposed to build a toll road. With the road, travelers, consumers, producers, and some landowners will gain, while transporters and other landowners will suffer loss. Tax revenues must cover the difference between the road cost and toll revenues. Road travel will create air pollution unpleasant to those living nearby. A regional government must somehow weight these diverse effects and decide whether or not to build the road.

Example 4: Subsidizing Disease Treatment

A government ponders whether it should cover the medical treatment costs for a certain disease. The disease may be fatal.

Example 5: Inoculation

A massive inoculation program is planned. It is intended to reduce the distress, deaths, and work days lost due to a disease. Not only will those vaccinated benefit, but the unvaccinated will also gain through the reduced contagion hazard. There is a slight risk of severe and possibly fatal reactions to the shots. The evaluator is asked to balance the prospective benefits against the costs and risks to determine whether the program should be enacted.

Example 6: Alternative Life-Saving Programs

A government with interest in saving lives must decide on the funding levels for such diverse programs as neonatal screening, atmospheric pollution control, mobile coronary care units, and road safety.

Example 7: Probation Programs

In comparing alternative programs for supervising adult probation, differential costs, recidivism rates, employment success, and welfare records provide pertinent information. Somehow, these various aspects of program performance must be weighed together to determine which program is best.

Example 8: Teacher Hiring

A school administrator must hire a teacher. He[1] cares about the abilities of the teacher to teach specific skills, to teach how to learn, to instill responsible social behavior, and to promote physical health. Different teachers emphasize and achieve these objectives differently. An evaluator might be asked to determine which of several teacher candidates represents the best choice.

Example 9: Lifting an Arms Embargo

A national government contemplates providing armaments to another country. Pertinent considerations include bilateral foreign relations, the balance of trade, and overall interest in promoting international disarmament.

1.2 WAYS FOR DEALING WITH MULTI-ATTRIBUTE PROBLEMS OF VALUATION

These examples have in common multiple dimensions or attributes of choice to be taken into account—according each its appropriate degree of influence—in decision-making. There are several ways to do this.

(1) Trade-offs. In considering several teacher candidates, their various advantages and disadvantages with respect to one another must be judged. Suppose first that the school administrator is interested only in two teacher attributes: enhancing

---

[1] In the interest of economy of language, all use of the pronoun "he" should be understood to be genderless.

cognitive skills and promoting affective growth (personality development). Five candidates, A, B, C, D, and E, apply for one teaching position and are ranked by the administrator as shown in Table 1.1. With such information, one can immediately eliminate the dominated candidates; a dominated candidate being one who in comparison to some other candidate is inferior to that candidate along at least one dimension of interest and is superior to that candidate along no dimensions. In this case, Candidate D is dominated by Candidate C and E is dominated by A. Therefore, Candidates D and E need no longer be considered.

The remaining candidates, A, B, and C, must now be compared. In each possible pair of these candidates, one is better than the other for cognitive growth and the other one better for affective growth. In choosing between A and B, the administrator must simply judge which is more important: A's advantage over B on the cognitive dimension or B's advantage over A on the affective dimension. This is a *trade-off* decision: weighing the advantages of one option along certain dimensions against the advantages of another option along other dimensions. A series of trade-off decisions (assuming consistency—or, in technical terms, transitivity) will indicate which is the best teacher candidate. As the number of dimensions of interest grows (perhaps taking into account salary demands or administrative abilities), trade-off decisions become more difficult: advantages along multiple dimensions must be traded off against disadvantages along other dimensions.

(2) Indifference curves. A common device used in microeconomic theory for resolving trade-off decisions is the *indifference map* composed of individual *indifference curves.* Figure 1.1 shows a possible set of indifference curves for the choice among teacher candidates with two dimensions of interest. The vertical scale in the diagram measures the ability to promote cognitive growth; the horizontal scale measures the ability to promote affective growth. Each scale may be set in whatever terms the decisionmaker thinks most appropriate: perhaps a subjective scale running from 1 to 10, perhaps test results from direct tests on the teachers or from tests on their students.

The positions of teacher candidates A, B, and C are shown in Figure 1.1—showing that A is better than C as a promoter of

TABLE 1.1   Ranking of Teacher Candidates Along Two
Dimensions of Decision Interest

Teacher Candidate	Rank among Other Candidates along Cognitive Dimension	Rank among Other Candidates along Affective Dimension
A	1	4
B	5	1
C	3	2
D	4	3
E	2	5

cognitive growth but worse than C as a promoter of affective growth, and that C is better than B along the cognitive dimension but worse along the affective dimension. An indifference curve through the point marked "A" can be constructed by asking a series of trade-off questions: "If a teacher candidate is one unit worse than A on the cognitive scale, how good need he be on the affective scale so that you will be indifferent between the two?" "If the candidate is two units worse?" "One unit better? Answers to these questions yield a series of points on the diagram, each representing a possible teacher candidate whom the decision actor considers just as good as A. Connecting these points gives an indifference curve shown as a solid line in Figure 1.1. Every point on the line represents a combination of teacher characteristics thought just as good as those of A. With the indifference curve, we can resolve the choice problem among A, B, and C. As the indifference curve through A passes below and to the right of C, A is inferior to C (possible teacher candidates thought just as good as A are dominated by C). The same indifference curve passes above B, indicating that A is considered better than B and hence that C is the best of the three.

General problems of choice may be resolved by selecting those options lying on the highest (most desired) indifference curves. If the administrator had to choose 10 teachers from 50 candidates, he could do it by selecting the 10 whose indifference curves lay furthest to the northeast on the diagram. Indifference curves thus provide a conceptually clear basis for choice but are at the same time not easy to use for actual decisions. Compared with all the trade-off questions that must be answered to obtain the indifference curves, a smaller number of trade-off questions in most cases can resolve the decision

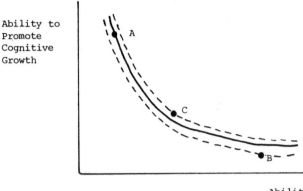

Ability to
Promote
Cognitive
Growth

Ability to Promote
Affective Growth

Figure 1.1: Indifference Curves Showing Trade—Offs Between Two Attributes

problem without reference to indifference curves. Like trade-off analysis, reasoning from indifference curves becomes much more complex as the number of attributes to be taken into account grows.

(3) Objective functions. Related to indifference curves are objective functions. In the case of teacher selection, the abilities to promote cognitive and affective growth might be seen as vital complements in the overall development of children, with one enhancing the other. While there is no single word—for example, "teacherness"—that captures both considerations, they may instead be appropriately reflected in an *objective function*: a formula for combining the attributes of different options (or outcomes) to tell how good the option is as a whole. Suppose the administrator in this case decided that an appropriate objective function (O.F.) in choosing teachers is

$$OF = (a_c)\,(a_a), \qquad [1.1]$$

where

a_c is the ability to promote cognitive growth, and

a_a is the ability to promote affective growth.

Suppose further that three teacher candidates have the various abilities show in Table 1.2. The last column shows the objective function ratings of the three candidates and indicates that C, with the highest rating, is the best.

(Objective functions—like indifference curves—usually are *ordinal*: One can tell which of two or more alternatives is better but not by how much. In this case, it does not follow from Table 1.2 that Candidate C is 22.36 ÷ 19.19 times better than Candidate B. Objective functions thus cannot necessarily be taken as measures of utility for purposes of decision analysis which requires *cardinal* utilities indicating by how much one outcome is better than another.)

One can always derive an indifference map from an objective function, and vice versa. Given an objective function, indifference curves are simply sets of points giving the same objective function ratings. Given an indifference map, one needs only some way for labeling the various indifference curves (perhaps according to how close they come to the origin) to have an objective function—considering the objective function rating of each point to be the label of the indifference curve it is on.

(4) Commensurability. Problems of choice are made easier when the various attributes affecting decisions are *commensurable*: if there is a simple rule relating two or more attributes to each other so that one can readily choose among various combinations of the attributes. A simple type of rule would be a ratio comparing them—for instance, valuing one unit of cognitive teaching ability as equivalent to 1.5 units of affective ability. But we can see in this example that this will not work. For candidates strong in promoting cognitive ability but weak in promoting affective ability—such as A—slight improvements along the affective dimension are highly prized: Candidate A could achieve his present objective function rating of 20.68 by giving up 2.94 units of cognitive ability while gaining one unit of affective ability. (An a_c of 6.46 [the present a_c of 9.4 less 2.94] and an a_a of 3.2 [the present a_a of 2.2 plus 1.0] give an OF of 20.68.) For Candidate B, weak for cognitive growth but strong for affective, the reverse is true: Slight gains on the cognitive dimension are more highly prized than those on the affective dimension. Candidate B could give up 3.48 units of affective ability to gain one unit of cognitive ability and still achieve the same objective function rating of 19.19.

TABLE 1.2   The Attributes of Teacher
Candidates Valued by an
Objective Function

Candidate	a_c	a_a	OF
A	9.4	2.2	20.68
B	1.9	10.1	19.19
C	4.3	5.2	22.36

The same conclusions could be drawn from the indifference map. The steep slope of the indifference curves near A means that many units of cognitive ability would be traded off for one additional unit of affective ability; the flatter slopes of the indifference curves near B mean that only small fractions of cognitive ability units would then be traded off for one additional unit of affective ability. A fixed ratio relating the value of the cognitive dimension to the value of the affective dimension will exist only if the indifference map is composed of parallel straight lines (because the slope of a straight line is constant and equal to the slopes of parallel lines).

(5) Collapsing attributes. In some cases where easy commensurability is not possible, the objective of commensurability—to reduce the number of attributes the decisionmaker has to worry about—may be achieved by *collapsing attributes*: expressing some number of attributes in terms of a smaller number of attributes.

Suppose, for instance, that a municipal transportation agency takes six factors—capacity, convenience, air pollution, noise effects, property values, and safety—into account in choosing the airport plan. The first two of these factors, capacity and convenience, cannot be related to one another by any fixed ratio: For an airport with high capacity (lots of runways and parking) and low convenience (access roads narrow and crowded, poor coordination of facilities within the airport), marginal improvements in convenience are valued much more highly relative to capacity than for an airport with low capacity and high convenience.

Despite the impossibility of relating the values of capacity and convenience by a fixed ratio, the two variables may be reduced to one by collapsing them. This could happen if airport planners only care about either capacity or convenience insofar as these factors affect profitability. The analyst may then collapse capacity and convenience into profitability: For any combination of the two, he would calculate the resulting profitability and report only that to decisionmakers. In this way, the number of variables that decisionmakers have to take into account is reduced from six to five. The more one can reduce the number of attributes to be considered, the easier will be the task of the decisionmakers. If all dimensions of interest can be collapsed into a single dimension, an objective function will have been achieved: Ratings of alternatives on that dimension may be taken as objective function ratings. Collapsing variables is thus a step toward formulating an objective function. (Collapsing variables is also a way of achieving commensurability, in that, for example, collapsing capacity and convenience into profitability means that one unit of capacity is equivalent to however many units of convenience yield the same amount of profitability.)

(6) Money valuation. Yet another way in which commensurability may be achieved is by valuing attributes in terms of money. Theoretically, this can always be done. To value an extra unit of cognitive teaching ability, the decisionmaker need only ask himself how much more of a salary he would be willing to pay a teacher if that teacher rated one unit higher on the cognitive scale. Yet, there are difficulties:

(a) this type of trade-off decision—cognitive ability versus money—is not easy to make nor is it frequently made;

(b) the values obtained are context-specific—the amounts of money that would be paid for an extra unit of airport capacity depend on whether one has a high-capacity, low-convenience airport or the reverse; and

(c) the value of money itself varies with context (see Section 7.2.3).

(7) Benefit-cost analysis. Money valuation is the soul of benefit-cost analysis: assessing the good and bad aspects of a decision alternative by valuing them in terms of money.

Benefit-cost analysis—synonymous with cost-benefit analysis and abbreviated as B/C or C/B—uses monetary valuation to achieve commensurability of all decision attributes. An attribute valued as equivalent to a one-dollar gain is usually considered to be canceled by another attribute valued as equivalent to a one-dollar loss. With this perspective, the difference between benefits (good attributes) and costs (bad attributes) is considered to be the objective function in benefit-cost analysis.

Benefit-cost analysis is soundest when the effects it values have monetary impact on one account. The profit-maximizing firm deciding on a plant site may value all aspects of sites in terms of their impact on its profits. Benefit-cost analysis for such a firm is the perfect analytic tool. Policymakers most often rely on benefit-cost analysis in prospectively evaluating programs, such as road construction, in which different program aspects have different effects, both good and bad, on different people. Such analyses suffer from all the problems with money valuation noted above. Societies usually care who realizes the benefits and costs and not just how large they are. Notwithstanding these defects, benefit-cost analysis is broadly considered a useful tool for evaluating multi-attribute public programs. This book will primarily address benefit-cost analysis—indicating how it should be performed, what correctable problems it has, and what its limitations are.

(8) Cost-effectiveness analysis. For certain types of problems, commensurability may be achieved in valuing many aspects of programs, yet valuation in money terms may be most difficult. A case in point is an inoculation program that saves some lives by protecting them from disease but whose adverse reactions endanger other lives. These effects may both be measured in terms of lives—saved or lost—and are therefore commensurable. However, most decisionmakers are extremely reluctant to place a dollar value on saving a life. In such cases, an appropriate tool is an offshoot of benefit-cost analysis,

> *cost-effectiveness analysis (C/E):* evaluating a decision alternative (1) by making all aspects commensurable in money terms or in terms of one output unit and (2) by comparing the two dimensions of impact.

For the inoculation program, the common unit of output used for valuation is the human life. In cost-effectiveness analysis, output effects in these terms (lives saved and lost) would be compared with net monetary effects.

1.3 COMPARING MULTI-ATTRIBUTE VALUATION PROBLEMS AND THEIR APPROPRIATE MODES OF ANALYSIS

Table 1.3 displays considerations in selecting the best form of analysis for the nine sample decision problems given earlier in this chapter. The first column lists the decisions and the second the types of attributes, other than costs (which are common to all nine decisions), that are of concern. In the third column are estimates of the ease of valuing the nonmonetary attributes in commensurable terms. The fourth column indicates how easy it would be to value the attributes in money terms. In the fifth column are suggested types of analysis; these are briefly commented on in the last column.

The first decision considered, plant site location for the profit-maximizing firm, is, as discussed above, tailor-made for benefit-cost analysis. The firm cares about the various attributes of alternative sites in precisely the measure that each attribute affects the firm's profits. It may be difficult to measure the various attributes—for instance, to estimate the likely effects on marketing that different site locations will have. However, once best estimates of the attributes are obtained (for instance, how many product units would be sold given different plant sites), they are readily translated into money terms. Easy valuation implies an easy commensurability of the nonmonetary attributes. (The converse, as the treatment and inoculation decisions below show, does not hold.) This decision situation will be used in Chapter 2 to introduce benefit-cost analysis.

In deciding on the airport plan and road, similar problems are faced: Impacts on many different populations must be estimated and valued. As Chapters 3, 4, and 5 will show, this is not easy. It nevertheless appears now that benefit-cost analysis offers the best prospect for guiding such decisions.

The decisions on subsidizing treatment for a potentially fatal disease and on the inoculation program must weigh the value of the lives saved against the cost of treatment. For simplicity, we assume that the lives are of comparable value to the policy-

TABLE 1.3 Multi-Attribute Policy Decisions and Their Appropriate Types of Analysis

Decision	Decision Attributes Other than Costs	Ease of Commensurability among Non-Monetary Attributes	Ease of Money Valuation	Appropriate Analysis	Comments
Plant location (see Ch. 2)	Costs of raw materials, marketing costs, tax gains and losses	Easy	Easy	B/C	An ideal situation for B/C
Airport planning	Capacity, convenience, noise and air pollution, property values, safety	Medium–hard	Medium–hard	B/C	Sophisticated techniques and understanding are required for B/C here but do not remedy all its defects. B/C nevertheless seems better than alternative types of analysis.
Road-building (see Ch. 3 to 5)	Travel ease, lower transportation costs, land appreciation, environmental effects	Medium–hard	Medium–hard	B/C	
Subsidizing disease treatment (see Ch. 8)	Lives saved	Trivial	Hard	C/E plus B/C plus some other ways of weighing the many different concerns in valuing lives	C/E is trivial or easy but problems of life valuation make B/C hard.
Inoculation	Lives saved, lives lost	Easy	Hard		
Alternative life preserving programs (see Ch. 9)	Lives saved, suffering caused and prevented	Medium–hard	Hard		Difficulties in commensurability complicate C/E; life valuation makes B/C hard.

TABLE 1.3 Multi-Attribute Policy Decisions and Their Appropriate Types of Analysis (Cont)

Decision	Decision Attributes Other than Costs	Ease of Commensurability among Non-Monetary Attributes	Ease of Money Valuation	Appropriate Analysis	Comments
Probation programs	Recidivism, employment success, welfare records	Hard	Hard	?	Difficulties in commensurability and money valuation owe to idiosyncrasies of context and to fundamental subjective disagreements on the philosophy of valuation and on the causal relationships.
Teacher hiring	Ability to achieve affective and cognitive gains, role model value, administrative ability	Hard	Hard	?	
Lifting an arms embargo	Competing considerations of relations with other countries, trade effects, overall policy aims	Hard	Hard	?	

maker (the disease afflicts only a narrow age range) and that he does not need to worry about such other attributes as pain caused by the disease. Commensurability among the non-monetary attributes is easy: For the treatment decision, life-saving is only one nonmonetary attribute; for the inoculation decision, lives lost due to adverse reactions are considered equal in value to lives saved via vaccination. The difficult part of each decision is the stark trade-off to be made between lives and money. The cost-effectiveness analysis leading up to this trade-off decision is easy; the benefit-cost analysis needed to resolve that decision is hard and, even when performed by the best of analysts, not wholly satisfying (as will be seen in Chapter 8).

In choosing among alternative life-preserving programs, com-mensurability becomes more difficult. Neonatal screening pro-grams save young lives and stroke prevention programs save old lives. Road safety programs often save perfectly healthy lives; mobile coronary care units often extend impaired lives. Finding a way to make these different lives commensurable is difficult but cost-effectiveness analysis, along the lines indicated in Chap-ter 9, has made some headway.

1.4 INTRACTABLE DECISIONS

Decisions on alternative probation programs, teacher hiring, and lifting an arms embargo are, like the others in Table 1.3, multi-attribute choices. Problems of commensurability among the attributes, however, are so great that neither benefit-cost nor cost-effectiveness analysis has been successful in such situa-tions. These problems derive from the following conditions.

(1) Fundamental lack of understanding about the cause and effect mechanisms. No one knows how much an improvement in the affective education of a fourth grader will be reflected in that person twenty years later, or how much more likely lifting an arms embargo will make World War III. Experimental deter-mination of the former would be too expensive, time-con-suming, and uncertain; of the latter, impossible.

(2) Subjective disagreements. Even though knowledge of the causal relationships is tenuous, people think they know and

disagree. The disagreements often reflect underlying and ineradicable philosophical differences. Some think that a nation of persons educated with a stress on affective development would be better than had cognitive development been stressed, and some think the reverse. Believers in the work ethic and the GNP will rate probation programs on their employment records. Believers in internal values will look to the results of attitudinal tests and recidivism records. Neither may be able to persuade the other.

(3) Contextual differences. Each of these decisions depends on context. They are likely to be resolved differently depending on whether recidivist crime is a major social problem, how much a society needs brain power relative to good temperament, and the likelihood of war. Evaluative context is discussed in Chapter 10.

Techniques of benefit-cost and cost-effectiveness analysis can be used to identify commensurable attributes, to collapse them, and thus to simplify decisions such as these. The more important modes of analysis will, however, involve substantive understanding of the problem and a sensitivity to what is in the hearts of the decision participants. Such analysis—while not as formal and as structured as benefit-cost analysis—may nevertheless be the more valuable in resolving the basic trade-offs in the decisions.

1.5 THIS CHAPTER AND OTHER WRITINGS

For good overviews of valuation problems—similar in many respects to that given here—the reader is referred to Keeney and Raiffa (1976) and to Stokey and Zeckhauser (1978). A slightly different approach describing how the values of different decision participants should be aggregated over multiple decision attributes is given by Edwards et al. (1975) and Edwards and Guttentag (1975). A variety of approaches to multi-attribute decision problems appears in Cochrane and Zeleny (1973). Further reading on objective functions is to be found in texts on operations research—such as Anderson et al. (1976). For an overview of the role of benefit-cost analysis, see Rothenberg (1975).

2

Monetary Benefit-Cost Analysis

2.1 CHAPTER OVERVIEW

In this chapter we analyze a hypothetical problem of multi-attribute valuation set in the private sector. The example will bring out many basic principles of benefit-cost analysis without becoming complicated by the difficult questions (such as handling of distributional issues or analysis of externalities) that must be faced in public benefit-cost studies.

We consider a decision on plant location—a decision involving many factors. The advantages and disadvantages of different sites are weighed against one another by calculating what effect each aspect has on company funds. Because the various effects occur at different times, money at one time must be related to money at another. This comparative valuation is achieved by discounting—whose two chief forms are present and future valuation. We see that these two forms are equivalent in the sense of leading to the same decision outcome. By first identifying, calculating, and discounting all decision aspects, the pros and cons of alternative sites can be combined and compared. The preferred site is that with best net effect on company funds.

2.2 COMPETING CONSIDERATIONS IN A DECISION

Example: Plant Siting

A company has decided to erect a plant to produce office machines. It is undecided whether to build the plant in State A or State B. Different attributes of the states that should be considered in the choice are that:

(1) Feasible capacities differ. In State A, a labor shortage makes it infeasible to construct a plant producing more than 200,000 units per year; if the plant were constructed in State B, it would have a capacity of 250,000 units per year.

(2) Construction costs differ. The State A plant (with capacity of 200,000 units per year) would cost $20 million. The State B plant (250,000 units of annual capacity) would cost $32 million.

(3) Production costs differ. The per-unit production cost in State A would be $260 in year 2, the first year of production; in State B, the figure would be $278 per unit.

(4) Transportation costs differ. The State A plant would be farther from the wholesalers for the machines and per-unit transportation costs of $40 in year 2 would be incurred. Per-unit transporation costs of $20 would be incurred for the State B plant in that year.

(5) Tax laws differ. The tax structures of the two states are the same except that State B has been designated a depressed state. It offers a credit on the national corporate profits tax equal to 10 percent of all capital investment expenditures in a year. State A offers only a five percent profits tax credit for capital spending. The company has sufficient profits from other dealings to be able to take full advantage of either tax credit.

(6) Finally, expected sale values differ. The plant, if constructed in State A, would be expected to be sold in five years for $12 million. The State B plant would be expected to sell for $14 million after five years.

2.3 THE CONTEXT OF THE DECISION

This is a multi-attribute decision problem with six important attributes or dimensions along which the two sites differ. Somehow the advantages that State A has along some (the second and third) dimensions have to be weighed against the advantages of State B along others (the first, fourth, fifth, and sixth). The importance of each of these differences between the states is measured in terms of their impact on the funds of the company. To calculate that impact, we must know more about the context of the decision: about the economic perspective of the company; about economic realities in producing office machines; about national economic conditions.

(1) The economic perspective of the company. The company is a profit maximizer. It cares about the differences between the two plant sites only insofar as those differences affect its profits. The company has many investment opportunities that would yield a 12 percent annual return. Any funds invested in the plant would involve taking money away from investments yielding an after-tax return of 12 percent.

(2) Economic realities in producing office machines. The plant would require one year to erect. The units to be produced by the plant would then be sold to wholesalers for $330 per unit—a price that would rise subsequently with inflation. The company could sell up to 250,000 units annually for the next four years, after which the units would become outmoded and the company would close down and sell the plant. Wholesalers pay for the office machines on the first day of the year in which they are produced.

The construction companies, transporters, suppliers, and plant workers insist on being paid on the first day of the year for all goods and services to be provided during the year. (This is a somewhat unrealistic condition, but one that simplifies the problem. Similarly, our neglect of complex depreciation options is for simplicity.)

(3) National economic conditions. The nation has a constant 7 percent inflation rate affecting equally all production costs, transportation costs, and product prices. National tax laws provide for a 50 percent tax on all company profits payable on the day that the profits are realized. A summary of the conditions for the decision problem is given in Table 2.1.

2.4 UNCERTAINTY

In the real world, companies cannot be as certain as the conditions given above indicate: future costs of production and transportation, plant resale price, machine wholesale price, and inflation rates are all likely to be subject to uncertainty. For illustrative purposes, our specifications are overcertain, yet this is also reflective of the prevailing attitude that the fundamental procedures of benefit-cost analysis are not appropriate mechanisms for dealing with uncertainty (see Feldstein, 1972; Sugden and Williams, 1978). One should not, for instance, consciously understate benefits or use an inflated discount rate to allow for uncertainty (although some analysts have done so). Instead, it seems better to carry through a benefit-cost analysis using best estimates of all parameters. If these best estimates are unsure, the analysis can be repeated using other values for the variables to see what effect on the overall analysis this had. This process amounts to a sensitivity analysis (see Section 5.19). Such an approach would provide decisionmakers with the best estimates of benefit-cost summary figures (for example, net benefits or the benefit-cost ratio) and with a sense of how these figures would vary depending on changes in assumptions. On this basis, they should be able to make good policy choices. Should greater formality or precision be desired in dealing with the uncertainty, decision analysis could be applied. To summarize, current preferred procedure is to perform the benefit-cost analysis as if certainty prevailed and, if some assumptions are uncertain, to redo the analysis treating alternative assumptions as certain.

2.5 THE STANDARD FOR EVALUATION

The company evaluates the two sites by measuring the effect of each on its money. For the sake of clarity, it designates the beginning of the construction as year 1, day 1. The construction companies must be paid on that day. Wholesalers pay for the second-year production on year 2, day 1—the same day that transporters, suppliers, and workers are paid for their goods and

TABLE 2.1   Summary of Parameters to be Considered in Selecting a
Plant Site

	State A	State B
Differences Between the States		
Annual plant production capacity	200,000 units	250,000 units
Plant construction costs in year 1	$20 million	$32 million
Per-unit production costs in year 2	$260	$278
Per-unit transportation costs in year 2	$40	$20
Investment tax credit for construction	5%	10%
Resale value of plant after five years	$12 million	$14 million
Conditions Common to Both States		
After-tax return obtainable by company on alternative investments	12%	
Time required for construction	1 year	
Unit price paid by wholesalers in year 2	$330	
Productive lifetime of plant	4 years	
Inflation rate affecting production costs, transportation costs, and product prices	7% annually	
Standard tax on all corporate profits	50%	

NOTE: The company seeks to maximize profits, which it will do by maximizing its money as of year 6, day 1. Payments for construction, transportation, products, and taxes are made on the first days of the years in which the goods or services are provided.

services provided in that year. Similar payments are made on the first days of years 3, 4, and 5. Sale of the plant is assumed to be made on year 6, day 1. On that day, all transactions having to do with the site choice will have been completed. The company decides to look at the effects on its accounts as of that day to evaluate the two sites.

2.6 IMMEDIATE EFFECTS

The State A plant costs $20 million to erect and hence would reduce year 1 profits by that amount. In reducing company profits by $20 million, profits taxes are reduced by $10 million—a gain to the company. The profits taxes are further reduced by the five percent tax credit for construction costs—a gain of $1 million (five percent of $20 million) to the company. If the plant is constructed in State B, the company would lose $32 million in construction costs, gain $16 million in consequently reduced profits taxes, and gain $3.2 million (10 percent of $32 million) through State B's 10 percent tax credit. These effects are summarized in Table 2.2 and show that the net effects of the construction as of year 1, day 1 are a loss of $9 million for the State A plant and of $12.8 million for the State B plant.

2.7 TAKING INTO ACCOUNT THE FACTOR OF TIME

How will these first-year costs be reflected in the company monies five years later? We compare the possibility of constructing the plant in either state with the alternative of not constructing the plant at all. We are focusing now on the effects of the construction costs and not on the profits that would be realized later. If a net company loss of $9 million were not incurred on year 1, day 1 to build the State A plant, that amount of money could be channeled into other investments yielding an annual after-tax return of 12 percent. By using $9 million in company money to cover the construction costs, that money no longer has the chance to grow annually at a rate of 12 percent and to amount to

$$(9)(1.12)^5 = 15.86 \qquad [2.1]$$

million dollars five years later. The company as of year 6, day 1 will have $15.86 million less because of the construction costs five years earlier. Similarly, the State B construction costs would reduce the company funds by

$$(12.8)(1.12)^5 = 22.56 \qquad [2.2]$$

million dollars on year 6, day 1. Since (having decided to build the plant in one of the states) we are most interested in the difference between the two sites, we see that the differential construction costs (taking into account the tax structure and the company's alternative uses for the money) give a net advantage to State A of

$$22.56 - 15.86 = 6.70 \qquad [2.3]$$

million dollars in terms of the company funds on year 6, day 1.

TABLE 2.2   Immediate Effects of Alternative Plants on Company Funds (in millions)

	State A	State B
Company loss due to construction costs	$20	$32
Company gain due to reduced profit taxes resulting from construction costs	$10	$16
Company gain due to tax credit for construction costs	$1	$3.2
Net company loss as of year 1, day 1	$9	$12.8

2.8 DISCOUNTING

We have, in the preceding section, made use of

discounting: translating effects valued in terms of the money (or other units of value such as utility units, but most commonly and conveniently money) at one time to valuation in terms of the money (or other units) at a different time.

Suppose that the company in our example might receive a windfall gain of $1,000 in three years and wants to know how much money it should give up today or in five years to achieve that gain (that is, how much that prospective gain is worth in terms of today's money or in terms of money in five years).

To solve this problem, we make use of the

discount rate: a number relating value in one year to value in the next year or the past year. A decisionmaker with a discount rate of d is (by definition) indifferent between (a) getting one dollar a year from today, (b) getting

$$1 \div (1 + d)$$

dollars today, and (c) getting

$$1 + d$$

dollars in two years.

The discount rate in the current example is 12 percent. The discount rate is commonly determined, as in this example, as the interest rate at which the decisionmaker can invest or borrow money.

2.9 OBTAINING PRESENT AND FUTURE VALUES BY DISCOUNTING

The value to the company of getting $1,000 in three years in terms of today's money is

$$\$1,000 \div (1.12)^3 = \$712. \qquad [2.4]$$

This is the *present value*—the value in terms of present money (or, occasionally, other units of value)—of getting $1,000 in three years. This amount of money, $712, received now and invested for three years, would be worth $1,000 three years from today.

The value to the company of getting $1,000 in three years in terms of the money in five years is

$$(\$1,000)(1.12)^2 = \$1,254. \qquad [2.5]$$

This is the *future value*—the value in terms of future money (in this case, money in five years)—five years hence of getting $1,000 in three years. If the company received $1,000 in three years and invested it at 12 percent, it would be worth $1,254 two years later.

These calculations show that the company should be willing to pay up to $712 (the present value) in this year's money to get $1,000 in three years. It should be willing to commit itself to paying up to $1,254 (the future value) five years from now in order to get $1,000 three years from now.

2.10 CONTRASTING PRESENT AND FUTURE VALUES

Future valuation is translating the known value of something at one time to valuation in the terms of a later time. Present valuation is translating the known value of something at one time to valuation in the terms of an earlier time. (Present valuation is a slight misnomer in that it need not be, although it usually is, set in present terms: Projects are often present-valued to the moment when they will begin operation. Both future and present valuation must specify the moment for which the valuation is made—be it now, last year, seven years in the future, or whenever.)

Using the discount rate d, the formula for the future value (FV) in n years of something worth S dollars now is given by

$$FV = (S)(1 + d)^n. \qquad [2.6]$$

The present value (PV) of something worth T dollars in m years is

$$PV = T \div (1 + d)^m. \qquad [2.7]$$

These formulae enable any decisionmaker with a known discount rate to make trade-off decisions concerning any values known at specific times.

2.11 PROFIT CALCULATIONS

The profits to be realized by the plant in year 2 in either state may be calculated from the information given. The State A plant incurs production costs of $260 per unit and transportation costs of $40 per unit. When these costs are subtracted from the wholesale price of $330 per unit, a per-unit profit of $30 remains. With production and sales of 200,000 units in year 2, the total before-tax profit is $6 million. After-tax profit is half of this, or $3 million. This money would be invested and four years later—on year 6, day 1—would amount to

$$(3)(1.12)^4 = 4.72 \qquad [2.8]$$

million dollars. That is, the year 6 future value of $3 million in year 2 is $4.72 million.

For the State B plant, production costs of $278 per unit and transportation costs of $20 per unit lead to a per-unit profit of $32 dollars. Realized on 250,000 units, this amounts to before-tax profits of $8 million and to after-tax profits of $4 million.

Future-valued to year 6, this is

$$(4)(1.12)^4 = 6.29 \qquad [2.9]$$

million dollars. This is summarized in Table 2.3.

2.12 FUTURE VALUATION OF PROFITS

Calculation of profits for years 3, 4, and 5 parallels that for year 2. The difference is that price to wholesalers, production costs, and transportation costs each grow by seven percent due to inflation. Profits will accordingly grow by seven percent annually. After-tax profits for the State A plant thus would be

$$(3)(1.07) = 3.21 \qquad [2.10]$$

million dollars in year 3,

$$(3)(1.07)^2 = 3.43 \qquad [2.11]$$

million dollars in year 4, and

$$(3)(1.07)^3 = 3.68 \qquad [2.12]$$

million dollars in year 5.

The \$3.21 million in after-tax year 3 profits will be invested at 12 percent for three years and will amount to

$$(3.21)(1.12)^3 = 4.51 \qquad [2.13]$$

million dollars on year 6, day 1. The year 6, day 1 future valuation for the fourth-year after-tax profits is

$$(3.43)(1.12)^2 = 4.31 \qquad [2.14]$$

million dollars. The year 6, day 1 future valuation for fifth-year after-tax profits is

$$(3.68)(1.12) = 4.12 \qquad [2.15]$$

TABLE 2.3   Summary of Profit Calculations For Year Two

	State A	State B
(E1) Unit price to wholesalers	$330	$330
(E2) Unit production costs	$260	$278
(E3) Unit transportation costs	$40	$20
(E4) Unit profit (= E1–E2–E3)	$30	$32
(E5) Number of units produced annually	200,000	250,000
(E6) Before-tax profit (= E4 times E5)	$6 million	$8 million
(E7) After-tax profit (= 1/2 of E6)	$3 million	$4 million
(E8) Value on year 6, day 1		
(= E7 times $(1.12)^4$)	$4.72 million	$6.29 million

million dollars. These calculations and comparable ones for the State B plant are summarized in Table 2.4.

2.13 COMBINING THE PARTS OF THE ANALYSIS

The State A plant would be expected to sell for $12 million on year 6, day 1; the State B plant, for $14 million. These amounts of money would contribute to profits in year 6 and would therefore be taxed at 50 percent. Only half of the amounts—$6 million and $7 million, respectively—would therefore go to increasing the company's monies as of year 6, day 1 (which is also the day of the sale of the plants).

We now have all the information needed to calculate the effects of plants in State A or State B on the amount of money the company has on year 6, day 1. Our calculations are summarized in Table 2.5. The first half of the table shows that the company will have $7.80 million more in its accounts on year 6, day 1 if it builds the plant in State A than if it does not build any plant (and instead invests its money in alternative projects yielding a return of 12 percent). The lower half of the table shows that the company will have $7.98 million more on year 6, day 1 if it builds the State B plant rather than no plant. This indicates that the company will have

$$7.98 - 7.80 = 0.18 \qquad [2.16]$$

million dollars more in year 6 if it builds in State B instead of in State A.

TABLE 2.4   After-Tax Profits in Years 2 Through 5 and Their Future
             Values in Year 6

	State A Plant	State B Plant
(E1) After-tax profits in year 2		
(From E7, Table 2.6)	$3 million	$4 million
(E2) After-tax profits in year 3		
(= E1 times 1.07)	$3.21 million	$4.28 million
(E3) After-tax profits in year 4		
(= E1 times $(1.07)^2$)	$3.43 million	$4.58 million
(E4) After-tax profits in year 5		
(= E1 times $(1.07)^3$)	$3.68 million	$4.90 million
(E5) Year 6 FV of after-tax profits in		
year 2 (= E1 times $(1.12)^4$)	$4.72 million	$6.29 million
(E6) Year 6 FV of after-tax profits in		
year 3 (= E2 times $(1.12)^3$)	$4.51 million	$6.01 million
(E7) Year 6 FV of after-tax profits in		
year 4 (= E3 times $(1.12)^2$)	$4.31 million	$5.74 million
(E8) Year 6 FV of after-tax profits in		
year 5 (= E4 times 1.12)	$4.12 million	$5.49 million

FV ≡ future values

2.14 THE ADVANTAGES OF
PRESENT AND FUTURE VALUATION

We have been able to demonstrate the superiority of building
in State B by future valuation—by translating all money effects
into their impacts on year 6 funds. This was done to establish
the soundness of our methods and results: Having carefully
worked through the arithmetic, there is no escaping the conclusion that the better of two projects is the one that leaves
$180,000 more in the accounts of the profit-maximizing com-
pany.

We could, however, have come to the same result by reasoning through present valuation. This would have had the disadvantage of being less concrete: Demonstrable impacts on
accounts on a specified day seem more real than present value
calculations (which are imputations of what future gains or
losses are worth in present terms). However, once the decisionmaker is convinced that present values are as valid as future
values, present values have the advantage of immediacy: Critical
and most immediate in many decisions are allocations of present resources which are most clearly valued as what they are

TABLE 2.5   Summary of the Calculated Monetary Effects for Plants in State A or State B

	Amount of Money ($000,000)	Effect on Company Funds of of Year 6, Day 1 ($000,000)
State A Plant		
Cost to the company of construction, incurred in year 1	−9	−15.86
After-tax profits realized in year 2	3	4.72
After-tax profits realized in year 3	3.21	4.51
After-tax profits realized in year 4	3.43	4.31
After-tax profits realized in year 5	3.68	4.12
After-tax return from sale of plant realized in year 6	6	6
Net gain to company as of year 6, day 1		7.80
State B Plant		
Cost to the company of construction, incurred in year 1	−12.8	−22.56
After-tax profits realized in year 2	4	6.29
After-tax profits realized in year 3	4.28	6.01
After-tax profits realized in year 4	4.58	5.74
After-tax profits realized in year 5	4.90	5.49
After-tax return from sale of plant in year 6	7	7
Net gain to company as of year 6, day 1		7.98

worth today. Also critical are obligated future resources and present and future benefits—which are most often made commensurate with present resources through present valuation.

2.15 THE EQUIVALENCE OF PRESENT AND FUTURE VALUATION

We can see that reasoning by present valuation is equivalent to reasoning by future valuation by examining the rightmost column in Table 2.5. Suppose that, instead of the effect on company funds as of year 6, day 1, we were interested in present values as of year 1, day 1. The present value of the first item is immediate: The present value of $9 million spent on the day of present valuation is $9 million. The year 1 present valuation of the second item—$3 million in year 2—is

$$3 \div 1.12 = 2.68 \qquad [2.17]$$

million dollars. This is

$$1 \div (1.12)^5 = .57 \qquad [2.18]$$

of the year 6 future valuation of the same item. The year 1 present valuation of every item in the table is just .57 ($= 1.12^{-5}$) of the year 6 future valuation. The present valuation of the net gain to the company from building the plant in State A is thus

$$7.80 \div (1.12)^5 = 4.43 \qquad [2.19]$$

million dollars and the net gain of building in State B is

$$7.98 \div (1.12)^5 = 4.53 \qquad [2.20]$$

million dollars. Present valuation leads to the same result as future valuation: finding that it is slightly better to build in State B than in State A.

2.16 PRIVATE AND PUBLIC BENEFIT-COST ANALYSIS

In solving this problem, we have used a simple and direct form of benefit-cost analysis. Benefits from the company's viewpoint are all happenings that increase its funds; costs are all happenings that decrease its funds. By discounting, all benefits and costs occurring at any time may be made commensurate. The actual discount rate used (here, 12 percent) reflects simultaneously inflation (seven percent) and the productive capacity of resources if in alternative use. (In many examples to come, for simplicity we will assume no inflation. Had we done so in this example, the discount rate would have represented only the rate at which real-valued amounts of money can be invested to obtain more money in the future. We will return to the issue of disentangling inflation from other effects bound up in the discount rate in Section 7.3.9.) For any contemplated action, the discounted costs may be subtracted from the discounted benefits (both being in commensurate terms) to see whether the action is better than no action. Of two or more alternative actions, that with largest benefits net of costs will contribute most to company funds and therefore is best.

For public program evaluation, benefit-cost analysis is less straightforward: it is not always clear who the decisionmaker is nor what are his criteria for choice; program effects are more difficult to translate into money values; and public valuation has many idiosyncrasies leading money values often to be inconsistent and misleading indicators of public concern. We turn now to face these problems.

2.17 THIS CHAPTER AND OTHER WRITINGS

The basic concepts in this chapter are covered in most texts on benefit-cost analysis (see Section 3.15). For more on the elements of benefit-cost analysis in the private, profit-making firm, see such works on capital budgeting as Bierman and Smidt (1975).

3

The Groundwork for
Public Benefit-Cost Analysis

3.1 CHAPTER OVERVIEW

We consider a hypothetical problem in multi-attribute valuation in the public sector: a decision on whether to build a road. It is tempting to transfer the techniques used in the previous chapter to this problem. Unfortunately, a variety of concerns (such as consumption, leisure, externalities, or equity) makes this impossible. An alternative methodology, based on the concept of the compensating variation (CV), leads directly to plausible but flawed criteria for public decision-making. The drawback to the methodology is its inability to reflect concerns of distributional equity. An eight-step methodology based on identifying compensating variations and separately considering equity is therefore recommended.

3.2 AN APPROACH TO EVALUATING
THE BUILDING OF A ROAD

Example. A regional government contemplates building a toll road across a desert. The toll is $1 for cars. The government can foresee the benefits of the road, including facilitating pleasure trips; reducing transportation costs for industry and agriculture, consequently leading to expansion of both sectors; and increasing the value of the desert land. Taxpayers, travelers, consumers, producers, transporters, road builders, landowners, entrepreneurs, and breathers are affected by the road. The authorities wish to know whether the region will benefit by building the road.

Strategy toward a solution. To assist decisionmakers in such situations, benefit-cost analysis has been developed and continues to be refined. For the company deciding on plant location, benefit-cost analysis was based on calculating what effects each of the decision alternatives would have on profits. This led to a direct and consistent analysis.

Perhaps the same approach should be taken in the regional evaluation of the road. One would first identify a set of monetary accounts taken to comprise the interests of the regional decisionmaker: This might be the total economic assets of the government. One would then estimate the effects of the road on these accounts. Costs come out of the accounts and benefits go into them. One could then decide that the road should be built if it has a net positive effect on the accounts and not built if the net effect is negative.

3.3 WHY THE ACCOUNTANCY APPROACH WILL NOT WORK

For a number of reasons, this monetary accountancy approach will not work in public decision-making.

(1) Consumption. People value consumption—the vacation, the good meal. These values should be taken into account by the regional government, but they will not be reflected in the assets of either the persons or the governments after the consumption has taken place.

(2) Leisure. When a person decides to stop working and to live off his savings, his assets will decline. The person is, however, rating his leisure—not reflected in the set of accounts—more highly than working and earning.

(3) Externalities. When a factory pollutes the air, breathers suffer. Suppose that this pollution occurs for five years, then stops. After that time, there will be no effect on property values (they would reflect only lasting damage or future pollution) yet those who suffered would strongly have preferred to breathe clean air.

(4) Distributional concerns. A policy might reduce the assets of the poor by $10 million and increase those of the rich by $11 million. Despite the overall increase in value, society may deem such policies unwise on the grounds of equity.

Neither consumption, leisure, externalities, nor distributional concerns are adequately reflected in an aggregated set of accounts. This means that the accountancy approach to benefit-cost analysis used for the company locating its plant is not good enough for most public decisions. (It might work for purely monetary decisions—for instance, in comparing alternative ways to finance a municipal budget deficit). We need, instead, stronger techniques for dealing with the broader concerns of public decisionmakers. The following two sections review alternative approaches for dealing with the values of many nonmonetary program effects, including consumption, leisure, and externalities. The methods discussed are not fully adequate for dealing with distributional concerns which, as shall be seen, remain among the least tractable aspects of benefit-cost analysis.

3.4 MONETARY AND NONMONETARY EFFECTS

A *benefit* occurs whenever a person is favorably affected by a program. *Cost*—or *disbenefit*—occurs whenever a person is unfavorably affected. (Costs are sometimes distinguished from disbenefits: costs being money the government pays for a program and disbenefits being unfavorable effects on private people. This distinction is not always a clear-cut and is not universally followed. We will here treat costs and disbenefits as roughly synonymous, but will later distinguish between public and private impacts.) Monetary effects are readily valued as the amounts of money gained or lost by those affected—although even this almost self-evident rule has its limitations (as will be seen in Chapter 7).

Nonmonetary effects—which are sometimes termed "intangible"—present more of a problem: We would like to express them in monetary terms, which would then make various nonmonetary effects commensurable not only with monetary effects, but also with each other. This would enable appropriate comparisons among the many types of effects and would accord each its due importance in decision-making. But monetary valuation of all effects is far from easy. For the decision on the road, it involves quantifying such consequences as greater convenience in pleasure travel (a benefit) or the unpleasantness in breathing polluted air (a cost). In evaluating crime control programs, such subtle effects as reduced fear of crime come into question. Disease control programs may both save money and make people feel better. To value suitably such nonmonetary effects is a long-standing challenge for benefit-cost analysts.

3.5 STRATEGIES FOR TREATING NONMONETARY EFFECTS

Three main approaches—nonquantification, shadow prices, and compensating variations—have been followed in dealing with nonmonetary effects.

Nonquantification. Many analysts take the attitude that nonmonetary effects are so difficult to value that it is better not to quantify them. One can describe the effects, mention their manifestations and consequences, while forbearing from placing numbers on them. This, for instance, is the tack taken toward decreased fear of crime by Friedman (1977). The drawback to this strategy is that nonmonetary effects are often critical, and that failure to quantify them even crudely may lead in decision-making either to overlooking them or to haphazardly allowing them too great or too small an influence.

Shadow prices. The original definition of a shadow price was the value that should be attributed to a constrained commodity in order to achieve optimal allocations (see, for instance, Anderson, 1976). Increasingly, shadow prices are taken to be any tenuously reasonable ascription of value to a good not traded in the market (Abt, 1977). In this vein, the value of reduced fear of crime might be somehow related to what people spend on crime-prevention or crime-protection devices. The dangers of this approach are seen in considering the value of assuring a continued water supply to a city. In fact, most cities pay little for their water. If deprived of it, the true value of water would be revealed by the vastly greater prices cities would pay to obtain it. True values are not the actual prices paid for similar goods in different situations—as shadow pricing assumes—but what people would pay for the goods in the situation in question.

Compensating variations. The optimal theoretical solution to valuation is the compensating variation (Mishan, 1976):

> A compensating variation (CV) is 1) for a program beneficiary, the amount of money he could pay so that, with the program but having paid this money, he would be just as well off as without the program and without the payment; and 2) for a person made worse off by a program, the amount of money he would have to be paid so that, with the program and the payment, he would be just as well off as without the program and the payment. CV's are taken to be positive for gainers and negative for losers.

The annual benefit to a pleasure traveler would thus be measured as the amount of money that could be taken from him annually and that would leave him indifferent between (1) making his pleasure trips, paying the tolls, and paying that amount of money and (2) not having the road built. This amount is his positive compensating variation: the most he would be willing to pay every year for the privilege of traveling on the road at the toll level of $1. The annual cost of the road to the breather of polluted air is the amount of money he would have to be paid so that he would be indifferent between (1) breathing the bad air and getting the money and (2) not having the road built. This amount is his negative compensating variation: the amount of money he would have to be paid each year so that he would be reconciled to the existence of the road. A primary shortcoming of CVs is the difficulty in measurement—since people have not thought through how much they would pay for nonmonetary effects, and, if questioned, give haphazard, inconsistent answers. A second drawback is the insensitivity of CVs to distributional issues. Rich people would generally pay more for the same benefits than would poor—implying that public services should be overwhelmingly directed to affluent neighborhoods and thus achieve greater benefits (as measured by CVs).

3.6 CHOICE OF STRATEGY

Drawbacks to nonquantification, shadow prices, and compensating variations have been mentioned and should guide the choice of method. Theoretically, the best approach uses compensating variations. To call limited effects unquantifiable is wrong theoretically since there should, in most cases, be some amounts of money that gainers would pay for their benefits or that would compensate losers for their disbenefit. These quantities refute the notion of fundamental unquantifiability. Shadow prices—for reasons mentioned above—are also clearly less valid than compensating variations.

We will accordingly, in conceptualizing most program effects, consider them to be quantifiable using compensating variations. The exceptions are disbenefits so large that they cannot be compensated and distributional effects. Nevertheless, while urging that we perceive effect values as compensating variations, we must recognize that, in many circumstances, they are pragmatically unworkable. Decisionmakers may prefer that nonmonetary values be mentioned but not quantified—thus avoiding the acrimonious debate that any concretely specified numbers might lead to. Similarly, decisionmakers may, at times, find shadow prices easier to relate to than compensating variations. An example might be valuation of a river clean-up enabling swimming: Valuation as the amounts paid to use swimming pools might be more readily accepted than the theoretically superior valuation as what people would be willing to pay for an unpolluted river.

Part of the theoretical appeal of compensating variations lies in their immediate applicability in resolving questions of economic efficiency. This is seen in the following section, which presents an important economic perspective in judging public programs.

3.7 CRITERIA FOR PUBLIC DECISION-MAKING

When all the compensating variations—both negative and positive—for a project are totaled, one will generally find either that

(1) the sum is positive, indicating that the gainers from the project could fully compensate all losers from the project (so that not one person would feel worse off with the project than without it) and some gainers would remain better off than without the project; or
(2) the sum is negative, indicating that there is no possible way that payments could be arranged so that after the payments there would not be at least some people worse off with the project.

The *Kaldor-Hicks criterion* for public decisions is that a net positive sum of the CVs (representing both monetary and nonmonetary effects) is a necessary and sufficient condition for enacting any project.

All projects meeting the Kaldor-Hicks criterion are *potential Pareto improvements* (pPi's). This is an extension of the economic notion of the *Pareto improvement* which is

> any change such that at least one person would be made better off and no one worse off.

A potential Pareto improvement is

> any change such that, *with suitable hypothetical redistributions,* at least one person would be made better off and no one worse off.

A potential Pareto improvement is obtained whenever the net sum of the CVs is positive.

3.8 PROBLEMS IN USING THE DECISION CRITERIA

The problem with a public strategy of enacting policies if and only if they are potential Pareto improvements is distributional: the suitable hypothetical redistributions postulated by the definition rarely occur. This means that some people lose. Defenders of the Kaldor-Hicks criterion argue that a strategy of enacting pPi's will generally cancel out the losses: People who are losers under some policies will be bigger gainers under others—making them, in sum, better off. It has not, however, been shown that such canceling of effects does, in fact, take place or, if it does take place, does so rapidly enough to satisfy social qualms about inflicting temporary net losses on people.

Decades of debate among economists have failed to resolve this conflict between efficiency (the Kaldor-Hicks criterion) and equity (the worry that the distribution of benefits and costs is uneven and unfair). Following the suggestion made by Little (1960), many economists think it best to treat the issues separately: to determine first whether a contemplated change is a pPi and then to see what its distributional implications are. With this analytic strategy, an action found to be a pPi might be rejected on the grounds of equity, the redistributions necessary to make the potential Pareto improvement a Pareto improvement not being practical. Conversely, an action that is not a pPi (that has net negative CVs) may be approved because its distributional effects are desirable.

Example. A public transportation authority contemplates a flight path change for incoming aircraft. The change would benefit airlines and air travelers but would be detrimental to the inhabitants of a town near the airport. With the change, the monthly effects would be that (1) the airlines would save $40,000 in costs—thus adding this amount to profits; (2) 50,000 air travelers would save five minutes each—for which they each would be willing to pay one dollar; and (3) 8000 townspeople would be aggravated by greater aircraft noise—to the extent that they would have to be paid $10 each (per month) to be as well off as without the change. (To determine the CVs for the travelers and townspeople, as will be seen in later chapters, is difficult. The point here is that, even if these determinations were made, subsequent decision-making would not be trivial.) What can we say about the proposed change on efficiency grounds? (Is it a pPi?) On equity grounds?

Solution. The numbers given are CVs. Combining them, we find that the benefits of $40,000 to the airlines and of $50,000 to the air travelers exceed by $10,000 each month the valued aggravation of the townspeople ($80,000). That is, the airlines and travelers could fully reimburse all those aggravated by the greater noise (so that with the change and the compensation they would each feel as well off as without the change) and have surplus benefits of $10,000. The change is a pPi and on efficiency grounds is clearly desirable.

Considering equity, the picture becomes cloudier. The compensations required to change the potential Pareto improvement into a Pareto improvement are unlikely to be made. They would be cumbersome and expensive to arrange (the procedural costs perhaps amounting to more than $10,000). A socially sensitive agency might decide that it is not just to cause the townspeople $80,000 worth of uncompensated noise annoyance in order to benefit airlines and travelers by $90,000. In other words, the efficiency advantages of the change might be judged to be outweighed by the equity disadvantages.

*3.9 EQUIVALENT VARIATIONS

For conceptual clarity, it is sometimes necessary to distinguish between compensating variations and *equivalent variations (EVs)*. CVs are hypothetical money amounts paid (to losers) or taken away (from gainers) to restore persons from their status with a program (SWP) to positions equivalent to their status without the program (SWOP). EVs are hypothetical money amounts paid to or taken away from persons without a program to bring them to their status with a program. In algebraic terms,

$$u(SWP - CV) = u(SWOP) \text{ and} \qquad [3.1]$$
$$u(SWOP + EV) = u(SWP), \qquad [3.2]$$

where u represents a person's judgment on his own utility. Both the CV and the EV are considered positive for a benefit and negative for a disbenefit.

For program effects that are monetary transfers, the CV and EV are identical: equal for each person to the amount received or taken away. For programs of limited impact, the differences between CVs and EVs are small. A person might, for instance, be willing to pay five dollars to have litter removed from a highway. This is his CV for a litter removal program [u (unlittered highway but with five dollars less) = u(littered highway)]. We would expect that the same person would consider his own position about as good with the highway unlittered as with the highway littered and with an extra five dollars in his pocket. If so, five dollars is also his EV for the program [u (littered highway but with five dollars more) = u(unlittered highway)].

*3.10 WHEN EVs AND CVs DIFFER

For programs with larger effects, CVs and EVs diverge. For program benefits, EVs may exceed CVs and, for disbenefits, the absolute magnitudes of CVs may exceed those of EVs. A person might think the opening of the public beach near his home equivalent to a sizable gift of money—for example, $1000 (his EV). Because of limited funds, he could not, however, pay any more than his CV of $600 for the beach. Similarly, persons may be adequately compensated (in the sense of reaching their previous utility levels) for increased airport noise only with payments of $500 (their negative CV) while they could, themselves, only afford to pay $350 (their negative EV) to keep the noise at its original level.

The discrepancies between CVs and EVs loom larger when lives and limbs are involved. Even though a person may only be able to pay $20,000 to save his legs from amputation, monetary compensation to make him as well off without his legs as with may be impossible. In this case, the CV of leg-saving action is $20,000, but the EV is infinite. For programs endangering lives, the CV to potential victims may be infinitely negative.

Unfortunately, the distinction between CVs and EVs is confusing, but this is why the distinction must be made. To determine whether a pPi exists and to maintain consistency in comparing the benefits and costs of different actions, benefit-cost analysis should be uniformly based on CVs. It is often tempting, however, to take EVs as values:

(1) If a pleasure traveler is indifferent between an annual gift (perhaps a tax rebate) of $50 and having the road built, the annual value of the road to him might be taken to be $50; and

(2) if a breather would pay $75 annually to keep the road from being built, that amount might be taken as the annual value of the road's cost to him.

Each of these EVs is likely to differ from the corresponding CVs: The pleasure traveler would probably pay a little less than $50 annually to have the road; the breather would probably require more than $75 yearly to reconcile himself to it. Whenever an EV differs from a CV, it is generally to the advantage of the change being considered. To mistakenly take an EV instead of a CV as a measure of a cost or benefit is to bias the analysis in favor of the change.

*3.11 WHEN COMPENSATING VARIATIONS
CANNOT IDENTIFY THE BETTER PROGRAM

The difference between CVs and EVs may confound even more the choice between two versions, A and B, of a program. Suppose that the versions are to be directly compared and that

A is taken as a reference point. The differential impacts on persons affected are measured as compensating variations: how much persons who prefer B would pay to have B instead of A; how much persons who prefer A would have to be paid to be reconciled to having B instead of A. Suppose further that the sum of such CVs is negative but that the sum of the corresponding EVs is positive—the differences between CVs and EVs make this possible, if not common. This indicates that changing from A to B is not a potential Pareto improvement.

The definitions of CVs and EVs are such that the positive EV in considering a change from A to B is the same as a negative CV in considering a change from B to A. Similarly, a negative EV for changing from A to B is a positive CV for changing from B to A. This and the supposition that the sum of the EVs is positive for a change from A to B indicate that the sum of the CVs for a change from B to A is negative. This implies that changing from B to A is also not a potential Pareto improvement.

In such a case, the choice between programs A and B cannot be made on efficiency grounds alone (even if the decision actor were willing to overlook equity), and distributional considerations become more critical than usual. This situation is one version of the Scitovsky Paradox. (For an alternative presentation of the paradox, see Sugden and Williams, 1978.)

3.12 A METHODOLOGY FOR BENEFIT-COST ANALYSIS

The notions of compensating variations and the potential Pareto improvement make possible an eight-step methodology for performing benefit-cost analysis—a methodology considered to represent best current practice.

(1) Identifying the decisionmakers and their values. This usually consists of indicating which people are to be considered in the analysis and how heavily the effects on different persons and different types of effects are to be weighted relative to each other. Some analysts (see Rossi et al. 1979) consider the possibility of adopting a societal perspective—asking what is good for society as a whole (somehow judged) as distinct from just aggregating what every person thinks is best for himself.

(2) Identifying alternatives. This requires understanding clearly what the decision choices are. Most resources, if not used in one program, will be used in other ways in either the public or private sectors. The benefits achieved via the program should, therefore, be compared with the benefits the resources would achieve in their alternative employments. When the alternative to Program A is Program B, choice should be made using benefit-cost ratios that compare the two programs directly—rather than using ratios comparing each program to the null alternative of no program. In this case, it is critical to compare the optimal versions of each program.

(3) Identifying costs. A cost is considered to be incurred for every person who feels himself worse off due to a program. Costs may be program expenses to be ultimately paid by tax-payers, or unwelcome effects—disbenefits—of the program, or benefits lost as resources are diverted from alternative uses to the program.

(4) Identifying benefits. Every person who is better off as the result of a program is a beneficiary. Direct costs and direct benefits are usually not hard to identify (often because the bearers of direct costs will be fighting against the program and the direct beneficiaries will be fighting for it). With less direct effects, identifying potential gainers and losers becomes more difficult.

(5) Valuing effects monetarily. All identified costs and benefits should be valued as compensating variations for each person affected by the program.

(6) Discounting. All identified and valued effects occurring at different times should be discounted at the appropriate discount rate to make them commensurable. (If all effects occur at about the same time, discounting is not needed.)

(7) Taking distributional effects into account. An understanding of decisionmaker values may enable the analyst to value distributional effects numerically. If not, the analyst may have just to describe as fully as possible the range of distribu-

tional effects and to leave all value judgments on these to the decisionmaker.

(8) Aggregating and interpreting the valued effects. The various valued effects of a program can be combined in a calculation of net benefits or of a benefit-cost ratio. These figures would then have to be interpreted in the light of distributional considerations and a sense of decisionmaker values. When uncertainty is present, interpretation is aided by *sensitivity analysis:* systematically varying uncertain parameters in the analysis to see what effect they have on decision-making criteria.

3.13 A POSSIBLE NINTH STEP

Many analysts would add a ninth step to the methodology above. They would differentiate not just between considerations of efficiency and equity—as the methodology above does. They would in addition distinguish issues that can be quantified with relative ease from those that cannot be. In this perspective, the eight-step methodology would first be carried through, whereupon, as a ninth step, the results of the methodology would be reexamined in the light of difficulties in quantifying program effects.

Examples of instances for which an additional step might be needed are various.

(1) When effects are not quantified. Whenever the analyst decides to mention but not to quantify certain effects, these should be considered along with the results of the analysis in decision-making.

(2) When quantification is subject to error. The analyst who quantifies effects using either shadow prices or compensating variations may obtain questionable results. These may be due to the conceptual defects of shadow prices or to the practical shortcomings of compensating variations.

(3) When a special societal perspective is needed. Sometimes the simple aggregation of effects on individuals is not considered sufficient. This might occur because the broader effects

of programs are only considered to be properly valued from a societal viewpoint. An example might be the symbolic effect of acting to demonstrate concern for the disadvantaged. Such effects—termed "global"—will be considered further in Sections 6.5.3 through 6.5.5. Another example concerns types of consumption that society might think good or bad. Societies may view spending on education in a favorable light (therefore often termed a "merit good") and spending on alcohol in an unfavorable light. If so, they may wish to value education more highly and alcohol consumption less highly than the sum of what consumers of either product would be willing to pay for it. (Such societal adjustments to individual values might also be analyzed as external or global effects.)

There is no single, broadly accepted way to integrate such concerns into benefit-cost analysis. The eight-step methodology above presumes that they will be addressed in the eighth step: by using sensitivity analysis to understand better what possible effects these unquantified aspects or errors in their quantification might have on the overall desirability of alternative policies. If, however, the analyst or decisionmaker believes that difficult-to-quantify aspects deserve special attention, this may be achieved by explicitly setting aside a ninth step in the process for it.

3.14 THE NUMERICAL FORMULATION FOR BENEFIT-COST ANALYSIS

The main numerical parts of the methodology above come in the middle steps, 3 through 6. Steps 1 and 2 set the stage; Steps 7 and 8 bring in the distributional concerns (often impractical to do numerically) and look ahead to the policy decision. The formulation for the product of Steps 3 through 6 is succinct: Present-valued net benefits are equal to the total of all program effects—good and bad, expressed as present-valued compensating variations—summed over all persons affected by the program and over all categories of program effects. The same thing can be said in algebraic notation:

$$\text{present-valued net benefits} = \sum_{i=1}^{n} \sum_{j=1}^{m} \frac{CV_{ij}}{(1+d)^{1_{ij}}}, \qquad [3.3]$$

where

CV_{ij} is the compensating variation of the jth category of effect on the ith person,

d is the discount rate,

l_{ij} is the number of years until the ith person is affected by the jth kind of effect,

m is the number of different categories of effect (for example, effect on a person as a taxpayer, as a traveler, as a breather), and

n is the number of persons affected by the program.

If the present-valued net benefits are positive, the program is a potential Pareto improvement.

Objections may be raised to the formulation in equation 3.3 of present-valued net benefits. Compensating variations may not be additive (as equation 3.3 implicitly assumes). If a person receives a $90 CV for pleasure trips made on the road and a $60 CV as a result of consumer products being made less expensive by the road, it does not necessarily follow that the combined CV is $150; it might be a little less. Summing the CVs for the different effects on a person represents, however, the best first approximation to the combined CV. We will proceed in the sections that follow as though CVs are additive, even though this is not strictly true.

A major problem in applying equation 3.3 is the lack of agreement on the appropriate discount rate. Different persons may have different rates—due to different opportunities for investment, or to different tax positions, or to tastes. Personal discount rates may differ from the governmental rate. That the governmental rate itself is not easily determined can be seen in the variety of official rates that have been used by or suggested for the U.S. government (see Staats, 1968).

For many benefit-cost analyses, these objections are quibbles. The overall accuracy of the analyses may depend much more on accurate identification and valuation of individual effects than on the combination of CVs or the choice of the discount rate. In such cases, equation 3.3 is fully adequate to evaluate the efficiency aspects of a program.

3.15 THIS CHAPTER AND OTHER WRITINGS

This chapter follows the approach of Mishan (1976) toward benefit-cost analysis. The classic paper discussing compensating and equivalent variations is Hicks (1943). A more recent critique of alternative compensation tests used in gauging program effects is by Boadway (1974). Keeney and Raiffa (1976) present formally the conditions that justify measuring program attributes via willingness to pay. Consideration of the distributional deficiences of potential Pareto improvements is found in Little (1960). Nath (1969), Winch (1971), and Fischhoff (1977) examine the underpinnings and the implications of welfare economics and of benefit-cost analysis as currently practiced. An overview and taxonomy of different kinds of program effects are given by Haveman and Weisbrod (1977). Various options and considerations in shadow pricing are discussed by McKean (1968) and Abt (1977).

A good general book introducing and explaining benefit-cost analysis is by Sugden and Williams (1978). For a briefer introduction, see Pliskin and Taylor (1977). Comprehensive treatment of project appraisal in developing countries is the subject of books by Little and Mirrlees (1974), Roemer and Stern (1975), and Squire and van der Tak (1975). Useful collections of papers on benefit-cost analysis providing a historical perspective are edited by Dorfman (1965), Chase (1968), Haveman and Margolis (1970, 1977), Kendall (1971), Layard (1972), and Zeckhauser (1975a).

4

Identifying and Valuing
Benefits and Costs

4.1 PLAN FOR THE CHAPTER

This chapter presents Steps 3 through 6—the most numerical steps—in the benefit-cost methodology as they apply to a regional decision on building a toll road across a desert. To resolve Step 1, we assume that decisionmakers care about the impact of the road on all persons whom it affects. Step 2 is trivial: The decision alternatives boil down to building or not building the road. We will examine steps 7 and 8 in Chapter 5.

Rather than proceeding step by step through the methodology—first identifying costs, then identifying benefits, then valuing both—these three steps will be intermingled. We shall progress generally from the more direct effects—whether they be costs or benefits—to the less direct. As each effect is identified, we shall consider how it should be valued. Discounting will not play a major role in the analysis of this situation.

4.2 BUDGETED COSTS, PRESENT-VALUED

Suppose that the construction cost of the road is $16,000,000, to which $400,000 in annual maintenance must be added. To simplify matters, we assume no inflation. The road takes one year to build and maintenance expenses commence in the second year. To make these two figures commensurable, either the lump sum of $16,000,000 (a *stock,* in economic terminology) must be converted to annual payment terms or the $400,000 annual costs (a *flow*) must be interpreted as an equivalent lump sum. Commensurability may be achieved by discounting—which can translate a long stream of future maintenance costs into their present-valued lump-sum equivalent. The current rate at which the government can lend or borrow money is 10 percent—which we take as its discount rate. (Discussion of other relevant determinants of the discount rate for public projects is deferred until Section 7.3.) With this rate, we can calculate the present value of the annual payments for maintenance. With adequate maintenance, the road is expected to last indefinitely, meaning that we seek the present value of an unending stream of $400,000 payments. To calculate this value, we use the formula for the sum of an infinitely long geometric series with first term, a, and constant ratio, r, between consecutive terms in the series:

$$a + ar + ar^2 + ar^3 \ldots = \frac{a}{1-r} . \qquad [4.1]$$

(The infinite geometric series on the left only converges to the righthand expression if the absolute value of r is less than 1.0.) This formula enables us to calculate the present value of an unending stream of $400,000 payments:

$$\sum_{i=1}^{\infty} \frac{\$400,000}{(1.10)^i} = \$4,000,000. \qquad [4.2]$$

That is, to have the money in hand when construction begins to pay all future annual maintenance costs, one must have $4 million. (These calculations may be checked. The present value

of two annual $400,000 payments starting next year is
$694,215; of five such payments, $1,516,315; of 10,
$2,457,827; of 20, $3,405,426; of 50, $3,965,926; of 100,
$3,999,710; of 150, $3,999,998.)

Combining this result with the construction costs shows that
a total of $20 million ($16 million for construction plus $4
million for all future maintenance) would cover all future costs
of the road. By present-valuing the future maintenance costs,
they have been made commensurable with the construction
costs.

4.3 AMORTIZATION

Most other effects of building the road are set in annual
terms. By present valuation, they could all be made commensurable with the $16 million initial cost of construction. It
would be easier, however, if the few costs (like construction)
that are given in lump-sum terms could be translated into an
equivalent stream of equal annual payments. The mathematical
technique for doing this is *amortization*. Whereas discounting
(either present or future valuation) achieves commensurability
among stocks and flows by expressing the flows as their equivalent stocks, amortization achieves the commensurability by
expressing stocks as their equivalent flows.

To amortize the $16 million construction cost, the analyst
must express it as a stream of constant annual amounts: the
way in which most of the benefits and other costs for the road
are expressed. For example, producer surplus amounts—as we
shall soon see—to $350,000 year after year. In amortizing
construction costs, we want to find out what constant annual
cost—recurring year after year—is equivalent to one lump-sum
cost of $16 million to be paid now. When we do identify this
level of constant recurring annual payments, it can then be
compared with maintenance costs, producer surplus, and other
costs and benefits originally set in such terms.

We amortize using algebra. We label as "x" the constant
annual payment such that a whole long, indefinite stream of
such payments is equivalent to one present payment of $16

million. We know from Chapter 2 that equivalence in terms of effects on the government's money means that the present values are equal. That is, the present value of the indefinite stream of equal payments must be $16 million. This gives the algebraic equation

$$\sum_{i=1}^{\infty} \frac{x}{(1.10)^i} = \$16,000,000. \qquad [4.3]$$

This can be solved, using the formula for the sum of an infinite geometric series, to find that x is $1.6 million. Amortization thus shows that paying $16,000,000 once is equivalent for the region to paying $1,600,000 the following year and then once per year indefinitely.

The total annual cost of the road is therefore $2 million: $1.6 million annually to cover the initial construction costs and $0.4 million to pay for yearly maintenance. Taxpayers (or, equivalently, public funds) need only provide one half this amount since $1,000,000 annually is collected as tolls for the road. Considering this group only as taxpayers—neglecting that taxpayers are also travelers, consumers, producers, and others affected by the road—an annual compensating variation of $1,000,000 is needed to make them as well off with the road as without it.

4.4 CONSUMER SURPLUS

Suppose that a given traveler would make 20 trips annually on the road and that the toll is $1 per trip. To calculate how much he would benefit from the road, we must know the maximum annual amount he would be willing to pay for its use. Suppose further that the traveler would be indifferent between (1) paying $36 and making 20 trips annually and (2) not using the road. The positive compensating variation of the traveler is the most he would pay to use the road ($36) minus what he actually pays ($20), or $16. That is, with the road and a toll of $1, the traveler considers himself better off by $16 annually than without the road. Equivalently, he would be willing to pay up to $16 annually for the right to travel on the road at a toll of $1.

The amount a user would be willing to pay for a good, a service, or a right less its cost to him is *consumer surplus.* Consumer surplus is, by this definition, a positive CV. For this traveler, the annual consumer surplus would be $16. We assume that the total consumer surplus for all travelers using the road is $1,400,000 annually. Section 4.11 shows how this determination may be derived from economic analysis of the demand curve.

4.5 DOUBLE COUNTING

A recurrent danger in benefit-cost analysis is *double counting*—effectively taking the same benefit or cost into the calculations more than once. Double counting would occur if we took the annual cost of the road to be $1,000,000 (costs less tolls) and if we counted the benefits to the given traveler as $36 (the most he would pay for use of the road). This reasoning is in error for counting the toll revenues twice: once to reduce the costs to taxpayers; a second time as part of the benefit to travelers.

Another type of double counting might occur in combining the consumer surplus of travelers with the appreciated value of land. Suppose that a given house is convenient to the road and that a frequent traveler would be willing to pay $500 more for the house with the road than without it. The reason is that he would have a consumer surplus of $50 annually in using the road: even after having bought the house at the higher price, he would be willing to pay $50 each year to use the road at a toll of $1. (The present value of $50 each year indefinitely is $500.) Suppose that the road is built and that the traveler does pay $500 more for the house with the road than he would have paid without it. How should these effects be taken into account?

One line of reasoning might be that the home seller has gained $500 (indisputably) and that the buyer/traveler has a consumer surplus in using the road of $500. The total gain would then be taken to be $1,000. This logic is wrong because it has subtly double counted the value of the road to the traveler: first, as the additional money paid for the house; second, as consumer surplus. The reason the traveler paid $500 more for the house was the anticipation of the consumer surplus.

4.6 CONSISTENT ACCOUNTING

The general, correct way to avoid double counting and to account consistently all effects is to determine compensating variations for all affected persons. In this case, the seller has a positive CV of $500. The traveler/buyer has a zero CV: he loses $500 in buying the house at the higher price and gains $500 in using the road. The net gain for both people involved is $500.

Such problems in actuality are fuzzy. Some of the gains of greater convenience in general will be reaped by the seller and some by the buyer/traveler. (For example, in the case above, the buyer might have paid only $250 more for the house with the road—making both persons better off by $250.) Neither gain is easy to estimate: the first requires knowing what the selling price would have been in a hypothetical case; the second a delicate determination of how much better off a person is. The conceptual approach for consistently accounting all effects nevertheless remains clear. One considers the relevant population individual by individual and determines the compensating variations—how much better or worse off each is in money terms with a program versus without a program.

4.7 CONSUMER SURPLUS FOR GOODS

The new road facilitates shipments of goods—both those produced outside the region and consumed inside and the reverse case. Air conditioners are purchased by regional inhabitants from producers outside the region. The road, even with the toll, reduces transport costs by $10 per air-conditioning unit. The retail price in a city of the region falls from $200 to $190. Every person in the city who would have bought an air conditioner with or without the road (that is, anyone willing to pay at least $200 for an air conditioner) gains $10 (per unit) with the road. To this consumer surplus is added that of consumers willing to pay amounts between $190 and $200 for the air conditioner. The consumer surplus of the person willing to pay no more than $194 for the unit is thus (with the road) $4. The total consumer surplus in the region for air conditioners and for all other items made less expensive by the road is (let us assume) $380,000.

4.8 PRODUCER SURPLUS

Producers within the region benefit from lower transportation costs. Suppose, for instance, that farmers within the region raise sugar beets for export and that the price for beets is $2.60 per bushel in a major distribution center outside the region. Without the road, shipment costs per bushel are $0.35 for farmers in the region. With the road, the costs fall to $0.20 per bushel. Regional farmers will thus realize $2.40 per bushel net of transportation costs with the road versus $2.25 without the road. Their gain—a *producer surplus*—is $0.15 for every bushel that would have been produced with or without the road.

To this producer surplus must be added the gains from beets that can be produced for $2.40 a bushel, but not for $2.25 a bushel. Without the road, farmers can afford to devote resources up to a rate of $2.25 per bushel for beet production. With the road, they can devote resources up to $2.40 per bushel for beet farming. This means that land that will yield beets at a total resource cost of $2.35 per bushel can be converted to that crop. The producer surplus for this land will be five cents ($2.40 minus $2.35) per bushel. The total annual producer surplus for beets and for other products grown and manufactured in the region is (again, by assumption) $350,000.

4.9 EXTERNAL CONSUMER SURPLUS

Regional production of beets is such a small fraction of national production that the national price of $2.60 is not affected as additional acreage in the region is devoted to beet raising. Such is not the case for mineral water. Half of the national supply comes from springs in the region. The national price of this water is $5.50 per bottle. When the road lowers transportation costs by $0.40 per bottle, the national price drops to $5.20 a bottle. Effectively, the national consumer has gained $0.30 of the $0.40-per-bottle saving and the producer the other $0.10. Such gains to consumers outside the region for all regional products whose cost is lowered by the road come to an annual consumer surplus of $250,000. The producer surplus on such products has been included in the figure of $350,000 given above.

4.10 LOSERS

While consumers and producers gain from lower transportation charges, the air cargo industry loses. Gross revenues are down by $2,300,000 annually with the road. However, this overstates the true loss since, with lower demand, the industry now has lower overhead expenses, cuts its annual spending on fuel and maintenance, lays off employees, and sells its equipment. Nevertheless, the net loss to the industry is substantial. Profits associated with the revenue drop are wholly lost, laid-off workers may have to take less remunerative and less pleasant jobs, equipment may have to be sold off at a loss. For owners and workers in the industry, the negative compensating variation resulting from the road amounts annually to $310,000.

Other persons made worse off by the road are producers who receive lower prices because the road lowers the transportation charges for their competitors. For instance, any local producer of air conditioners makes $10 less per unit with the road. Similarly, producers of mineral water outside the region are hurt as they make $0.30 less per bottle. Total producer losses of this nature are $90,000 annually.

*4.11 GRAPHICAL DEPICTION OF CONSUMER SURPLUS

Calculation of consumer surplus, producer surplus, and producer loss can be illustrated and calculated by referring to

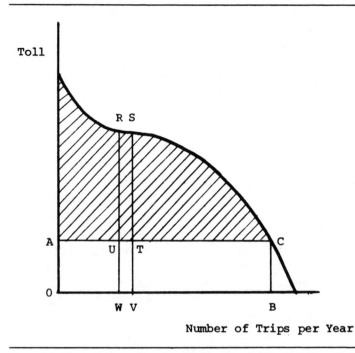

Figure 4.1: Demand Curve Showing the Number of Trips Taken at Various Toll Levels

The shaded area represents consumer surplus at the actual toll level.

demand curves and supply curves. Figure 4.1 depicts the demand curve for travelers using the toll road. For each possible toll on the vertical axis, the demand curve indicates how many trips would be taken at that toll. With the toll level set at OA—equal, for example, to $1—one reads off the curve that a total of OB (equal to 1,000,000) pleasure trips would be taken each year.

The trips generate annual toll revenues of $1,000,000: OA multiplied by OB which gives the area of rectangle OACB. But almost all the trips made are worth more than $1 apiece to the travelers themselves. This can be seen by visualizing the trips as lined up on the horizontal axis. Those that would be made at the highest toll are closest to the origin; the less a traveler would pay to make a given trip, the farther it is from the origin. A thin vertical segment of the demand curve—for instance, the near-trapezoid RSVW—then represents the trips (WV in number) that would be taken at a toll of SV but not at a toll of RW.

Suppose that SV is $3.40 and RW is $3.41. SV and RW intersect AC—the line representing a toll of $1.00—at T and U, respectively. Consumer surplus for each trip designated by segment WV is between $2.40 (the length of ST) and $2.41 (RU). Total consumer surplus for all trips on WV is therefore roughly WV (the number of trips) times $2.405 (the approximate average consumer surplus for these trips) which is roughly the area of the near-trapezoid RSTU (a near-trapezoid because the demand curve need not be perfectly straight between R and S). Total consumer surplus at a toll of $1.00 is the area of a sequence of vertical trapezoids like RSTU lined up along segment AC. The area of all the trapezoids is the shaded area right of the vertical axis, below the demand curve and above the horizontal line (AUTC) showing the actual toll level. This is the general graphical representation of consumer surplus: area beneath the demand curve but above the price line.

This representation of consumer surplus is inaccurate when income effects are present: when paying a high price for the first unit of a good reduces the amounts one would pay for subsequent units. For instance, if one would buy one car at a $13,000 price and two at $5,000, one might not, having bought a first car at $13,000, pay $5,000 for a second. The income effect is not likely to be large in the case of tolls. Travelers represented at different points on the curve—for example, at $4.00 and $2.00—are unlikely to alter the amounts they would pay for the $2.00 trips just because they were charged $4.00 for the others. Willig (1976) shows that income effects in most instances are not large enough to worry about. The representation in Figure 4.1 may also be inaccurate if consumers care about congestion. A traveler willing to pay a $7.00 toll might not get a $5.00 consumer surplus at a toll of $2.00 because increased use of the road diminishes its value to him.

*4.12 CONSUMER SURPLUS FOR A TRANSPORTED GOOD

We consider now refrigerators manufactured at one end of the road and consumed at the other. The supply and demand curves for refrigerators are shown in Figure 4.2. At an initial unit transportation price of BE (=GJ), BJ units would be produced and sold. Producers would realize price OB per unit and consumers would pay price OE. At this price, taking transport costs into account, supply equals demand.

When the road lowers transportation costs from BE to CD, an additional IL (=HK) units will be produced and sold. The price for producers (how much money they receive for each unit) rises to OC and for consumers falls to OD. Consumer surplus under the higher price was the near-triangle EFG. With the lower price, consumer surplus grows to near-triangle DFK. The difference is the trapezoidal figure DEGK which represents consumer gain (increase in consumer surplus) due to the road. This gain is composed of that realized by consumers who would have bought refrigerators at the higher price (rectangle DEGH) plus gains to persons who would only purchase refrigerators at the lower price (triangle GHK).

*4.13 PRODUCER SURPLUS FOR A TRANSPORTED GOOD

Producer surplus for the refrigerators grows from near-triangle ABJ at the higher transport cost to near-triangle ACL as transport costs are lowered. The difference is trapezoid BCLJ—the gain to producers. Like consumer gain, the producer gain can be partitioned into that realized on all units that would have been sold at the higher transport cost (rectangle BCIJ) plus that associated with increased production (triangle ILJ). (That total producer surplus is the area right of the vertical axis, below the line of price realized by producers, and above the supply curve can be shown by reasoning parallel to that used in identifying the total consumer surplus.)

The increase in producer surplus is partly higher profits and partly increased payments to the factors of production. Wages,

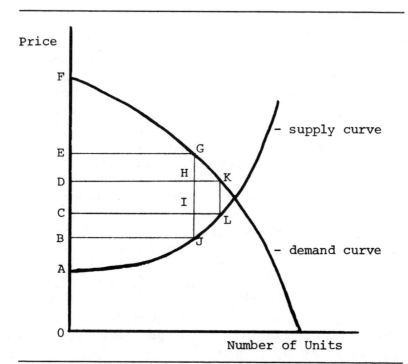

Figure 4.2: Demand and Supply Curves Indicating Consumer and Producer Surplus for a Transported Good

for instance, may have to rise to attract the additional workers needed to increase production. Workers previously employed may demand parity and would thus realize a portion of the gain represented by rectangle BCIJ. The prices on equipment and facilities (whether purchased or rented) may similarly rise with the implication that part of the increment in producer surplus would accrue to these suppliers and renters. In determining whether the road is a potential Pareto improvement, we need not identify the ultimate gainers. It suffices to know that the total gain to all parties engaged in producing refrigerators is given by trapezoid BCLJ.

*4.14 PRODUCER LOSS

The air cargo industry loses revenues with the construction of the road. The seriousness of this loss can be seen by referring to

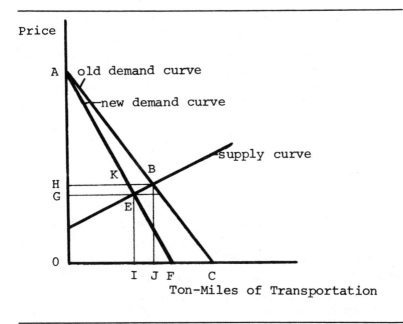

Figure 4.3: Disbenefits to Industries for which Demand Drops

its supply curve and its old and new demand curves. These are shown in Figure 4.3.

The new road reduces demand for air transport from curve ABC to curve AKEF. This brings about a drop in the price of air cargo from OH to OG and in ton-miles contracted for from OJ to OI. The decrease in revenues is the difference between rectangles OHBJ and OGEI. This is the irregular concave hexagon GHBJIE which may be analyzed in three parts: trapezoid EBJI, trapezoid HKEG, and triangle KBE. The first of these represents (theoretically, at least) no loss to the air cargo industry. This is the amount of revenues the extra capacity needed to increase ton-mile volume from OI to OJ would have earned in other employment. With the drop in demand, the resources should return to their alternative uses and once again earn revenue equal to trapezoid EBJI.

The loss in producer surplus is trapezoid HBEG—the negative counterpart of trapezoid BCLJ in Figure 4.2. If the wages or hours of air cargo workers are cut (demand for them drops), they will bear part of the loss. This loss to the air cargo industry is balanced by a corresponding amount of gain to the users of air cargo. These users include consumers who get an increased consumer surplus and producers whose producer surplus rises. The gain to all those using air cargo transport after construction of the road is trapezoid HKEG. Triangle KBE represents the gain to all those who would use air cargo transport at a price of OH if there were no road but who switch to using the road instead. These users have additional gain that would appear as consumer surplus in a diagram depicting the total demand (demand of producer users and of travelers) for the road.

We see thus that followers of the Kaldor-Hicks criterion would not be interested in Figure 4.3. The loss to the air cargo industry is for them canceled by the corresponding gain to their customers and potential customers. These effects do not influence whether the road is a potential Pareto improvement. If only economic efficiency is a concern, Figure 4.3 is irrelevant. If, however, distributional equity is considered important, then the benefit-cost analyst will want to use such figures to measure the disbenefit to the air cargo industry.

*4.15 DIFFICULTIES IN REDIRECTING RESOURCES

The flatter the supply curve, the greater is the proportion of revenue losses recouped by turning resources to other uses (the greater is trapezoid EBJI in contrast to trapezoid HBEG). This theoretical finding may, however, overlook the irreversibility of resource commitment. The supply curve may be flat because additional resources cost little more than initial resources—the hundredth plane purchased having a price little higher (lower, with volume discounts) than the first. However, if the plane may not be used or sold for alternative purposes, then the revenue loss represented by trapezoid EBJI will not be recouped. Warehousing too may be hard to turn to alternate uses. A vacant warehouse may at a loss be converted into a hockey rink, razed, or held until demand grows. In such cases, focusing theoretically on lost producer surplus is insufficient. To determine the negative compensating variation, one must recognize that the area beneath the demand curve (trapezoid

EBJI) may not reflect the difficulties and costs encountered in shifting resources to other uses.

4.16 THE CONSTRUCTION INDUSTRY

If the road is not built, the construction firm that would build and maintain it would undertake a variety of smaller projects. The bid submitted for the road work would yield the firm $90,000 more in annual profits than its alternatives. In order to muster the manpower to build the road, construction wages must be raised from $4.00 per hour to $4.20 per hour. Those workers who would be in the industry whether or not the road is built gain $0.20 per hour. The brewery worker who would be indifferent between that job and construction at a wage of $4.13 per hour would switch jobs and gain a positive compensating variation of $0.07 per hour. The former construction worker who would come out of retirement for any construction wage above $4.13 per hour gains the same amount. The total positive compensating variations for construction workers are $110,000 annually. Owners and workers in the construction industry (those who would be in it if the road is built) thus would gain a yearly total of $200,000. (This figure represents many lump-sum gains realized only in the year of construction that have been amortized into gains occurring every year so as to be commensurable with the other effects of the road.)

4.17 LAND VALUATION

When the road is built, land convenient to it appreciates. A barren desert tract, for instance, becomes an ideal site for a restaurant. Its value then jumps from $5,000 to $50,000—a gain realized by the owner of the land at the time of the decision to build the road. The entrepreneur who buys the land realizes as a compensating variation gain only $10,000 annually. This is the difference between the profits realized with the restaurant and those he would have obtained if, without the road, he had taken his capital and energy elsewhere.

Land that can produce beets at a resource cost of less than $2.40 per bushel grows in value with construction of the road. If this land was already owned by the potential beet farmer (though perhaps used for other purposes) the gain is all his. If the farmer buys or rents this farm from another landowner, the breakdown of the gain depends on the bargaining abilities of the two. Land converted to beet farming is essentially bid away from other uses. The amount paid for the land must at least equal the return obtained by the land in its alternative employment.

For this problem, all compensating variations gained by producers have been included in the producer surplus. All gains by landowners who rent or sell their land to producers or consumers are considered land appreciation gains: They amount to $4,500,000. Expressed in annual terms (that is, amortizing), they are equivalent to a yearly gain of $450,000.

When a popular restaurant is established on the new road, other restaurants lose business. The land that restaurant entrepreneurs and home purchasers might have coveted in the absence of the road loses value. The total annual amount of loss to the owners of these properties is $170,000.

4.18 CONSUMER SURPLUS AND DOUBLE COUNTING

Many of the effects we have been considering would show up in the estimated total consumer surplus for the road. Sloppy thinking could lead to double counting of effects in several ways:

(1) Land value. People may pay more for land due to anticipated consumer surplus. This—as discussed in Sections 4.5 and 4.6—should not be counted twice.

(2) Consumer surplus for goods and producer surplus. The total demand curve for the road includes that of individual travelers and of goods transporters. We have above considered only the former component in estimating the consumer surplus for travel. The total demand curve could be used as the basis for

calculating consumer surplus—in which case the maximal tolls that the goods transporters could pay would be included. These tolls, however, would reflect the amounts of consumer surplus for goods and producer surplus realized by consumers and producers at various toll levels. It would be double counting to calculate total consumer surplus in this way and also to include consumer surplus for goods and producer surplus.

(3) Consumer surplus for the restaurant. A consumer surplus would be associated with the restaurant. The same consumer surplus would, however, be associated with the use of the road. People pay to use the road to get to the restaurant—a fact reflected in the demand curve for the road. This consumer surplus should not be counted twice—as demand for the restaurant and for the road.

*4.19 ALTERNATIVE APPROACHES

Examining the total demand curve for the road would lead to appropriate calculation of the net effects on traveler consumer surplus, consumer surplus for goods (inside and outside the region), producer surplus and loss, the restaurateur's gain, and appreciation and depreciation of land and business. Why not then, one might ask, simply examine the total demand curve for the road instead of considering separately the various effects as we have done?

First, the decisionmakers may be interested in distributional effects. It may not suffice for them to know that what the air cargo industry loses their customers gain. They may want to know how much the industry loses.

Second, the total demand curve is not immediately known. Rather, it is estimated by aggregating the effects we have considered separately: how much consumer surplus for goods there would be, how much people would be willing to pay to live near the road, to use its restaurant, and the like. We have to examine the separate effects in order to get a notion of the total demand curve.

4.20 EXTERNALITIES

An Indian community near the road does not travel and will not sell or move from its land (even though the land appreciates with the road). The main effect of the road to the community is the pollution caused by vehicle exhaust. We suppose that the Indians consider this annoyance equivalent to an annual negative compensating variation of $190,000.

The incidental impact of an action in the private sector on persons with no decision control over it is termed an *external effect* or *externality*. Externalities are also known as side-effects, spillovers, or neighborhood effects. The concept of the externality is clearest in the case of private actions (your neighbor paints his house, making you better off), where the term originated. Indirect effects—such as the loss of business to previously existing restaurants—have also been considered externalities. The critical aspect of externalities in the private sector is that one unit (person or firm), in doing what is best for itself, influences the well-being of others—a consideration that it has no incentive to heed.

In public decisions, the concept of an externality is murkier. For even the most direct consequences, those affected (such primary beneficiaries as road travelers) may not be consulted and may thus feel that they have no control over the decision. On the other hand, a responsible sensitive government may well decide to measure and to take into account the most indirect and subtle effects of its actions. We will take externalities in the public sector to be the incidental or secondary effects of public actions. These often occur as effects on the environment.

4.21 THIS CHAPTER AND OTHER WRITINGS

The main concepts in this chapter—measurement of program effects as consumer surplus and producer surplus, avoidance of double counting, externalities—are to be found in most texts on benefit-cost analysis. Particularly recommended are Mishan (1976) and Sugden and Williams (1978). Standard microeconomic treatment of these themes is to be found in Scitovsky (1971) and Mansfield (1975). Mishan (1971b) reviews current concepts in dealing with externalities.

5

Interpreting Benefit-Cost Calculations

5.1 PLAN FOR THE CHAPTER

It is often taken on faith that benefits and costs, once they have been calculated (as in Chapter 4), are easy to use in decision-making. However, the number of mistakes and misconceptions occurring in interpreting benefit-cost calculations for decision-making is vast. In the simplest situations, either the difference or the quotient (ratio) of benefits and costs may be an adequate basis for decision. When true alternatives (recognizing, for instance, what would be done with the resources if not spent on one program) are identified, complications ensue. Sometimes the differences, sometimes the quotients are good decision guides; sometimes neither are. The first part of the chapter, Sections 5.2 to 5.10, considers simple ways of using benefit-cost figures in decision-making and points out their pitfalls.

In Sections 5.11 to 5.18, the different ways of combining estimates of benefits and costs into benefit-cost ratios are examined. Only recently have analysts recognized the possibility that alternative, reasonably justified, ratios can be derived for the same project. The different numbers obtained can lead to different decisions. We will consider the arguments for focusing on each of our main ratios and see that the inclusion or exclusion of certain program effects in the ratios may depend on discretionary value judgments of decisionmakers. Section 5.19 shows how uncertainty regarding some elements in the benefit-cost ratio can be reflected using sensitivity analysis.

Finally, in Sections 5.20 to 5.23, we consider general, recommended ways to use benefit-cost numbers in decision-making. These procedures avoid the pitfalls seen in Sections 5.2 through 5.5.

5.2 NET BENEFITS AND THE BENEFIT-COST RATIO

Benefits and costs associated with road construction are laid out in Table 5.1. While Chapter 4 discussed the derivation of these figures, here we will look into how they should be combined and interpreted for decision-making.

A common tack is to denote the sum of the positive compensating variations (benefits) as "B" and the sum of all negative CVs (costs) as "C." Table 5.1 shows that B is $4.04 million and that C is $2.76 million. Net benefits are then defined as

$$B - C \qquad\qquad [5.1]$$

and the benefit-cost ratio as

$$B \div C. \qquad\qquad [5.2]$$

(We shall see below that other formulations of the benefit-cost ratio are possible, but restrict ourselves for the moment to this one.) In the present example,

$$
\begin{aligned}
B - C \quad &= \$4.04 \text{ million} - \$2.76 \text{ million} \\
&= \$1.28 \text{ million, and} \qquad\qquad\qquad [5.3]
\end{aligned}
$$

$$
\begin{aligned}
B \div C \quad &= \$4.04 \text{ million} \div \$2.76 \text{ million} \\
&= 1.46. \qquad\qquad\qquad\qquad\qquad [5.4]
\end{aligned}
$$

TABLE 5.1 Comparison of Gains and Losses for Road Construction in Annual Terms

Effects	Accruing to	Annual Amount of Gains	Losses
Cost of construction and upkeep	Taxpayers		$2,000,000
Toll revenues	Taxpayers	$1,000,000	
Consumer surplus for travel	Travelers	1,400,000	
Consumer surplus for goods	Consumers in region	380,000	
Producer surplus	Producers	350,000	
Consumer surplus for goods	Consumers outside of region	250,000	
Loss of transporters	Air cargo industry		310,000
Producer loss	Producers		90,000
Gain of constructors	Construction industry	200,000	
Restaurant bonus	Restaurateur	10,000	
Land appreciation	Lucky landowners	450,000	
Land and business depreciation	Unlucky owners		170,000
Pollution	Indian breathers		190,000
Total	All affected persons	$4,040,000	$2,760,000

The more or less standard rules for using these figures are that

(1) for choices between spending resources on a program and not doing so (the "go-no-go" decisions), the program should be enacted if and only if net benefits are positive, which occurs precisely when the benefit-cost ratio exceeds 1.0; and

(2) for choices among mutually exclusive, competing programs, that with the highest net benefits is to be preferred.

The first rule may be applied for the decision on building the road. This rule is based on the Kaldor-Hicks criterion: that programs that are potential Pareto improvements should be enacted. Both the net benefits of $1.28 million and the benefit-cost ratio of 1.46 indicate that the road is a potential Pareto improvement: The gainers due to the road could hypothetically compensate the losers in such a way that, after compensation, there would still be net gainers but no net losers. On efficiency grounds, it is better to build the road than not to.

5.3 WHEN NET BENEFITS ARE A GOOD GUIDE

A modified decision situation illustrates the second rule. Suppose that a choice is to be made among three different (and mutually exclusive) versions for the road as shown in Table 5.2. Which version of the road is best?

Focusing only on the benefit-cost ratios, the third version of the road appears best. Its benefit-cost ratio of 1.50 is higher than those for Versions 1 and 2. Version 3 might be argued for on the grounds that it brings the greatest return for the resource allocations: $1.50 in benefits for each dollar spent.

That this reasoning may be specious is seen by comparing Versions 1 and 3. By spending another $560,000 under Version 1, a further $740,000 in benefits are received in comparison with Version 3. This indicates that Version 1 is, with respect to Version 3, a potential Pareto improvement: Those who gain by having 1 instead of 3 could fully compensate those who lose and be better off in the end by $180,000. The same reasoning shows Version 2—that with the worst benefit-cost ratio—to be better than Version 1, and, hence, the best of the three. In general, we find that any project version with greater net benefits than another is a potential Pareto improvement with respect to the other—arguing that maximizing net benefits should guide decision-making.

5.4 THE BENEFIT-COST RATIO: PROBLEMS AND ALTERNATIVES

The disadvantage of the benefit-cost ratio is that it effectively compares possible projects to the null alternative of doing nothing (somewhat like trying to compare the best two teams in the league by seeing how well they did against the worst team). A better and generally more reliable analytic technique is to compare best alternatives directly (have the two best teams play each other).

TABLE 5.2 Comparing Net Benefits and the Benefit-Cost Ratio for
Mutually Exclusive Projects

Road Version	Benefits (= Gains)	Costs (= Losses)	Net Benefits	Benefit-Cost Ratio
1	$4,040,000	$2,760,000	$1,280,000	1.46
2	5,000,000	3,500,000	1,500,000	1.43
3	3,300,000	2,200,000	1,100,000	1.50

Unfortunately, this is unwieldy: To select one project from
among n possible projects, it is necessary to make n-1 comparisons. This problem would be avoided if there was an objective
function reflecting all concerns of the decision actor. We would
then simply select the project rated highest by the objective
function without having to compare each project against at least
one other. Both the benefit-cost ratio and net benefits have
been taken as objective functions. We have seen, however, above
that the benefit-cost ratio is an imperfect objective function;
indeed that, in our example, the project with the worst benefit-
cost ratio was truly best. We will soon see that net benefits, too,
are an imperfect objective function.

5.5 WHEN THE BENEFIT-COST RATIO
IS A GOOD GUIDE

We consider now the problem of a department of public
works which must allocate its annual budget of $5,000,000
among a group of proposed projects (such as improving parks,
widening roads, and installing sidewalks) which have been prospectively evaluated as shown in Table 5.3. There are 26 possible projects labeled A through Z, of which only five are shown.
How should the department decide which to undertake?

Reasonable decisions may here be based on the benefit-cost
ratios. One should first choose the project with the highest
ratio, then that with the next highest ratio, and so on until the
budget is fully allocated. (Since this decision rule might not
exactly exhaust the budget, one might choose to spend slightly
less or more than the budget or to try variations on the last few
projects chosen so as to meet the budget limit better.) The five

TABLE 5.3   Comparing Net Benefits and the Benefit-Cost Ratio in
            Choosing a Group of Projects

Project	Benefits	Costs	Net Benefits	Benefit-Cost Ratio
A	$ 420,000	$ 300,000	$120,000	1.4
B	1,350,000	1,000,000	350,000	1.35
C	350,000	200,000	150,000	1.75
D	900,000	600,000	300,000	1.5
.	.	.	.	.
.	.	.	.	.
Z	640,000	400,000	240,000	1.6

projects shown would thus be chosen in the order C, Z, D, A, B. The project with highest net benefits (B) would be the last chosen of the five and hence the least likely to be included on the list of projects selected for implementation. This occurs because we are choosing projects to maximize the benefits per dollar of cost. Project C secures $1.75 of benefits per dollar of cost, whereas with B a dollar of costs returns only $1.35 in benefits. This decision process—which focuses on benefit-cost ratios—concludes with that roster of projects yielding highest total benefits for total costs of $5,000,000. This roster, of all possible rosters of projects, consequently will have both the highest benefit-cost ratio and the highest level of net benefits. In similar decision situations, benefit-cost ratios have been useful in selecting projects for the U.S. Corps of Engineers.

5.6 WHEN NEITHER NET BENEFITS NOR THE BENEFIT-COST RATIO WILL DO

The types of reasoning used in these two examples are now reasonably well understood.[1] This logic fails, however, when program funds, if not spent on one program, can go to others with positive benefit-cost ratios. This means that the funds have "opportunity costs"—a concept to be considered in more detail in Sections 6.4.2 through 6.4.8. This situation is not well understood or even widely recognized.

Suppose that any funds not spent on one project could be allocated to other projects with benefit-cost ratios of 1.4.

---

[1] They are, for instance, well explained in Stokey and Zeckhauser (1978). They do not broach in this context the question of the opportunity costs of public funds.

Assume further that the projects under consideration have no disbenefits for private persons and that all costs in question are budgetary. Choice must be made among three project versions: P, Q, and R. One and only one version is to be chosen. The versions have been prospectively evaluated with the results shown in Table 5.4. Should choice be made according to the benefit-cost ratio (in which case R would be preferred) or according to net benefits (in which case, Q would be preferred), or by some other mode of analysis?

We first note that, since all projects have benefit-cost ratios larger than those for alternate uses of the money (that is, greater than 1.4), one of them should be funded. We discover which of the three is best by comparing the alternatives directly. We first compare P and Q to see what is obtained for the additional costs of Q. Version Q costs $100,000 more than P and yields $125,000 in additional benefits. The benefit-cost ratio for the difference between the programs is 1.25: For the $100,000 spent to get Q instead of P, an average of $1.25 in benefits is secured for every $1.00 in additional cost. But this $100,000 could have been spent on projects with benefit-cost ratios of 1.4—thus earning total benefits of $140,000. In the choice between P and Q, it is best to implement P and to spend the $100,000 that might have gone to Q on other projects.

Comparing P and R, we see that the $100,000 spent on P above and beyond the costs of R would yield an additional $150,000 ($800,000 - $650,000) in benefits. The benefit-cost ratio for these monies is thus 1.5—indicating that one can get $0.10 more in benefits per dollar of this money by using it to get P instead of R than by implementing R and allocating the $100,000 to other projects. Project Version P is thus better than both Q and R—even though Q offered greater net benefits and R a better benefit-cost ratio. We found this by focusing on the most relevant benefit-cost ratios—those on the differences between the projects.

5.7 SOLUTION USING AN OBJECTIVE FUNCTION

The problem could alternatively have been solved by introducing an objective function. This function would treat program costs as their opportunity costs in terms of benefits

TABLE 5.4   Seeking the Best Project Version when Public Funds Have
            Opportunity Costs

Project Version	Benefits	Costs	Net Benefits	Benefit-Cost Ratio
P	$800,000	$500,000	$300,000	1.6
Q	925,000	600,000	325,000	1.54
R	650,000	400,000	250,000	1.625

forgone. That is, each dollar of costs would be treated as
equivalent to the $1.40 of benefits it would achieve if not spent
on P, Q, or R. The objective function (O.F.), for each program
version, subtracts 1.4 times the costs from the benefits. The
objective function valuations of the versions are:

O.F. (P) = $800,000 - (1.4) ($500,000) = $100,000;

O.F. (Q) = $925,000 - (1.4) ($600,000) = $ 85,000; and

O.F. (R) = $650,000 - (1.4) ($400,000) = $ 90,000.   [5.5]

We see, as before, that P is best and further that R is better than
Q (which could have been found by comparing the two
directly).

5.8 SUMMARY: BENEFIT-COST GUIDANCE FOR DECISIONS

The conclusions drawn from these examples are shown in
Table 5.5. At times, depending on the circumstances, either net
benefits or the benefit-cost ratio is an appropriate decision
criterion; at other times, either figure but not the other will
serve; at still other times, neither is appropriate.

The table and the example on which it is based indicate the
difficulties in using either net benefits or the benefit-cost ratio
as the decision criterion. Benefit-cost ratios are deceptive in
choosing among project versions in that they capture the differences between each version and the null alternative of doing
nothing. More valuable would be benefit-cost ratios depicting
the differences between the most reasonable alternatives. Net
benefits mislead because they often implicitly misstate the
opportunity costs of resources. The true cost of mounting a
project is not just its budgeted monies but whatever benefits
would otherwise have been obtained with the resources it uses.

TABLE 5.5   Conditions under which Various Decision Criteria
Based on Benefit-Cost Analyses are Appropriate

Decision Conditions	Appropriate Decision Criterion: $B - C$ or $B \div C$
Go-no-go decision presuming that potential Pareto improvements (other things being equal) are good	either
Decision on mutually exclusive alternate project versions presuming that potential Pareto improvements are good	$B - C$
Decision on projects to complete a roster of fixed total budget size	$B \div C$
Decision on alternate project versions presuming that all unspent monies can go to other projects (otherwise unfunded) with net benefits	neither

When completing a roster of projects, the opportunity costs of one project are the benefits not realized by other projects because they no longer can be funded.

5.9 ALTERNATIVE ANALYTIC APPROACHES

The shortcomings of net benefits ($B - C$) and the benefit-cost ratio ($B \div C$) as decision guides raise questions of how analysis generally should proceed after benefits and costs have been calculated. Several approaches are possible.

(1) Categorizing the decisions. By first identifying the type of decision (asking, for instance, whether it is go-no-go, or whether the projects considered are mutually exclusive, or whether opportunity costs are important), one can determine whether $B - C$ and/or $B \div C$ should be taken into account. This unfortunately may require a complicated set of rules for determining when either $B - C$ or $B \div C$ should be calculated and is of limited help when neither $B - C$ nor $B \div C$ is an appropriate guide.

(2) Referring to an objective function. Objective function ratings of the benefits and costs will tell which decision alternative is best. This approach might be useful for many decisions to

be guided by the same considerations, but, in general, the different concerns require that different objective functions be set up for each decision. Formulating an objective function is usually an arduous and sensitive task not worth the effort for a single decision.

(3) Comparing alternatives directly. The best simple rule for decision-making is to compare competing alternatives directly. That is, if each of two mutually exclusive programs is better than no program, the differences between the two (for example, how much additional cost gains how much additional benefits) should be examined. This avoids the misleading aspects of $B \div C$ that come from having the null, do-nothing alternative as the implicit reference point. Benefit-cost ratios on differences between projects can enable useful comparisons with opportunity costs of the resources. The technique of comparing best alternatives directly was basically what we followed in the previous sections in pointing out the problems with $B - C$ and $B \div C$.

(4) Analyzing marginal differences. A common variant in economics of comparing alternatives directly is analyzing marginal differences. Best modifications of a program (including determination of optimal budget size) can be found by analyzing marginal differences: A marginal change is good if the benefits at the margin outweigh the marginal costs (opportunity costs being taken into account).

(5) Using a more general decision rule. We will present in Sections 5.20 to 5.23 below a more general decision rule for project selection after calculating benefits and costs. This rule requires some categorization of alternative programs (for instance, whether or not they are mutually exclusive) in focusing on the overall objective of achieving maximum benefits for the total budgetary outlay. The rule yields decisions consistent with those obtained by comparing alternatives directly or by analyzing marginal differences.

(6) Not combining the separate benefits and costs. When the analyst is unsure about the values of the decision actor, he may do best just to report his best estimates of the various benefits

and costs (collapsing only those that are clearly commensurable) and to leave the assignment of values for the benefits and costs to the decisionmaker.

5.10 WHEN THE AGGREGATION OF EFFECTS BREAKS DOWN

It is tempting for benefit-cost analysts to focus on net benefits which, if positive, indicate that the program evaluated is a potential Pareto improvement. This attitude presumes that positive compensating variations cancel out negative compensating variations of the same size. If the hypothetical redistributions needed to change a potential Pareto improvement into a Pareto improvement actually took place, no quarrel could be made with this position. Without these redistributions, however, we cannot assume that, for instance, a $5,000 gain to a landowner cancels out a $5,000 loss to a trucker (although we could if the same person filled both roles).

Without the redistribution, a decisionmaker might value differently each of the 13 categories of benefit and cost (cost to taxpayers, toll revenues, traveler consumer surplus, and so on) shown in Table 5.1. The analyst may know how each is valued: for instance, that a dollar of traveler consumer surplus is considered equivalent to $0.85 of toll revenue, that a dollar loss in compensating variation to truckers is as bad as a $1.15 drop in tolls, or that a dollar of land appreciation is thought equal to $0.55 of toll revenue. With such information, the analyst could construct an objective function [for example, O.F. (road) = toll revenues, plus 0.85 of traveler consumer surplus, minus 1.15 times the loss to truckers, plus 0.55 of land appreciation, and so on]. Without such information, the analyst may do best simply to transmit Table 5.1 in its entirety to the decisionmakers.

5.11 REDUCING THE NUMBER OF PROGRAM ATTRIBUTES

The latter solution brings us back to the full multi-attribute decision problem. All the analyst does is describe effects along 13 dimensions, leaving the difficult problem of valuation to the decisionmaker. The analyst can transmit a tidier package if he can reduce the number of dimensions—for instance, by deciding that consumer surplus for travel and for goods are equally important and thus lumping them together. An ideal number of dimensions to reduce the problem to is two: One dimension should then show a net good effect (benefits), the other a net bad effect (costs). Dividing the benefits by the costs will then achieve

the goal of the benefit-cost ratio: concisely comparing what one pays with what one gets in return.

We shall see later that this is also the goal of the cost-effectiveness ratio. Ratios with three or more terms cannot present as clear a distinction between what is paid and what is received as can a two-term ratio.

The best way to reduce many dimensions of program effects to two dimensions has not been agreed on. We will, continuing with the example of road-building, consider arguments for alternative ways of doing this. We first classify the 13 dimensions of effect shown in Table 5.1 into four groups depending on whether the effect is a gain or a loss and on whether its impact is on governmental funds or on private persons. The four groups of effects—private gain (PRG), private loss (PRL), public gain (PUG), and public loss (PUL)—are shown in Table 5.6.

5.12 ALTERNATIVE BENEFIT-COST RATIOS

A long-running controversy in benefit-cost analysis (see, for example, Feldstein, 1972) concerns whether a private loss (PRL) should be thought of as a negative benefit (in which case, it should be subtracted from other benefits in the numerator of the benefit-cost ratio) or as an added cost (in which case, it should be added to other costs in the denominator). Numerically, this choice makes a difference in the size of the ratio—even though it does not affect the calculation of net benefits. Similarly, it is not clear whether public gains (PUG) should be added to the numerator or subtracted from the denominator of the benefit-cost ratio. This choice, too, makes a numerical difference.

In the four sections that follow, we consider the alternative benefit-cost ratios that result depending on how these choices

TABLE 5.6   Breakdown of Effects of Road Building Project into Four
              Main Groups

Private Gain (PRG)

Traveler consumer surplus	$1,400,000
Internal consumer surplus for goods	380,000
Producer surplus	350,000
External consumer surplus for goods	250,000
Constructor gain	200,000
Restaurateur's gain	10,000
Land appreciation	450,000
Total Private Gain	**$3,040,000**

Private Loss (PRL)

Transporter loss	$ 310,000
Producer loss	90,000
Land depreciation	170,000
Pollution	190,000
Total Private Loss	**$ 760,000**

Public Gain (PUG)

Toll revenues	$1,000,000

Public Loss (PUL)

Costs	$2,000,000

are made. We will argue for one specific version of the ratio—
while recognizing that cases can be made for other versions.

5.13 THE GAIN-LOSS RATIO

One straightforward calculation of a benefit-cost ratio is
obtained by dividing private and public gains by private and
public losses. This we term the *gain-loss* benefit-cost ratio and
compute (in million-dollar units) as

$$\text{Gain-Loss } B \div C = \frac{PRG + PUG}{PRL + PUL}$$
$$= \frac{3.04 + 1.0}{0.76 + 2.0} = 1.46. \qquad [5.6]$$

The justification for focusing on the gain-loss ratio is the sense
that the most important differences between the various effects
is whether they are gains or losses. Societies often take the
attitude that private losses hurt more than private gains help: A
program benefiting one man by $100 and hurting another in

similar financial status by the same amount is not equivalent to no program. Society may be more concerned with the $100 injury—both for the injury per se and for the unfairness it represents—than it is pleased by the $100 gain. With all gains valued equally and all losses valued equally, one might determine the amount of gain necessary (other things being equal) to cancel $1 of loss. Projects with gain-loss benefit-cost ratios greater than this number should be funded; those with smaller gain-loss ratios should not be.

Societies, on the other hand, may adopt the Kaldor-Hicks perspective—assuming that gains and losses even out over different people and different programs and thus tend to cancel one another. In this case, the societies only care whether the gain-loss ratio exceeds 1.0—which happens precisely when there are net benefits (indicating that the Kaldor-Hicks criterion has been met).

5.14 THE CONSOLIDATED RATIO

The gain-loss ratio is most meaningful when only net gains are considered for each individual. A person who gains $10 annually as a consumer and who loses $7 as compensating variation for breathing polluted air ought to enter the calculations only as a net gainer of $3. The benefit-cost ratio figured by including individuals and governments only as net gainers or losers is the *consolidated* benefit-cost ratio. In determining whether a program has net benefits (is a potential Pareto improvement) it does not matter if one person straddles many categories of effect. The benefit-cost ratio will, however, be affected if the gains and losses of an individual appear in both the numerator and the denominator.

Computationally, this realization is difficult to apply. It requires knowing the overlapping and partial canceling of effects for the affected population. One can, however, combine the effects for public gains and losses by subtracting the one from the other. In this case, construction and upkeep costs less tolls are $2 million minus $1 million, or $1 million. Public funds need only provide annually this amount. A partially consolidated benefit-cost ratio (consolidated for public effects but not for private) is calculated as:

$$\text{Partially consolidated } B \div C = \frac{PRG}{PRL + PUL - PUG}$$
$$= \frac{3.04}{0.76 + 2.0 - 1.0}$$
$$= 1.73. \qquad [5.7]$$

5.15 THE PUBLIC-PRIVATE RATIO

Another approach to the benefit-cost calculation is to differentiate between public and private effects. This is justified by two factors that may make a dollar of public gains more valuable than a dollar of private gains:

(1) In spending public dollars, there are unlimited opportunities to allocate monies to projects with net benefits. Suppose that projects at the margin return $1.20 in private gain for $1.00 of public cost. This suggests that obtaining a benefit of $1,200,000 in private benefits is equivalent to obtaining a gain of $1,000,000 in public monies (which can then be turned into $1,200,000 in private benefits).

(2) More than $1.00 in private gain must be forgone to put $1.00 in the public treasury. Revenue service personnel have to be paid and economic dislocations suffered to raise public money.

Distinguishing public and private effects, we obtain the *public-private* benefit-cost ratio by dividing net private gains by net public costs:

$$\text{Public-private } B \div C = \frac{PRG - PRL}{PUL - PUG}$$
$$= \frac{3.04 - 0.76}{2.0 - 1.0} = 2.28. \qquad [5.8]$$

This ratio indicates that the road should be preferred to projects securing net private gains of less than $2.28 per public dollar and should be considered inferior to projects returning more than that.

5.16 THE BUDGETARY RATIO

Yet another benefit-cost ratio is obtained if one simply seeks to maximize total net benefits for a fixed budgetary outlay. In this case, each project should be rated according to net private gain plus public gain per budgeted dollar. This is the *budgetary* benefit-cost ratio, computed as

$$\text{Budgetary B} \div \text{C} = \frac{\text{PRG} - \text{PRL} + \text{PUG}}{\text{PUL}}$$

$$= \frac{3.04 - 0.76 + 1.0}{2.0}$$

$$= 1.64^2. \tag{5.9}$$

To include public gains (= \$1 million) in the numerator of the budgetary benefit-cost ratio essentially assumes (1) that they are commensurable with private gains and losses and (2) that they are not commensurable with public losses. The second assumption might hold because the regional government treats toll revenues as money separate from the funds budgeted for construction and holds firmly to a total budget for all road construction projects (not allowing tolls to count toward increasing the construction budget). (Such separation between incoming and outgoing public funds would be more likely if the public fund gains were income taxes realized on increased economic activity due to the road or reduced welfare payments due to construction industry hiring among the unemployed.) Transportation planners in such a situation might take their goal to be maximizing net benefits for their fixed total budget. In this case, they would focus on the budgetary benefit-cost ratios of projects: The road would be preferred to projects with budgetary ratios greater than 1.64 and should have preference over those with budgetary ratios less than 1.64.

---

[2] The public losses in the denominator of (5.9) should comprise only the budgetary outlay. Other public losses—for instance, drops in other public revenues due to a program (tolls on an old road may decline when a new road is opened)—should appear in the numerator of the budgetary ratio (the point of which, after all, is to compare all other effects to the budgetary outlay). That is, differentiating budgetary public losses (BPUL) from nonbudgetary (NBPUL), the budgetary benefit-cost ratio becomes

$$\text{Budgetary B} \div \text{C} = \frac{\text{PRG} - \text{PRL} + \text{PUG} - \text{NBPUL}}{\text{BPUL}} \tag{5.10}$$

5.17 CHOOSING AMONG ALTERNATIVE RATIOS

Formulae for calculating the gain-loss, partially consolidated, public-private, and budgetary benefit-cost ratios are given in Table 5.7. Each of these ratios has at times been put forward by analysts as the uniquely correct formulation. The consolidated ratio, due to computational difficulties, has probably never been calculated—despite its superiority to the gain-loss ratio. With the simpler programs that have been the staple for benefit-cost analysts, there was in the past little need to distinguish among the ratios. For these programs, private losses and public gains were often thought inconsequential—with the result that the four alternative ways of computing the ratio yielded the same figure. As these effects are increasingly deemed important and as techniques of program evaluation are refined and made more accurate, it is necessary to specify the type of benefit-cost ratio to be computed. We have shown above that four significantly different figures are derived as gain-loss, consolidated, public-private, and budgetary ratios for the same project.

Determining which ratio is best depends on knowing the decision criteria. The partially consolidated gain-loss ratio is superior to the gain-loss ratio for the same reason that the public-private ratio is superior to the budgetary: Only the net effects on public funds are considered. The budgetary ratio would be preferred to the public-private only if restrictive regulations or narrow analytic vision prevented seeing public fund gains as equivalent to cost reductions. Whether the partially consolidated ratio is preferable to the public-private ratio depends on which is deemed the more crucial distinction: between gains and losses or between public monies and private effects. To maintain both distinctions is to exceed the capacity of the two-term ratio whose great advantage is concisely comparing what is received to the cost incurred.

The more crucial distinction in most governmental programs seems to be between public monies and private effects. This argues for concentrating on the public-private ratio. In most of the examples that follow, the public-private ratio will be considered the relevant indicator for decisionmakers.

TABLE 5.7   Formulae for Calculating
Different Benefit-Cost
Ratios

$$\text{Gain–Loss B} \div \text{C} = \frac{\text{PRG} + \text{PUG}}{\text{PRL} + \text{PUL}}$$

$$\text{Partially Consolidated B} \div \text{C} = \frac{\text{PRG}}{\text{PRL} + \text{PUL} - \text{PUG}}$$

$$\text{Public–Private B} \div \text{C} = \frac{\text{PRG} - \text{PRL}}{\text{PUL} - \text{PUG}}$$

$$\text{Budgetary B} \div \text{C} = \frac{\text{PRG} - \text{PRL} + \text{PUG}}{\text{PUL}}$$

PRG ≡ Private gain   PUG ≡ Public gain
PRL ≡ Private loss   PUL ≡ Public loss

Private gains and losses are effects on individuals
as compensating variations.

Public gains and losses are defined as gains and
losses of public funds.

5.18 OTHER BENEFIT-COST RATIOS

The values of the decision participants may lead to still other, numerically different, benefit-cost ratios. As an example, a political public figure helping to make the road decision might consider his constituency to include the poor Indians and to exclude the rich producers and landowners. He would compute his own benefit-cost ratio to guide his personal actions by focusing only on the impact on his constituency (which would require estimating how much of the taxpayer burden his constituents would bear, how much of the consumer surplus they would realize, and so on).

Other benefit-cost ratios are obtained by analyzing the road from an exclusively regional perspective. The analysis above has been nationally based. If the regional government sees itself narrowly as the agent for its citizens—and not for national citizens outside the region—it might break down all gains and losses into their regional and extraregional components. Regional gains and losses are positive and negative CVs for regional citizens.

Suppose, for illustration, that this breakdown is as shown in Table 5.8. The region would now compute its own public-

TABLE 5.8   Gains and Losses Due to Road Project Falling Within or
             Outside the Region

	Gains Within Region	Gains Outside Region
Toll revenues	$1,000,000	$ 0
Traveler consumer surplus	560,000	840,000
Internal consumer surplus for goods	380,000	0
Producer surplus	250,000	100,000
External consumer surplus for goods	0	250,000
Constructor gain	200,000	0
Restaurateur's gain	0	10,000
Land appreciation	360,000	90,000
Total	**$2,750,000**	**$1,290,000**
	Losses Within Region	Losses Outside Region
Costs	$2,000,000	$ 0
Transporter loss	270,000	40,000
Producer loss	50,000	40,000
Depreciation	120,000	50,000
Pollution	190,000	0
Total	**$2,630,000**	**$ 130,000**

private benefit-cost ratio as the net private gain within the
region divided by the net public cost. This is

$$\$1,120,000 \div \$1,000,000 = 1.12. \qquad [5.11]$$

Should the region have other possible uses for its funds yielding
greater private return per public dollar, it may choose not to
construct the road.

The national government, however, is guided by its own
estimation of the public-private benefit-cost ratio as 2.28. It
may wish to build the road itself. It could alternatively offer to
subsidize one quarter of the construction and upkeep costs
($500,000 annually). With this subsidy (and neglecting that the
region, as part of the nation, effectively bears part of it), the
region's calculation of the public-private ratio is

$$\$1,120,000 \div \$500,000 = 2.24. \qquad [5.12]$$

The subsidy offer could induce the region to build the road.

Distributional concerns may also be catered to in calculating
the benefit-cost ratio. A government with a strong interest in

improving the welfare of the poor at the expense of the rich may decide to weight the benefits and costs accruing to the different groups accordingly. In computing a benefit-cost ratio, the government might multiply all compensating variations (negative and positive) of poor families by 2.0, of middle-income families by 1.0, and of rich families by 0.5.

The many alternative benefit-cost ratios for a given project depend on the perspective and values of the decision actor. One cannot say that certain approaches are right and others wrong. The varying approaches instead point out the primary necessity of determining who the decisionmaker is and what his values are before appropriate and useful benefit-cost ratios can be derived.

5.19 SENSITIVITY ANALYSIS

There is frequently uncertainty concerning many of the numbers used in benefit-cost analyses. This may be handled by *sensitivity analysis*: deliberately varying the uncertain factors to examine their effect on the decision criterion.

Methods for estimating traveler consumer surplus (TCS), for example, might be inexact. We have presumed above that TCS is $1.4 million annually. However, this might just be the best estimate of an amount that is thought possible to range from $1.1 to $1.8 million. Suppose that the decision guide is the public-private ratio. Taking the TCS to be $1.1 million leads to a public-private ratio of

$$\frac{2.74 - 0.76}{2.0 - 1.0} = 1.98. \qquad [5.13]$$

With TCS at $1.8 million, the ratio would be

$$\frac{3.44 - 0.76}{2.0 - 1.0} = 2.68. \qquad [5.14]$$

This sensitivity analysis thus indicates that, depending on the somewhat uncertain value of traveler consumer surplus, the public-private benefit-cost ratio could vary from 1.98 to 2.68.

A variant of sensitivity analysis is *threshold analysis*: determining how much variation in individual elements of the analysis is necessary to affect the decision. In the more standard example of sensitivity analysis given above, a range of uncertainty for the value of TCS was identified, whereupon the effects on the ratio of variation within this range were determined.

In threshold analysis, instead of estimating a range of uncertainty and calculating its effects, one would start by identifying the decision criterion. Suppose that decisionmakers wish to build the road only if the public-private ratio exceeds 1.8. To reduce the public-private ratio to this value, private gains (PRG) would have to fall to $2.56 million—instead of the $3.04 million originally estimated. This would happen if TCS, instead of being the $1.4 originally estimated, were only $920,000 annually. Threshold analysis thus indicates that, for any value of TCS greater than $920,000, decisionmakers will wish to build the road. The decisionmakers use this result of threshold analysis by estimating the likelihood that TCS will be less than the threshold value of $920,000 annually. If they judge the likelihood small, they will go ahead with the road with confidence (unless uncertainty about other parts of the analysis shakes this confidence); if they judge the likelihood large, they will proceed more cautiously (perhaps commissioning further study of TCS to reduce the uncertainty concerning it before deciding whether or not to build the road).

5.20 A GENERAL RECOMMENDED PROCEDURE FOR PROJECT SELECTION

We can now present a general procedure for project selection following calculation of benefits and costs. The goal is presumed to be to obtain maximum private benefits for a given public outlay. The procedure may also—as indicated in Step 1—be used to help determine the most appropriate level of public outlay. A variant of the procedure—for use when spending is determined not by a preset limit but by a rule such as the Kaldor-Hicks criterion—will be presented in Section 5.22. The main procedure consists of seven steps, which we first describe, then illustratively apply. All references in these steps to benefit-cost ratios (or marginal ratios) pertain to the public-private ratios.

(1) Determine the total budget available. With predetermined budgetary limits, this requirement is met. With a more elastic budget, alternative budget limits may be tried. For example, the limit might first be set at $5 million and the appropriate

roster of projects for this limit selected. The limit could then be changed to $6 million, a new roster chosen, and the marginal expenditure of $1 million examined. If this marginal expenditure seems reasonable, the budget limit of $6 million would be preferable to one of $5 million; if this expenditure seems unjustifiable, the limit would be better set at $5 million.

(2) Eliminate infeasible or clearly undesirable alternatives. Alternatives costing more than the budget limit or with benefit-cost ratios less than 1.0 can be dropped from consideration.

(3) Determine best ratios among mutually exclusive alternatives. Among each group of remaining, mutually exclusive, project alternatives, that project with the highest benefit-cost ratio should be selected and the others may be temporarily ignored. Alternative funding levels for a given project represent, essentially, mutually exclusive projects. In this step, the level of funding with highest ratio should be identified, and this funding level should be considered alone for the moment in competition with other projects.

(4) Of alternative projects under consideration, select that with the highest benefit-cost ratio. Projects with ratios or marginal ratios less than 1.0 should not be chosen.

(5) Revise determination of best ratios among mutually exclusive projects. Every time a project is selected for implementation, two types of changes may be made among the projects under consideration. The first is that more expensive versions of the project chosen may now be considered. Their relevant ratios for comparison with other projects are the marginal benefit-cost ratios—comparing marginal benefits and costs beyond their levels in the project version selected. The more expensive project version with highest marginal ratio is identified and compared with other projects. The second type of revision is to reflect the reduced budget monies available. All project versions requiring expenditures or marginal expenditures exceeding the remaining budget limit are dropped from consideration. This may require redetermining which among the remaining, mutually exclusive project alternatives had the highest benefit-cost ratio (or marginal ratio, if a less expensive alternative has already been selected for implementation).

(6) Repeat steps 4 and 5 as long as possible. This process concludes when there are no further possible expenditures requiring less than the remaining budgetary funds and with ratios greater than 1.0.

(7) Consider adjustments to the list of selected projects. The first six steps may leave some money left over or may, at some stage, have eliminated a desirable project costing just more than the budget monies then remaining. In these cases, it may be possible by trial-and-error substitutions to arrive at a list of projects with higher total private benefits than that originally obtained.

Example: Applying the Procedure
for Project Selection

Suppose that a public works department with a budget limit of $1 million is deciding which projects to fund. Project alternatives are shown in Table 5.9, where each group of mutually exclusive projects is labeled by the same letter. Projects A_1, A_2, A_3, and A_4 are thus mutually exclusive—perhaps because they represent different funding levels for the same project, perhaps because they represent alternative uses of the same land. For simplicity, the projects are assumed to offer no public gains. (If PUG were not zero for various projects, one reasonable way to proceed is to determine the average public-private ratio for government-wide marginal programs that might be funded if there were a bit more public money—call this ratio k; to consider all public gains, PUG, equivalent to k·PUG of private gains; and to proceed as indicated in the example.) The general recommended procedure for project selection may now be followed to determine the list of projects yielding maximum net private benefits within the budget limit.

Solution. Steps 1 and 2 are immediate. The budget limit has been set at $1 million and no projects in Table 5.9 can be immediately eliminated since none has costs of more than $1 million or a ratio less than 1.0. In step 3, we merely identify the project among the four A projects (A_1, A_2, A_3, A_4) with the best ratio, and similarly among the Cs, Ds, and Es. This reduces the projects under consideration to the following six.

TABLE 5.9   Costs, Benefits, and Public-Private Benefit-Cost Ratios for
a List of Alternative Projects

Project	Public Cost ($000) (= PUL)	Net Private Gain ($000) (= PRG–PRL)	Public-Private Benefit-Cost Ratio*
A_1	135	280	2.07
A_2	170	370	2.18
A_3	210	440	2.10
A_4	270	530	1.96
B	150	250	1.67
C_1	250	315	1.26
C_2	280	405	1.45
C_3	600	890	1.48
D_1	110	175	1.59
D_2	150	235	1.57
E_1	100	220	2.20
E_2	200	480	2.40
E_3	300	670	2.23
E_4	400	830	2.08
E_5	500	1030	2.06
E_6	600	1170	1.95
F	60	140	2.33

*PUG = 0 for all projects

Project	Public Cost ($000)	Net Private Gain ($000)	B ÷ C
A_2	170	370	2.18
B	150	250	1.67
C_3	600	890	1.48
D_1	110	175	1.59
E_2	200	480	2.40
F	60	140	2.33

In Step 4, we now select the project among these six with the best ratio. This is E_2. Having chosen E_2, we now consider whether more expensive projects in the E group should be funded—in competition with the other five groups of projects for funding. We examine marginal benefit-cost ratios—spending beyond the limits of E_2 to obtain benefits beyond those of E_2. E_3, for example, costs $100,000 more than E_2 and obtains $190,000 more ($670,000 - $480,000) in benefits. Its marginal ratio is 1.9 (= $190,000 ÷ $100,000). The marginal figures for the four projects in the E group more expensive than E_2 are:

Project	Marginal Public Cost ($000)	Marginal Net Private Gain ($000)	Marginal B ÷ C
E_3-E_2	100	190	1.90
E_4-E_2	200	350	1.75
E_5-E_2	300	550	1.83
E_6-E_2	400	690	1.72

Of these, Project E_3-E_2 (that is, substituting E_3 for E_2) has the highest ratio and should be considered in comparison with the other projects. We note that $800,000 (= $1 million minus the $200,000 to be spent on E_2) remains to be spent. Since all projects cost less than this, none are eliminated due to exceeding the remaining budget limit.

The six alternatives now under consideration are shown below.

Project	Public Cost ($000)	Net Private Gain ($000)	B ÷ C
A_2	170	370	2.18
B	150	250	1.67
C_3	600	890	1.48
D_1	110	175	1.59
E_3-E_2	100	190	1.90
F	60	140	2.33

Project F has the best ratio among these and is next selected. This reduces the list of projects under consideration to the other five shown above—none of which costs more than the $740,000 remaining in the budget. The next project to be picked is that with the best ratio of the remaining five. This is A_2. A_3 and A_4 now come into consideration. A_3 has a marginal ratio of

$$(440\text{-}370) \div (210\text{-}170) = 1.75; \qquad [5.15]$$

and A_4 of

$$(530\text{-}370) \div (270\text{-}170) = 1.6. \qquad [5.16]$$

Since the first of these is higher, we will now consider Project A_3-A_2 in comparison with the other projects.

We have, at this point in the procedure, decided to spend at least $170,000 on A-group products, at least $200,000 on E-group projects, and $60,000 on Project F. This leaves $570,000 to be allocated. Since Project C_3 costs more than this, it is eliminated. C_2, because it has a higher ratio than C_1, takes the place of C_3 in comparison against other projects. The list of projects under consideration now consists of the following.

Project	Public Cost ($000)	Net Private Gain ($000)	B ÷ C
A_3-A_2	40	70	1.75
B	150	250	1.67
C_2	280	405	1.45
D_1	110	175	1.59
E_3-E_2	100	190	1.90

Among these, Project E_3-E_2 has the best ratio. E_3 accordingly replaces E_2 on the list of projects tentatively selected at a cost of an additional $100,000—leaving $470,000 to be allocated. Projects E_4-E_3, E_5-E_3, and E_6-E_3 have marginal ratios of

$$(830-670) \div (400-300) = 1.60,$$

$$(1030-670) \div (500-300) = 1.80, \text{ and}$$

$$(1170-670) \div (600-300) = 1.67, \qquad\qquad [5.17]$$

respectively. The second is best, making the list of competing projects:

Project	Public Cost ($000)	Net Private Gain ($000)	B ÷ C
A_3-A_2	40	70	1.75
B	150	250	1.67
C_2	280	405	1.45
D_1	110	175	1.59
E_5-E_3	200	360	1.80

Project E_5-E_3 has the best ratio on this list—implying that E_5 should be substituted for E_3 at a further cost of $200,000. Now only $270,000 is left to be spent, requiring that C_2 be replaced by C_1 on the list of competing projects.

Project	Public Cost ($000)	Net Private Gain ($000)	B ÷ C
A_3–A_2	40	70	1.75
B	150	250	1.67
C_1	250	315	1.26
D_1	110	175	1.59
E_6–E_5	100	140	1.40

Project A_3 is now chosen to replace A_2. Disposable monies are reduced by $40,000 to $230,000. This eliminates C_1 from consideration. The projects under consideration are shown below.

Project	Public Cost ($000)	Net Private Gain ($000)	B ÷ C
A_4–A_3	60	90	1.50
B	150	250	1.67
D_1	110	175	1.59
E_6–E_5	100	140	1.40

We now pick Project B, leaving $80,000 to be allocated. Since only A_4-A_3 of the projects remaining under consideration costs less than $80,000, A_4 would replace A_3 —at a cost of $60,000 and leaving $20,000 unallocated. This completes Steps 1 through 6 of the procedure. So far, it has been decided to fund Projects A_4, B, E_5 and F—achieving total net private benefits of $1,950,000 at a total cost of $980,000.

In Step 7, we examine whether minor adjustments to fit excluded projects under the budget limit could increase total net private benefits. The most attractive (best ratio) project excluded because of the budget limit was D_1. Enough money to fund D_1 could be made available by funding Project A_2 instead of A_4. Projects A_2, B, D_1, E_5, and F would yield total net private benefits of $1,965,000 at a total of $990,000. This roster of projects obtains $15,000 more in benefits for $10,000 more in costs. As this is a desirable change, the final list of projects chosen is A_2, B, D_1, E_5, and F.

5.21 RATIONALE FOR THE PROCEDURE

This somewhat complicated procedure has a fairly simple rationale: At all times, the decisionmaker is simply trying to get the greatest per-dollar return for the marginal dollars allocated. The best return available at the outset was $2.40 in benefits per dollar spent on E_2, so $200,000 was allocated to E_2. Next, $2.30 in benefits per dollar spent was available with Project F, then $2.18 per dollar with Project A_2, then $1.90 per dollar by substituting E_3 for E_2, and so on. In this way, a final list of projects offering greatest net benefits (total net private benefits minus total costs) is obtained.

5.22 A PROCEDURE FOR SELECTING PROJECTS WITH A FUNDING RULE

Suppose now that there is no predetermined limit on public spending, but instead a rule for identifying desirable and undesirable projects. Such a rule might be that expenditures obtaining $1.30 or more in benefits per dollar of cost are justifiable. A rule following Kaldor-Hicks would be that marginal expenditures with net benefits (ratios greater than 1.0) should be approved.

With such a rule guiding spending, the procedure for project selection becomes simpler than with a budget limit. Groups of mutually exclusive projects no longer compete with one another for funding. The procedure therefore may be applied to each such group separately. The procedure has four steps.

Step 1. Select the project version with the best benefit-cost ratio.

Step 2. If the ratio or marginal ratio satisfies the rule for a justifiable expenditure, funding at at least the level of the project considered is justifiable.

Step 3. After a project is judged justified, select from the remaining, more expensive projects in the group of mutually exclusive projects that with the highest marginal ratio—the marginal ratio comparing benefits and costs beyond the levels of the last project judged justified. Return to Step 2.

Step 4. Repeat Steps 2 and 3 until there are no projects more expensive than the last judged justified with marginal ratios satisfying the spending rule.

TABLE 5.10   Costs, Benefits, and Public-Private Benefit-Cost Ratios
for a List of Alternative Projects

Project	Net Public Cost ($000) (= PUL–PUG)	Net Private Gain ($000) (= PRG–PRL)	Public-Private Benefit-Cost Ratio
G_1	20	38	1.90
G_2	30	63	2.10
G_3	38	77	2.03
G_4	52	98	1.88
G_5	58	109	1.88
G_6	67	121	1.81
G_7	72	128	1.78

Example: Selecting Projects with a Funding Rule

One government considers expenditures justified if and only if their benefit-cost ratios exceed 1.5. This government must decide which among the mutually exclusive projects, G_1 to G_7 as shown in Table 5.10, it would fund.

Solution. In Step 1, we identify G_2 as having the best ratio and, in Step 2, verify that its ratio of 2.1 is greater than 1.5. This leads us to examine the marginal ratios for the more expensive projects, G_3 through G_7.

Project	Marginal Net Public Cost ($000)	Marginal Net Private Gain ($000)	Marginal B ÷ C
G_3-G_2	8	14	1.75
G_4-G_2	22	35	1.59
G_5-G_2	28	46	1.64
G_6-G_2	37	58	1.57
G_7-G_2	42	65	1.55

Project G_3 has the best marginal ratio of 1.75 and is therefore considered justified. Marginal benefits and costs for projects more expensive than G_3 are shown below.

Project	Marginal Net Public Cost ($000)	Marginal Net Private Gain ($000)	B ÷ C
G_4-G_3	14	21	1.50
G_5-G_3	20	32	1.60
G_6-G_3	29	44	1.52
G_7-G_3	34	51	1.50

In this list, G_5 has the best ratio of 1.60—which exceeds 1.5. The marginal ratios for spending beyond the level of G_5 for G_6 and for G_7 are

$$(121-109) \div (67-58) = 1.33, \text{ and}$$
$$(128-109) \div (72-58) = 1.36. \tag{5.18}$$

Since these are both less than 1.5, neither is justified. Project G_5 is therefore selected for implementation.

5.23 JUSTIFICATION AND VARIANTS OF THE DECISION RULE

The rule that expenditures are justified if and only if their benefit-cost ratios exceed 1.5 could be based on a sense that money not spent could go to any of a large number of projects with ratios of 1.5. The rule alternatively could derive from estimating that $1.50 in private benefits must be forgone on average to enable the government to spend $1.00. If this is true, the alternative of not spending could be seen as a project of leaving the money in the private sector with a benefit-cost ratio of 1.5.

Note that the rule states that expenditures, not projects, are justified if their ratio exceeds 1.5. All seven projects, G_1 to G_7, have ratios greater than 1.5. Each, if the others did not exist, would be justified. However, since G_5 exists, G_6 and G_7 can no longer be justified: They only yield $1.33 and $1.36 in benefits per dollar spent in excess of that required for G_5. This marginal money would be better not spent (and, perhaps, gain benefits of $1.50 per dollar not spent by remaining in the private sector).

A rule based on the benefit-cost ratio could easily be combined with a spending limit. Thus, the conditions could be that expenditures with benefit-cost ratios greater than 1.5 are justified but only up to a budget limit of $1 million. To meet these conditions, Steps 2 and 4 in the procedure of Section 5.20 would be modified to prohibit selecting projects with ratios or marginal ratios less than 1.5.

5.24 THIS CHAPTER AND OTHER WRITINGS

Benefit-cost practitioners have long recognized that benefit-cost ratios are inappropriate criteria for choosing among mutually exclusive projects. The frequently recommended remedy for this, as formulated by Stokey and Zeckhauser (1978), is their "*Fundamental Rule*: In any choice situation, select the alternative that produces the greatest net benefit." Indeed, appropriately identifying and maximizing total benefits is the universally acknowledged goal for benefit-cost analysis—in which light it may seem strange that our recommended procedure for project selection makes extensive use of benefit-cost ratios. The reason is that total benefits are best maximized by applying marginal criteria in project selection: by making sure that each succeeding dollar allocated to projects is obtaining maximum possible benefits. This chapter spells out in greater detail than other works a procedure for doing this.

The notion that alternative judgments and perspectives by the decisionmaker can lead to different benefit-cost ratios can be seen in such applied work as that of Friedman (1977). The distinctions between public and private effects are made in Rossi et al. (1979), where the triple perspective of private, governmental, and social effects is adopted. Sugden and Williams (1978) acknowledge the difference in value between public and private monies: "£1 in the hands of the government has a greater social value than £1 in the hands of the taxpayers." A number of applied works (for example, Hanke and Walker, 1974) recognize that the crucial distinction is between net private effects and net public effects. This is seen in that privately borne disbenefits are subtracted from the numerator of the benefit-cost ratio (as in the public-private ratio) rather than added to the denominator (as in the gain-loss ratio). The critical underlying premise—with which we agree—is that the goal of public programs is to turn public funds into maximal, privately sensed benefits.

Notwithstanding these other works, this book—in this and the next two chapters—diverges from the standard literature in explicitly distinguishing between public and private monies and in allowing for the possibility that they have different values. Most texts implicitly find that a program with a (public-private) benefit-cost ratio of 1.02 is a good thing. We do not, first, because there virtually always are programs with better ratios that can be funded in its stead, and, second, because putting $1.00 in the public treasury may cost the private sector more than $1.02 (as will be argued in the next chapter). This we take to indicate that a public dollar is worth more than 1.02 private dollars—a distinction that should be consistently maintained throughout benefit-cost analysis.

Currently disputed among analysts is the relative weighting of private gains and losses. The Kaldor-Hicks criterion implies that doing someone harm of $100 is exactly balanced by doing another person in the same general circumstances the good of $100 (both figures are CVs.) Some analysts, on the other hand, argue that equal amounts of good and bad do not cancel. For large changes, the declining marginal utility of money (Friedman and Savage, 1948; Raiffa, 1968) makes this undisputed. For small changes, investigators (Hammond, 1967; Kahneman and Tversky, 1979) report that people consider slight amounts of harm (for example, losing $10) to be much more serious than comparable amounts of good. Equal chances of harm and gain of the same size do not, in their minds, even approximately cancel. Although inconsistencies can be shown in such attitudes, the fact remains that people—including many decisionmakers—tend to regard a CV of harm as more important than an equal CV of good. If and when the numerical ratio giving the relative importance of the two is worked out, the gain-loss benefit-cost ratio becomes a useful tool in basing decisions on this distinction.

Classification of benefit-cost ratios by their treatment of public gains and private losses—as gain-loss, partially consolidated, public-private, and budgetary ratios—represents new terminology. It is introduced because there have been inconsistent arithmetic computations of the ratios and because different circumstances and values can make the various formulations more or less relevant for decisionmakers.

The problem our taxonomy is designed to combat has been described by Feldstein (1972) in explaining why he does not focus on the benefit-cost ratio:

Although valuing projects by the ratio of discounted benefits and costs provides an equivalent criterion of admissibility (i.e., the benefit-cost ratio exceeds one if and only if the present value is positive), the benefit-cost ratio cannot be used to choose among mutually exclusive alternatives. Any benefit-cost ratio can be substantially raised by reclassifying a "cost" as a "reduction in benefits"; such classification decisions are arbitrary and do not affect the present value of a project.

Our aim has been to invalidate this criticism of Feldstein: By defining different benefit-cost ratios based on explicit rules, arbitrary shifting between the numerator and denominator is no longer possible. With this change, the benefit-cost ratio can be used to choose among mutually exclusive alternatives.

6

Identifying the Decisionmaker, the Values, the Alternatives, the Costs, and the Benefits

6.1 CHAPTER OVERVIEW

In the examples of Chapters 2 through 5 we have not had to face certain analytic difficulties that may arise in Steps 1 through 4 of the general procedure for benefit-cost analysis. In Section 6.2 we consider cases where the specification of the decisionmaker and the pertinent structure of values is not altogether clear. Possible problems in laying out the alternatives for benefit-cost analysis are the subject of Section 6.3. The complexities of determining costs—when the given price misstates true value and when the act of resource procurement causes subtle (but important) changes—are discussed in Section 6.4. In the following section, 6.5., we examine a range of program effects that are difficult to identify because of their indirectness and diffuseness. To address all these effects in a benefit-cost analysis may not be worth the effort of the analyst. This question of practicality is raised in Section 6.6 for the context of the road-building example. Among the possible refinements, some seem to be desirable and feasible for this case; others are desirable but not feasible; still others turn out not to be important.

6.2 IDENTIFYING THE DECISIONMAKER
AND HIS VALUES

We have seen that the benefit-cost analysis of a project may vary depending on whether the local, state, or national government is the decisionmaker (since any government may care little about benefits to noninhabitants). Even within one government, the values assigned to different effects (for example, benefits to business, harm to the environment) will vary according to its composition and to changing individual attitudes. For a benefit-cost analysis to serve decisionmakers best, it must accurately reflect their values.

Example: Alternative Valuations of Health Clinic Effects

A clinic may be established in a hospital. It would cost $1 million per year and would bring the hospital an additional $1.4 million in annual revenues. The convenience of the clinic would save time for prospective patients—time valued (as compensating variations) at $650,000 each year. The clinic would cause previously existing clinics in surrounding neighborhoods annual profit reductions of $300,000. Focusing only on these effects, what would the gain-loss benefit-cost ratio be:

(a) if the hospital is a private, for-profit institution with no concern for the time savings of its patients (except perhaps as they affect profits) or the profit margins of other clinics?

(b) if the hospital is part of a health maintenance organization (HMO) that also operates the clinics in the surrounding neighborhoods but that does not care about the time of its patients?

(c) if the hospital is run by the national government which cares about effects of the clinic on all institutions and persons?

Solution.

(a) The decisionmaker is the hospital. The gain-loss B/C is simply

$$\frac{\$1,400,000}{\$1,000,000} = 1.4. \qquad [6.1]$$

(b) The decisionmaker is the HMO:

$$\text{G-L B/C} = \frac{\$\,1,400,000}{\$1,000,000 + \$300,000} = 1.08. \qquad [6.2]$$

(c) The decisionmaker is the government:

$$\text{G-L B/C} = \frac{\$1,400,000 + \$650,000}{\$1,000,000 + \$300,000} = 1.58. \qquad [6.3]$$

Depending on the values of the decisionmakers, the benefit-cost ratios can, as in this example, vary markedly.

6.3 IDENTIFYING ALTERNATIVES

Accurate benefit-cost analysis requires understanding the decision alternatives: the range of possible actions and the constraints on them. We have seen that both benefit-cost ratios and net benefits may mislead if each essentially compares each decision alternative to doing nothing. Such results can be avoided if the competing decision alternatives are compared directly—a method that depends on clear perception of the choices.

A common error is to analyze suboptimal versions of alternatives. When one feature of one alternative makes that alternative look· bad in comparative benefit-cost analyses, the alternative should not be summarily discarded. Instead, the analyst should see whether modifications of the bad feature can substantially improve the alternative.

Identifying alternatives often becomes a problem of design or of systems analysis. Design is necessary to determine the range of feasible alternatives: For instance, can an airport be designed so that access problems are minimized, capacity is maximized, safety is adequate, and noise primarily affects uninhabited areas?

Systems analysis plays a similar role in manipulating program parameters in quest of an optimal formulation. For a program of vaccination against rubella, for example, alternatives vary according to the various ages at which persons would be vaccinated, to the possibility of vaccinating different sexes at different ages (or males not at all), and to the methods of pursuing those who miss the vaccinations. More complex programs can vary many more parameters. Systems analysis is responsible for ensuring, in an efficient way, that all program formulations that might be optimal are considered.

As the number of dimensions for program modification grows, it often becomes impossible to perform a benefit-cost analysis for each variant. Instead, benefit-cost considerations must guide design and systems analysis in formulating alternatives. By feeding back to these disciplines information on how various factors affect benefits and costs, more efficient searches for best program formulations can be conducted. This implies that identification of alternatives—the second step in the method—may not be concluded early in a benefit-cost analysis but may be reiterated using information fed back by Steps 3 through 7.

6.4 IDENTIFYING COSTS

6.4.1 Summary of Conclusions on Costs

This section will consider program costs in terms of money or other resources that are diverted to programs. Program costs that arise as negative effects of the program itself—often termed disbenefits—will be considered along with program benefits in the following section. Much of this section covers technical details that will not interest the nontechnical practitioner. Such readers should, however, note the operational conclusions reached in the technical sections:

(1) Resource costs are not always accurately given by their prices. In imperfect markets, it is often better to take into account the opportunity costs of resources—the benefits the resources would achieve in alternative employments. Still more accurate is the tracing through of all effects—who gains and who loses—as the result of obtaining resources for programs.

(2) The process of getting money from the private sector for the public sector causes many hidden costs and dislocations. Such effects include collection costs for public funds, the

unseen effects of government procurement in lending and resource markets, excess burden (loss due to behavioral distortion caused by taxes), excess unburden (gain via the same type of distortion), and the loss of private consumer surplus. Each of these influences the true costs of obtaining public funds.

(3) It is hard to take these diverse effects into account in decisions. Most benefit-cost analyses do not attempt to estimate these effects; however, they can be substantial. In particular, the true opportunity cost for a dollar of public money seems to be much greater than a dollar in terms of the private benefits that have to be forgone to get the public dollar. (All the effects in 2 above, except excess unburden, indicate that private opportunity costs exceed the public budgetary costs of programs.) Perhaps the best analytic reflection of this is not at great difficulty to estimate all these effects but instead to segregate effects on public and private monies and to focus on public-private benefit-cost ratios. This will enable identification of projects with greatest private benefit per public dollar but will not (until the opportunity cost of the public dollar is accurately estimated) tell whether a given project (with public-private benefit-cost ratio of, for example, 1.4) represents a net benefit or a net cost (the former if the public dollar opportunity cost is less than 1.4, the latter if it exceeds 1.4).

6.4.2 Opportunity Costs

When resources are traded in imperfect markets, their worth may not be accurately reflected as their monetary price. Economists often look instead to their

Opportunity costs: the benefits resources would achieve in alternative employments.

We have already seen opportunity costs of money in two examples:

(1) In the plant relocation problem, we did not simply take the costs of initial construction to be their immediate impact on company funds—$9 million for the State A plant and $12.8

million for the State B plant. Instead, by discounting, we took
into account what these funds would have achieved in alternative employment—a return of 12 percent per year. The opportunity cost for the $9 million for the State A plant was thus
seen in terms of the company's money as equivalent to

$$(9) (1.12)^5 = 15.86 \qquad\qquad [6.4]$$

million dollars five years later. In alternative employment, the
$9 million would have grown to $15.86 million five years later.
Discounting effectively captured this opportunity cost.

(2) In the example on the choice of program versions (in
Section 5.6), we saw the inadequacy of taking only the budgeted costs of the programs into account. The budgeted cost for
Program Version P was $500,000, but that money in alternative
employment could have gone to projects with a benefit-cost
ratio of 1.4. This meant that, to fund P,

$$(\$500,000) (1.4) = \$700,000 \qquad\qquad [6.5]$$

in benefits received under alternative use of the funds—the
opportunity cost of the money—would have been forgone.

6.4.3 Examples of Opportunity Costs

Opportunity costs for any resource can be calculated by
asking what gain (net benefits) would have been created by the
resource in its alternative employment.

Example: The Opportunity Cost of Land

In evaluating the plan for an energy plant, one must assign a
cost to the land it requires. The plan calls for the plant to use
half the land of a park. This amount of parkland could be sold
for $250,000 to private purchasers. The present-valued net
benefits for the park with all its land are $1,000,000 and with
only half its land are $600,000. Suppose that increasing public
funds by $1 is considered just as good as increasing net benefits
by $1. What value should be placed on the half of the park
required for the energy plant?

Solution. To answer this, we first must know what the alternative use of the land would be if not used for the energy plant. Given the potential sales price of $250,000, the land is worth a minimum of $250,000. If maintained as parkland, the half of the park in question would increase present-valued net benefits by $400,000 (= $1,000,000 minus $600,000). The land is thus worth $400,000 if maintained as parkland: That amount of additional benefit is created by keeping the land in the park. Since this is more than the $250,000 that would be received if the land were sold, the land—if not used for the energy plant—should be kept as parkland. The net benefit forgone by taking the land from the park—$400,000—is the opportunity cost of the land. The energy plant evaluators should take the cost of the land as its opportunity cost of $400,000, not as its potential sales price of $250,000, as is commonly done. (The opportunity cost of the land would be $250,000 only if the public authorities would, irrationally, sell the land rather than keep it in the park if the energy plant is not built. Opportunity costs are based on what would—not on what should—be done with the resources.)

Example: The Opportunity Cost of Labor

A typical worker for the energy plant would be paid $11,000 annually. If not hired for the plant, the worker would earn $10,000 per year in a can opener factory. If the wages were equal in the two sites, the worker would be indifferent between them. He can make 6,000 can openers in a year which sell for $3 apiece. The owner must pay $1 in materials and overhead costs to produce and to sell each can opener. The owner cannot replace workers hired by the plant. (This consideration indicates a market imperfection: In a well-functioning market, the owner should attract new workers, or keep old workers, by increasing wages.) What is the annual opportunity cost of the worker to be calculated by evaluators of the energy plant?

Solution methods. When one resource is combined with other resources to yield a product, either of two methods may be used to calculate its opportunity cost in being removed from that use.

Method 1: Subtract from the value of the product the costs of all other resources.

We thus calculate the opportunity cost of the workers as

O.C. = (6,000) ($3) of product value, less (6,000) ($1) in materials and overhead

= $12,000 per worker per year. [6.6]

Method 2: Sum the gross benefits the resource brings to its owner plus the net benefits to all other affected parties.

The labor of each worker creates gross annual benefits of $10,000 (the pay) for himself plus $2,000 in profits for the factory owner. These sum to $12,000.

6.4.4 Features of Opportunity Costs

Four general aspects of opportunity costs can be seen in this example.

(1) The actual price of the resource misstates true social costs. To have taken the cost of the worker simply as his $11,000 wage at the plant would have overlooked the fact that his labor could have created $12,000 in output value in another setting.

(2) Under perfect market conditions, the actual price of the resource would be the opportunity cost. An operational rule is: In the absence of clear-cut market imperfection, actual prices may be taken to be true costs and opportunity costs may be ignored. In perfect competition, the worker would be paid the value he produces ($12,000 = his marginal revenue product). The plant would have to pay him this wage to hire him. (The factory owner could profitably meet or beat any offer up to $12,000 per year. Perhaps he would not better the energy plant's offer because he knows that the plant could bid more than $12,000 if it had to. Perhaps he wishes to keep paying the workers who remain at the factory $10,000.) Many analysts (such as Harberger, 1972) urge, using theoretical arguments, that the value of resources be taken as their price and that opportunity costs should not be allowed to muddy the picture. When markets are perfect or nearly perfect, this posture works

well; when markets are imperfect, use of actual prices leads to substantial errors in benefit-cost analysis.

(3) Full identification of all effects captures opportunity costs. The evaluators of the plant could have just noted the effects caused by hiring the worker away from the factory: public funds lose $11,000 (PUL); the worker gains a positive compensating variation of $1,000 (PRG); and the owner loses a negative CV of $2,000 (PRL). These can be combined (assuming them commensurable) to a net negative CV of $12,000—the opportunity cost.

(4) Opportunity costs may be oversimplifications. If public loss (PUL) and private gain and loss (PRG and PRL) are valued differently, these different CVs cannot be simply combined. Their aggregate valuation depends on the values of the decision-maker. Identifying a single opportunity cost for a resource tends to gloss over these problems of valuation. Full identification of all effects due to obtaining a resource is more accurate than just quantifying a single opportunity cost, which in turn is more accurate than accepting the price of a resource as its value.

An added wrinkle is introduced if the workers have a preference for one type of work or another—independent from monetary considerations. For instance, the workers might prefer energy plant work to factory work and thus be indifferent between working at the energy plant for $11,500 per year and at the factory for $12,000 per year. In this case, it would appear to make sense to subtract $500 from the opportunity cost of the workers. If, on the other hand, they preferred the factory to the energy plant by, for example, the same amount, it would seem sensible to add $500 to the opportunity cost.

The problem with such adjustments to opportunity costs to reflect the preferences of the resources is that opportunity costs would then depend not just on· where the resource is coming from but also on where it might go. The opportunity cost would be lower if workers moved to more desirable work than if the same workers moved to less desirable work. Opportunity cost methods have traditionally neglected the preferences of human resources and have thus risked overlooking a possibly important welfare effect. The alternative methodology of fully identifying all effects and valuing them as compensating variations accurately captures all such effects.

6.4.5 Manifestations of Opportunity Costs

Opportunity costs have various manifestations.

(1) Limited budget monies. The opportunity costs of budget funds are not the nominal amounts but the benefits that could be realized if these funds were devoted to other programs.

(2) Limited physical resources. Suppose that open land is in short supply and might be used for a road or for a park. In deciding whether to build the road, the land value should be taken as the benefits it would create when used as a park.

(3) Market valuation as opportunity cost. When the alternative employment for a resource is in the private sector and when perfect competition prevails, market valuation should approximate the opportunity cost. In the previous example, the land in question might, if not used for the road, be privately developed. The private developers in this case should bid the price of the land to a level reflecting the profits they would reap from it. This level would approach the true opportunity cost (but fall short of it for failing to reflect the consumer surplus associated with the land development).

(4) Limited labor. With labor in short supply, its opportunity cost is the benefit it would return in alternative employment. With perfect competition in the labor market, the wage should be close to the opportunity cost.

(5) Slack factors. When the resources needed for a program would otherwise not be used, they are *slack factors,* with their cost best considered to be their opportunity cost of zero.

(6) Leisure as the slack factor. When the labor used by a program would otherwise not be employed, its effective cost to the government is the difference between the unemployment payments and the program wage. Should personnel be paid the program wage while unemployed, they would constitute a truly slack factor and have zero opportunity cost. When unemployed persons work, they lose leisure that may be of value to them but of no value to the government. In this case, the value of

leisure to the unemployed may be paid by governments as the necessary monetary inducement to work.

(7) Time of program participants. When manpower training or higher education upgrades work skills, the trainees or students must forgo the income they would have received if instead they had worked. When a patient waits to be treated in a health clinic, the work he could have done during that time is lost (to him if self-employed or not paid for sick-time; to his employer if paid for sick-time). These are opportunity costs.

(8) Shadow prices. Developing countries may have at their disposal limited amounts of convertible currencies. A project requiring convertible currencies may then force other spenders of these currencies to adjust to reduce their need for them. The opportunity cost is the total loss caused by these adjustments. In a constrained situation, the *shadow price* is the total change in benefits (or objective function) associated with a unit change in the constrained good. The opportunity cost of limited currencies is thus a shadow price. (This is the more restricted definition of a shadow price. Some economists—as seen in Section 3.5—use the term to refer to any imputed price for any commodity not traded in a market and hence not having a market price.)

In each of these cases, the opportunity cost reflects the value of resources more accurately than their prices. However, the most precise way to reckon costs is to note all effects due to removing a resource from its alternative employment. In the sections that follow we shall pursue this more general perspective on costs.

6.4.6 Using Opportunity Costs

Example: A Summer Recreation Program

A city considers organizing an eight-week summer recreation program for children. It would be staffed by 10 social workers whose wages for the period amount to $16,000. If they did not staff the recreation program, these workers would create $23,000 in benefits for the city through regular social work activities. The program would require daytime use of a building for which the city holds a long-term lease. Rent on the building is $3,000 for eight weeks. If the program is not undertaken, the building would be used as a senior citizen social center. As such, it would bring the elderly $5,000 in benefits. The families of the 150 children who would attend the recreation program would be willing to pay an average of $20 per child per week for it. There is no charge for the program. Is the recreation program net beneficial (a potential Pareto improvement)?

Missolution and solution. Neglecting opportunity costs, the analyst would figure program costs at

$16,000 for the social workers plus

$ 3,000 for the building, equalling

$19,000   [6.7]

Since this is less than the program benefit of

$ 20   times

150   children, times

8   weeks, equalling

$24,000;   [6.8]

the program appears to have net benefits of $5,000.

This analysis has gone astray in not taking into account the alternative uses of the workers and of the building if there were no recreation program. It is implicitly assuming that the services of the workers and use of the building, without the program, would not be bought by the city. If this were so (or, indeed, if the city could hire more social workers and another building at these prices), the analysis would be accurate and pertinent.

Focusing not on the actual budgeted costs of the resources but on their opportunity costs yields different calculations. The program costs taking alternative resource uses into account are

$23,000   in benefits that would be forgone if the
social workers staff the program, plus

$ 5,000   in benefits that would be forgone if the
building cannot be used by the senior
citizens, equalling

$28,000   [6.9]

In this light, the program is net disbeneficial. The net costs are $4,000.

6.4.7 How to Avoid Using Opportunity Costs

As an alternative to determining opportunity costs, the analyst can always (1) specify the true alternatives and (2) calculate their consequences for all affected parties. The analysis neglecting opportunity costs goes wrong in misperceiving the alternatives and their effects. It erroneously compares the program alternative with the null alternative over three effects:

(1) *costs of social workers:* it costs $16,000 to pay the social workers under the program alternative versus nothing to pay the workers under the null alternative;

(2) *costs of the buildings:* rent of $3,000 under the program alternative versus no rent under the null alternative; and

(3) *benefits:* $24,000 in benefits with the program versus no benefits without the program.

More accurate analysis focuses on two alternative states of the world: Alternative 1—the way the world would be with the program; and Alternative 2—the way the world would be without it. Alternative 1 comprises the program, less social work being done, and no space for senior citizen social activities. Alternative 2 comprises no recreation program, more social work, and a senior citizens' activity center. Benefits and costs are differentiated by whom they affect:

(1) The city budget—no effect since the city pays the same amounts to the social workers and for the building under either alternative. The incorrect analysis is wrong in assuming that, if the recreation program is not implemented, the money paid as salary and rent would be saved by the city;

(2) the social work of the city—less benefits by $23,000 under Alternative 1 than under Alternative 2;

(3) the senior citizens—less benefits by $5,000 under Alternative 1 compared with Alternative 2; and

(4) the children—$24,000 more benefits with Alternative 1 than with Alternative 2.

Summing these effects shows that Alternative 2 is a $4,000 potential Pareto improvement with respect to Alternative 1—as we found in the previous section using opportunity costs. Identifying and combining all effects is equivalent to using opportunity costs. The former method is often conceptually clearer and may be used to check whether opportunity costs have been appropriately determined. The opportunity cost method may enable quicker and more concise calculations.

6.4.8 Rules for Using Opportunity Costs

Three steps are involved in using opportunity costs for the profit-maximizing private firm:

(1) Determining what the resources would do if not used in the application being contemplated. If any resource would not be purchased, then the opportunity cost and the price would be identical. (For a public firm in imperfect markets—for example, the can opener factory above—this may not be true, as the government may try to take into account possible discrepancies between the price and the value of the resource in its alternative situation.);

(2) calculating the opportunity costs as the net benefits—as valued by the decisionmaker—that would be realized using the resources in their alternative applications neglecting the costs of the resources in question; and

(3) considering the opportunity costs of the resources as their costs.

Example: Agribusiness

A profit-maximizing farm wonders whether it should raise onions. The onions would be raised on marshy land owned by the farm on which $3,000 in taxes are paid annually. If not used for onions, the land would lie fallow but would be kept by the farm. Onion farming would require $5,000 in annual payments for equipment and seeds. Labor for the onion-raising would be provided by five farm workers recently hired for $5,000 each per annual farming season. No other workers are available (a market imperfection). The farm could sell the onions for $50,000. If not used to raise onions, the farm workers could be used to raise corn, tomatoes, or lettuce. The corn raised annually would be sold for $63,000 and would require the outlay of $25,000 for land rental, seeds, and equipment; tomatoes would sell for $77,000 and would require an outlay of $18,000; lettuce would sell for $41,000 and would require an outlay of $21,000. Should the farm raise onions?

Solution. In the first step, we determine that the land, if onions are not raised, would lie fallow and that the equipment and seeds would not be bought. The opportunity cost for the equipment and seeds is their cost. For the farm workers, we must examine the net benefits they would earn in alternative uses. Raising corn, their net benefits (neglecting their own cost) would be $38,000; raising tomatoes, $59,000; and raising lettuce, $20,000. If they did not raise onions, the workers should raise tomatoes.

Opportunity costs may now be calculated. The opportunity cost of the marshland is zero: If not used for onions, it would yield no benefits. This land is a slack factor. The opportunity cost of the workers is the net benefit they would earn, neglecting their own cost, in alternative uses. This is the net benefit of $59,000 they would earn raising tomatoes.

Taking, in the third step, opportunity costs as costs, we find that the costs of onion-raising are nothing for the land, $5,000 for equipment and seeds, and $59,000 for labor. These sum to $64,000—more than the $50,000 selling price for the onions. The farm should not raise onions.

*6.4.9 Collection Costs for Public Funds

The value of public funds reflects not only the benefits lost when they are removed from their alternative employment but also the cost of collecting them. Suppose that it costs three cents to raise an additional dollar of public funds. The three cents might represent the costs of toll booths, or of sales tax administration, or of property assessments. This means that, for every additional dollar raised, only $0.97 is available for public programs. A program costing $100,000 that is to be raised by additional taxation thus requires that

$$\$100,000 \div .97 = \$103,093 \qquad [6.10]$$

be removed from the private sector to pay both for the program and to raise its funding.

The additional $3,093 paid to raise the program funding probably represents a social loss. It means that work that would have produced about this amount of benefits in the private sector must now be shifted to obtaining money to pay for a program. This money would not be a real social cost only if the workers would otherwise have been unemployed (a slack factor in that they would not have been producing other benefits).

*6.4.10 The Invisible Interest Costs
for Public Funds

Example: Unseen Interest

A project requires $500,000 from public budgets. This amount would be raised by borrowing on national capital markets. The prevailing interest rate is seven percent and the interest rate elasticity of capital is 2.6. (The meaning of this figure is explained below. The actual number used represents the best estimate of one economist who has researched the problem.) The capital markets provide $1 billion to the government, the interest rates for which are renegotiated each year. What is the cost of the project during its first year in terms of public funds?

Solution. The interest paid on the monies runs to $35,000 (seven percent of $500,000) during the first year. One is tempted (especially if an advocate of the project) to end the cost analysis there. After all, borrowing an additional $500,000 in a market of $1 billion can hardly change the interest rate enough to matter. Or can it?

An interest rate elasticity of 2.6 means (by definition) that

$$\frac{\Delta s}{s} \div \frac{\Delta r}{r} = 2.6, \qquad [6.11]$$

where:

s is the supply of funds provided by the market and Δ s, the change in s; and

r is the interest rate and Δ r, the change in it.

Without the project, s is $1 billion and r, seven percent. The change in s, Δ s, is the amount of funds—$500,000—that would additionally have to be supplied by the capital market to support the project. We can now use 6.11 to compute Δ r:

$$\Delta r = \frac{\Delta s \cdot r}{s \quad 2.6}$$
$$= \frac{5 \times 10^5}{10^9} \cdot \frac{.07}{2.6}$$
$$= .0000135. \qquad\qquad\qquad\qquad\qquad [6.12]$$

The project would thus raise the interest rate from seven to 7.00135 percent—on the surface, not a great change. However, this new rate must, if the project goes into effect, be paid on $1 billion. The additional cost during the year is 0.00135 percent of $1 billion or $13,500—an amount equal to 38 percent of the basic interest payment of $35,000 yearly for the $500,000. (Calculating things finely, the higher interest rate would also be paid on the $500,000—yielding annual interest of $35,007 [.0700135 of $500,000]. We shall ignore the extra $7.) From 6.11, we see that the cost incurred by raising the interest rate is

$$\Delta r \cdot s = \Delta s \cdot \frac{r}{2.6}, \qquad\qquad\qquad [6.13]$$

while Δ s $\cdot$ r is the interest paid on the additional funds raised in the market (here $35,000 annually). Of the basic interest charge, 38 percent (or 1/2.6) is thus additionally, if less visibly, lost by the government. No matter what schedule is arranged for repaying the money to the market, the costs due to raising the interest rate will amount to 38 percent (more generally, one divided by the supply elasticity of funds) of the interest paid on the money.

*6.4.11 Invisible Costs

The unseen interest costs of public funds, in a sense, are not as serious as they may seem. Unlike collection costs, they do not represent a direct social loss in forfeiting the benefits real resources would achieve in other situations. Instead, they are an additional transfer: Along with the evident transfer of $35,000

that the public sector pays the private for the $500,000 goes
another transfer of $13,500. Each transfer is a negative com-
pensating variation for public funds and a positive CV for
private lenders. Most governments do not feel that a $1 loss in
its funds is adequately compensated by a $1 gain to money
lenders. To take these effects appropriately into account in
decision-making, it is necessary first to recognize their full
extent—in this case a total transfer of

$$\$35,000 + \$13,500 = \$48,500. \qquad [6.14]$$

With this recognition, the decision maker can better evaluate
how important the transfer is.

A yet less visible effect should also be noted. To some extent,
governmental and private borrowing compete for the same
funds. Increased governmental borrowing will therefore increase
not only the interest rate paid by the government but also the
rate paid by private borrowers. New home owners and all other
private borrowers will have to (1) pay marginally more for their
mortgages and loans, (2) borrow less, or (3) give up on the
projects for which they would have borrowed. Any additional
transfers from borrowers to lenders must be recognized by all
governments that care about the distributional effects of their
policies.

While the example focused on interest rate effects in the
capital market, similar price effects may occur for other
resources. When the government secures land, it may marginally
nudge up the price of land for subsequent land acquisitions of
its own and for private purchasers. This price rise transfers
money from the purchasers to the sellers of the land. The
general effect is that governmental acquisition of any resource
tends to raise the resource price and thus to transfer funds from
other purchasers (private persons or other governmental programs) to the sellers.

*6.4.12 Excess Burden

Suppose that, instead of raising money by borrowing, the
government taxes. If taxes could be obtained by confiscating

private money without changing private behavior, the negative compensating variation associated with a tax would be the tax amount. In actuality, taxes change behavior. Suppose that a 10 percent tax on bicycles increases the price on one model from $100 to $110. The person willing to pay more than $110 for the bicycle simply transfers $10 of his consumer surplus to the government. This effect is foreknown: A government knows that, to raise a sum of money, it must cause citizens losses of that amount.

Now consider the person willing to spend only $105 for the bicycle and who therefore will not buy it with the tax. That person loses the $5 consumer surplus he would have had without the tax, while the government gains nothing. This loss due to taxation effects on behavior is *excess burden*. Governments know that, to obtain $1 million by taxation, the private sector must lose that amount. They often fail to see, however, that the private sector often loses more than just the tax revenue gained by the governments. The welfare lost by the private sector in excess of its evident tax burden—what it actually pays to the government—is excess burden.

Excess burden occurs only when taxes change behavior. If all persons who would have bought bicycles without the tax buy them with it, there is no excess burden (just burden). However, whenever a tax affects behavior, it creates excess burden. (Like many concepts in benefit-cost analysis, excess burden has variant definitions. Sugden and Williams [1978] for instance, consider any excess of forgone private resources [such as the collection costs considered in Section 6.4.9] over disposable public funds obtained to be excess burden [even though there is no behavioral distortion]. The usage here follows that in standard welfare economics [Musgrave, 1959].)

Raising tax rates to increase public funds also increases excess burden. The more inelastic is the demand (and the supply) for the item taxed, the lower are these additional costs. While this argues for taxing goods with inelastic rather than elastic demand, problems of equity will ensue if consumers of the former are too heavily taxed.

An effect like that of excess burden occurs when government borrowing raises interest rates. We noted in Section 6.4.11 that this transfers money from borrowers to lenders. A further effect, however, is that people who would have borrowed at lower interest rates will not do so at higher rates and will therefore lose their associated consumer's (borrower's) surpluses. An example of this effect is given in Section 6.4.20.

*6.4.13 Graphical Representation of Excess Burden

Example: An Ice Cream Tax

A city decides to raise money by levying a 20-cent tax on ice cream cones. The demand curve for ice cream cones is given by

$$q = 200{,}000 - 200{,}000 \, p \qquad [6.15]$$

where q is the number of ice cream cones that would be bought per month at a given price p (in dollars). The supply curve is

$$q = 200{,}000 \, p: \qquad [6.16]$$

that is, ice cream cone makers will produce 200,000 cones monthly for every $1 in the price of the cones. How much money will be raised by the tax? What will be the excess burden?

Solution. We graph the demand and supply curves in Figure 6.1. ABCD is the original (pretax) demand curve and OFC is the original supply curve. They intersect at C, which can be found graphically or algebraically to be the point where 100,000 cones are sold monthly at a price of $0.50.

When the tax is imposed, the effect as seen by the producers is that the demand curve is lowered by $0.20—from ABCD to EFG. From the consumers' viewpoint, the supply curve is raised by $0.20. To avoid cluttering the figure, we show only the modified demand curve—as the producers see it. With the tax, production and consumption drop to point F: 80,000 cones produced and sold each month at a price of $0.40 (but purchased at a price of $0.60) with the tax. Consumer surplus declines from triangle AIC ($25,000 monthly) to AHB

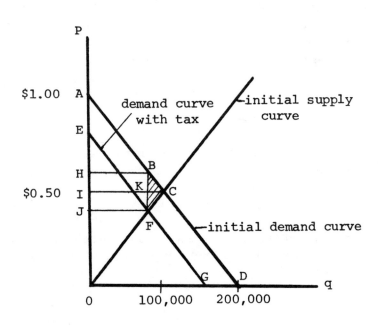

Figure 6.1: Diagram of Supply and Demand Curves Illustrating Excess Burden
The shaded triangle is the excess burden.

($16,000); producer surplus declines from triangle OIC ($25,000) to OJF ($16,000); and the city gains rectangle HBFJ ($16,000). The producers and consumers thus lose more—a total of $18,000 in reduction of producer and consumer surpluses—than the $16,000 that the city gains in taxes. The difference between what the producers and consumers lose and what the city gains is the excess burden—$2,000. The excess burden is shown in Figure 6.1 as the shaded triangle BCF. This can be broken down into two parts: triangle BKC ($1,000) representing the reduction in consumer surplus not gained by the city in taxes; and triangle FKC ($1,000)—lost producer surplus that is not gained by the city.

6.4.14 Excess Burden and the Supply of Labor

The same diagram, Figure 6.1, can be relabeled to depict excess burden occurring as people decide how much they would like to work. Let the horizontal axis represent hours of work and the vertical axis represent the wage—ignoring the actual numbers on the axes. Line OFC can be taken as the supply curve for labor and ABCD as the original demand curve for labor. Suppose now that a tax on income effectively lowers the demand curve as seen by workers to EFG. The gross wage (what the employer pays) then rises to HO. The net wage (what the worker gets after taxes) falls to JO. The employers are the consumers of labor and their consumer surplus (as in the ice cream cone example) declines from triangle AIC to AHB. The workers are the producers of labor and their producer surplus falls from triangle OIC to OJF. The tax revenues amount to rectangle HBFJ and the excess burden, as before, is triangle BCF. This triangle represents labor that employers would have been willing to pay for and that workers would have been willing to provide—at a clear net gain for each. This labor, however, ends up not being contracted for or provided because the government demands its cut: a tax amount for this labor greater than the net gains of the employers and workers combined.

*6.4.15 Excess Burden as Inefficient Production

To tax some items and not others or to tax them unequally leads to inefficient production.

Example: Taxing Wine

Suppose that a region consumes a fixed total amount of wine—both red and white—each year. As far as the wine drinkers are concerned, the two types are perfect substitutes for one another. We display the situation as in Figure 6.2. where the vertical axis measures the price. Line segment OP represents the total amount of wine consumed. The horizontal distance to O is the amount of red wine consumed; the horizontal distance to P,

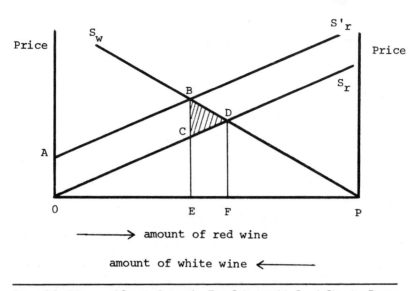

Figure 6.2: Diagram of Supply Curves for Two Substitutable Goods Showing Excess Burden Resulting from Unequal Taxation

S_r = initial supply curve for red wine.

S_r' = supply curve for red wine with tax, as seen by consumers.

S_w = supply curve for white wine.

The shaded triangle is the excess burden.

the amount of white. Line OCD is the supply curve for red wine; PDB is the supply curve for white.

Without any tax, consumers will consume OF of red wine and FP of white. In this situation, the prices of the two would be equal. (If production were to differ from these proportions, the prices would become unequal, people would drink the cheaper wine, and consumption would return to OF of red and FP of white--the equilibrium situation.) Total cost of production is the area under each supply curve: triangle OFD for red wine and PFD for white—for a total cost equal to triangle ODP.

Suppose now that red wine is taxed a constant amount. This raises the supply curve of red wine by consumers from OCD to AB. Being indifferent between the two types, consumers will always prefer the wine cheaper to them—thus leading to a situation in which the prices to them are equal. This occurs with consumption of OE of red wine and EP of white. The total production cost of red wine falls to triangle OEC, and of white wine rises to triangle PEB. The government raises the parallelogram OABC in tax.

The excess burden now is represented by triangle BCD. This can be seen by looking at production costs. The region could have produced the required amount of wine at a total cost equal to triangle ODP. With the tax, its total production costs rise to quadrilateral OCBP—an increase of triangle BCD. This indicates that resources are not being used in the most efficient way to produce the set amount of wine. The amount of inefficiency is measured by the excess burden triangle BCD.

Example: Plumbing

The same type of situation arises when you need to have a plumbing job done. The most efficient solution is to have it done at minimal resource cost—valuing both the plumber's and your time appropriately. If he can do it more cheaply, he should; if you can, you should. However, if there is an income tax, the plumber must be paid it in addition to his take-home pay. It may then well happen that (1) the plumber can repair your pipes at lower total resource cost than you can; but, (2) having to pay an income tax for what he earns, it becomes cheaper to do it yourself. In this case, as with the wine tax, the unequal taxation leads to an outcome that is inefficient in terms of the resources used.

Example: Tax Shelters

Some investments offer greater tax advantages than others. Tax shelter investments typically allow paper losses to enable the overall reduction of the individual's tax bill. One consequence is that the government loses taxes—what the individual saves, the government loses. A second result is excess burden: Since some forms of investments are better tax shelters than others, this consideration distorts investment from its optimal allocation under perfect competition. In addition, lawyers and accountants have to be hired to figure out the best tax angles. The net effect is that the governments lose more through the

existence of tax shelter opportunities than persons gain from
using them.

*6.4.16 Excess Unburden

Taxes may, at times, modify behavior favorably—perhaps by
fining behavior with negative externality effects. Examples are
fines for reckless driving, penalties for environmental pollution,
and congestion charges (for instance, for use of a highway or of
an airport at peak periods). As in the case of excess burden,
taxes may not be realized in such cases due to behavior altera-
tion: people drive less recklessly, firms pollute less, drivers avoid
peak hours. In contrast to excess burden, these changes achieve
net benefits—the loss to the firm from reducing its pollution
being exceeded (if the fine is appropriate) by the good done the
environment. Favorable modification of behavior due to taxes
or fines is *excess unburden.*

*6.4.17 Second Best

Commonly cited examples of excess unburden are *second-
best* phenomena: instances where policies that would work best
in a perfectly competitive world are no longer optimal due to
market imperfections. We saw above that introducing a tax in a
perfectly competitive world tends to lead to excess burden
distortions: changed patterns of consumption and production
such that the private sector loses more than the public sector
gains in taxes. But the real world, instead of being perfectly
competitive, already has many taxes in place and is thus a
second-best situation. To introduce taxes in a second-best world
may not be as bad as to introduce them in a perfectly competitive world since the distortions caused by the new taxes might
partially reverse distortions caused by the old taxes. When the
behavioral responses to taxes in a second-best world lead to
improved resource allocations, excess unburden (really the
removal of previous excess burden) occurs.

Example: Taxing Wine Twice

Suppose in our previous example of wine consumption that
the tax on red wine is well established. To raise more revenue,

the region considers taxing white wine by the same amount. Taxes on both types of wine are shown in Figure 6.3. With the new tax, the supply curve of white wine as seen by consumers is line GH. Consumers again alter their consumption in a way that makes the prices of two wines equal to them. This occurs at the consumption of OF of red wine and of FP of white—the original proportions of consumption. The new tax has thus undone the distortions of the old tax. Total resource costs for wine production drop from quadrilateral OCBP to ODP—a drop of triangle BCD, the excess unburden. In first taxing red wine, the tax cost consumers and producers combined a total of quadrilateral OABD—more by triangle BCD than the quadrilateral OABC of taxes gained by the government. In later taxing white wine, the government gains more (hexagon BCDPHG) than the consumers and producers together lose (quadrilateral BPHG).

*6.4.18 The Net Effect of Distortions Caused by Taxation

It is tempting, following the previous example, to argue that all activities should just be taxed equally—whereupon there would be no behavioral distortions. But this is impossible. Leisure cannot be taxed the same as work: implying that any taxation of work will lead to undesirable promotion of leisure. We cannot tax a man for fixing his own plumbing. Other taxes—as well as tax reduction opportunities—are hard to distribute equally.

The net effect is that taxes distort behavior unfavorably. Resources are overallocated to activities with tax advantages—with often significant transaction costs (tax lawyer fees) for doing so. Higher taxes will in general tend to be spread as unevenly as lower taxes, meaning that, with tax increases, excess burden will rise (excess unburden in second-best situations is the exception, not the rule). To obtain the marginal public dollar through raising taxes is thus to raise marginally the total level of excess burden and therefore to cost the private sector somewhat more than one dollar.

*6.4.19 Private Consumer Surplus

While it has become customary to include consumer surplus as part of public project benefits, forgone private consumer

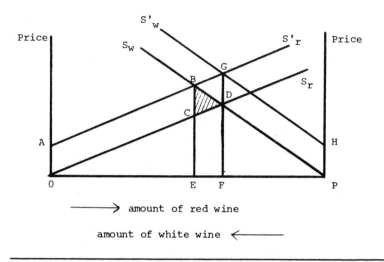

Figure 6.3: Diagram of Supply Curves for Two Substitutable Goods Showing Excess Unburden Resulting from Equalizing Taxation

S_r = initial supply curve for red wine.

S_r' = supply curve for red wine with tax, as seen by consumers.

S_w = initial supply curve for white wine.

S_w' = supply curve for white wine with tax, as seen by consumer.

The shaded triangle is the excess unburden.

surplus is less frequently noted. When resources are taxed or bid away from the private sector, the private production of goods and services is lowered. These goods would inevitably have had some consumer surplus. This would not, however, affect resource prices: The developer who bids for land does not stand to reap the consumer surplus and hence does not reflect it in his bids. As a result, the market price for land understates the true opportunity cost to the private sector. The forgone consumer surplus is thus a further invisible cost incurred when money and other resources are taken from the private domain for public use.

Example: Private Consumer Surplus for Land

Suppose that a public program wishes to use a tract of land. A private developer could subdivide the land into 50 lots and could build houses on them at a cost of $40,000 per house. The demand curve for these houses is given by

$$p = 59{,}000 - 180q, \qquad [6.17]$$

where p is the house price in dollars and q is the number of houses that could be sold at that price. That is, if the developer were to build one house, he could sell it for

$$\$59{,}000 - \$180 = \$58{,}820; \qquad [6.18]$$

two houses could be sold for $58,640; and so on. What is the most the developer could bid for the land and not show a loss? How much consumer surplus would there be if the developer buys the land and maximizes profits? What is the true opportunity cost of using the land for the public program?

Solution. For every house the developer builds and sells at a price of at least $40,000, he achieves a profit of the price minus $40,000 minus the cost of the land. In deciding how many houses to build once he owns the land, the developer can neglect the price of the land and hence should maximize

$$(q)\,(p - 40{,}000). \qquad [6.19]$$

This is maximized when

$$q = 50 \text{ and}$$
$$p = 50{,}000. \qquad [6.20]$$

At this number of houses and price, the developer obtains a profit of $500,000, from which the price of the land must be subtracted. This indicates that he could bid any amount up to $500,000 for the land and still show a profit.

At a house price of $50,000, the person who would have paid $58,820 for a house gets a consumer surplus of $8,820. Forty-eight other house buyers get consumer surpluses of declining amounts; the fiftieth buyer gets no consumer surplus. The total consumer surplus amounts to

$$\$8,820 + \$8,640 + \ldots + \$180 + 0 = \$220,500. \qquad [6.21]$$

We use the second method of Section 6.4.3 for calculating opportunity cost: gross benefits to the owner plus the net benefits to others. These are $500,000 gross benefit for the developer and $220,500 for the house buyers. The true opportunity cost is $720,500.

This analysis indicates that, if the public program were to bid $500,001 for the land, no developer could match the bid. Suppose that net benefits of the program exclusive of the land were $600,001. Taking just the cost of land into account, the program might think itself a potential Pareto improvement with net benefits of $100,000. However, considering the forfeited consumer surpluses, the program is really net disbeneficial— having a net cost of $120,499.

*6.4.20 Forgone Private Consumer Surplus Due to Interest Rate Effects

The same kind of effect occurs when the public sector borrows and thus bids money away from the private sector. Suppose that the price of the land is set in the private sector at $400,000 but that the developer must borrow $1 million for one year in order to build 50 houses. To show a profit on the development, the builder can pay no more than $100,000 in interest. If public borrowing derives the interest rate above 10 percent, the houses will not be built and $220,500 in consumer surplus will again be lost.

6.4.21 Arguments for Analyzing Forgone Consumer Surplus

The consequences of neglecting forgone private consumer surplus would be reduced if public consumer surplus was also left out of the calculations. The two oversights would then, to some extent, cancel one another. But it is hard not to include the consumer surplus of public goods since so many of them are unpriced or priced low and consumer surplus constitutes the bulk of the benefits. Forgone private consumer surplus—like many opportunity costs—is less visible and often ignored. To do so, however, as this example shows, is to bias the analysis in favor of public use of resources.

6.5 IDENTIFYING BENEFITS

6.5.1 General Strategy

In identifying costs, the surest way to be consistent and accurate is to look at all persons conceivably affected by resource procurement for a program and ask how much better or worse off they are as a result. The same tack may be followed in identifying benefits—as well as costs in the form of negative program effects (often termed "disbenefits") which will also be dealt with in this section. The main conceptual and practical problem is that such benefits and costs may be diffusely spread over many people. Types of diffuse effects are external effects, global effects, effects on rates and prices, displacements, and multiplier effects (effects springing from more direct effects).

6.5.2 External Effects

External effects are the secondary and the incidental impacts of actions—often occurring through effects on the environment. Examples are displeasure due to the noise near a new airport; the reduction in contagion risk that an inoculation program brings those not inoculated; the benefits of breathing better air experienced by both smokers and nonsmokers when the excise tax on cigarettes is doubled; the rise in your property value when the school near your home is renovated; the various disbenefits downstream when an upstream community decides not to process its sewage.

6.5.3 Global Effects

Global effects derive from impacts on individuals, institutions, conditions, and concepts. They occur, separately from the direct and indirect effects of these impacts, simply when people know about the impacts.

(1) Impacts on individuals. Unemployment compensation directly benefits the recipients and indirectly benefits the merchants who sell to the recipients. Still other people support unemployment compensation not because they gain either directly or indirectly by it but from the satisfaction they take in knowing that the unemployed are cared for. The latter effect is a global benefit.

(2) Impacts on institutions. Suppose that a crime control program improves the efficiency of a police department and thus reduces crime. Some people will value the program because it reduces the chance that they will be victims of crime. This direct effect may be measured as positive compensating variations—how much money people would pay for their greater safety. Other people may not stand to gain by being safer but instead are just proud to live in a city, state, or nation with efficient police departments. Such pride is a global effect and may be measured also as positive CVs—how much people would pay in order to have a police department they can be proud of.

(3) Impacts on conditions. Public works programs have as specific benefits their finished products—roads, parks, or whatever. The programs may also stimulate the economy and thus increase the gross national product (GNP). Two types of benefits will then occur. The first is the indirect effect that a more vital economy will mean more business and income for many people (this could be measured as a multiplier effect, as in Sections 6.5.10 and 6.5.11). The second benefit is global in that people, quite apart from their own monetary gains, may derive satisfaction from having a high rate of GNP growth—to the extent that they would be willing to pay something for that satisfaction.

(4) Impacts on concepts. Many citizens are willing to pay to preserve or to enhance their cherished concepts. An example might be equality before the law—a concept that would lead many citizens to support a program providing legal support for the indigent.

Global effects can benefit all members of a society (although individuals will value them differently), whereas externality benefits usually involve specific groups (for instance, people living near enough to an airport to be affected by its noise). Unlike externality effects, global effects cease to exist if people do not know about the impacts on which they are based.

6.5.4 Salience and Identifiability

When society subsidizes treatment for a child with kidney failure, much of the benefit is global: contentment in knowing that children requiring expensive medical treatment are not allowed to die. In such cases, global values are influenced by:

(1) *Salience*—the global benefit derived disappears if the public does not know of the instance or the policy (and would not know if such children were permitted to die). The better publicized such a case is, the greater are the global benefits (the total amount of money people would pay to avoid the death of the child).
(2) *Identifiability*—people care more about the sharp-edged drama (the young leukemic, the trapped miner) than about comparably important but less dramatic events (lives shortened by radiation exposure).

6.5.5 Measuring Global Effects

Theoretically, all global effects can be valued as CVs: how much one would pay to reduce inflation by one percent; to preserve a free, irreverent press; to save a dying child. Practically, such value measurement is dangerous. Global effects are not bartered and indeed are even further removed from market valuation than externalities. Measurement by direct questioning founders on the lack of thought given to it (who has considered how much he personally should pay to feed a hungry child in Africa?) and on disincentives for honest responses (people may understate the amounts they would pay if they actually have to and if they think it likely that the child would be fed even without their donations).

Many analysts (such as Rossi, 1979) do not believe that such global effects as equity considerations and distributional ramifications can be quantified by merely summing individual judgments. Instead, they argue that such global effects have to be viewed and valued from the perspective of society as a whole. In any case, it is evident that valuing global effects is among the most difficult tasks of the benefit-cost analyst.

6.5.6 Effects on Rates and Prices

In considering costs, we saw that a variety of effects arises when a government competes with the private sector for resources and thus raises the prices: Sellers gain and buyers and prospective buyers (those who would have bought without the price rise) lose. Similar effects occur when the outputs of a program alter prices. When an irrigation project lowers the cost of raising corn in one area, the national price of corn should also be marginally lowered. This helps all corn buyers but hurts other sellers. To some extent, these cancel: What one gains another loses. This and the difficulty in measuring such effects have often been taken as pretexts for neglecting them. Yet, two points argue for more precise analysis to take such price effects into account. First, the canceling of effects is exact only for sellers and buyers who do not change the amount they sell or buy. Production will be marginally lowered in other areas and consumption will rise—meaning that the increase in consumer surplus will exceed the drop in producer surplus. Second, distributional considerations may enter in: society may think it bad or good—depending on its values—to shift from sellers to buyers. This distributional effect must be measured to be appropriately taken into account. Note that although the marginal decrease in price may be minimal, it will be spread over so large a market that the total effects will be of the same order of magnitude as the direct effects of the irrigation program. Estimating these effect sizes will be considered further.

*6.5.7 Are Effects on Rates and Prices Worth Calculating?

Many authors (for example, Harberger, 1971) argue that effects on rates and prices are second-order effects and simple transfers and hence not worth worrying about. To examine this proposition, we consider the situation of a government irrigation program that increases crop yields.

Example: Governmentally Increased Supply

Suppose that the original demand curve for a crop is given by line ABCD in Figure 6.4 and that a governmental irrigation program yields an additional harvest of KL = Δ q bushels. This has the effect of shifting the demand curve for all other farmers to EFGH. This intersects their supply curve, OGB, at G. Without the governmental program, the other farmers would produce IB bushels at a price of IO; with the program, they would produce JG bushels at a price of JO. Call IB, q; IO, p; JG, q′; and JO, p′. Call p - p′, Δ p.

Aside from the cost of producing the crop under the irrigation program, there are three effects of its production:

(1) sales value of the new crop—the new crop is sold for an amount equal to rectangle GCLK = Δ q $\cdot$ p′;

(2) loss of other producers—their producer surplus drops from triangle IBO to JGO, a drop of trapezoid IBGJ = 1/2 Δ p $\cdot$ (q + q′); and

(3) gain of consumers—consumer surplus rises from triangle ABI to ACJ, a gain of trapezoid IBCJ = 1/2 Δ p (q + q′ + Δ q).

The simple way to value the crop is at its sales value (= Δ q $\cdot$ p′) ignoring all other effects. The argument is that other effects largely cancel: the producer loss being nearly equal to the consumer gain—with the discrepancy between the two being negligible. We examine this argument more closely.

Most of the gain to consumers is just a transfer to them from producers. The irrigation program transfers trapezoid IBGJ = 1/2 Δ p (q + q′) from producers to consumers. The size of the effect is of the first order. (The loose rule of thumb is that the order of the effect is given by the number of Δs multiplied together to calculate it.) It might thus be as large as the sales value. If the society cares about distributional effects and, does not simply assume that transferring money from producers to consumers has zero net effect, then this transfer should be reflected in the analysis. If supply is highly elastic, IBGJ will be much smaller than GCLK (because the change in price will be proportionately much smaller than the change in

Price

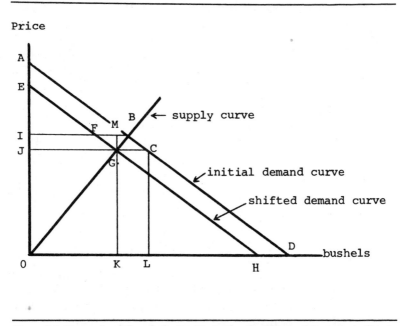

Figure 6.4: Demand and Supply Curves Illustrating the Effects of Increases in Supply
Brought about by Governmental Programs

quantity). In this case, the size of the transfer from producer to consumer will be small and may perhaps be neglected.

The amount by which the consumer gain exceeds producer loss is triangle BCG. This has a value of $1/2 \, \Delta p \, \Delta q$ and is a second-order effect (two Δs). Unless Δp is large compared with p (for example, at least five percent of p), this effect will be quantitatively negligible (equal to less than three percent of the sales value). Another even smaller second-order effect is the loss associated with production cutbacks, including the loss of farmers forced out of business by the new production. Their loss is only triangle MBG, a small part of the total trapezoid (IBGJ) of producer loss.

*6.5.8 Guidelines for Calculating Effects

Governmental effects on rates and prices occur whenever a governmental program increases or decreases the supply or demand of a good. Governmental procurement (demand increase) could be analyzed in much the same way that we have here examined governmentally induced supply growth. The guidelines for including all these effects in the analysis distinguish among three types of effect.

Primary effects. These include the sales value of changes in supply and procurement costs. These effects must be included in the analysis—with possible adjustments to reflect opportunity costs or pricing anomalies.

Primary transfers. Governmentally induced price changes cause transfers between buyers and sellers. These should be included in the analysis unless (1) society feels that the gains and losses involved in the transfers cancel one another, or (2) it feels that the transfers are not important in that they mainly affect those whom the government does not care greatly about (maybe those outside its jurisdiction), or (3) supply elasticity makes these effects numerically negligible.

Secondary effects. These may usually be neglected. The exception occurs when the changes in price or quantity are significant proportions (perhaps five or more percent) of price or quantity.

*6.5.9 Displacements and Opportunity Disbenefits

Example: Displacement Creating a Benefit

When a road is built, it may divert traffic from preexisting roads. Persons who switch to the new road will realize some consumer surplus. People who continue to drive on the old roads will have an increased consumer surplus because those roads will become less congested. (People who begin to drive on the old roads because of the building of the new get a smaller consumer surplus.) These are benefits achieved through *displacements*: behavioral shifts caused by programs.

Example: Displacement Creating
Opportunity Disbenefits

Suppose that a community health clinic is opened. Net public costs are operating expenses less fees received. The fees in this view constitute a benefit. They may, however, represent a displacement or transfer of fees from preexisting public or private facilities. The transfer may thus disbenefit one clinic in the same amount as it benefits another. The disbeneficial effect is an *opportunity disbenefit:* the lost opportunity to achieve a benefit (here, fees) in one place because benefits are transferred elsewhere. In the broader public analysis of the clinic, it is not sufficient to calculate net public costs by subtracting fees from expenses for the new clinic alone: Opportunity disbenefits to other public institutions must also be taken into account. Opportunity disbenefits for private institutions should be similarly reflected in the calculations of net private benefits.

An opportunity disbenefit is often hard to see because, from the viewpoint of program users, there is no loss: All patients may be better off with the opening of the new clinic. The disbenefit is seen in thinking in terms of clinics rather than of patients.

Displacements and opportunity disbenefits may occur through a price effect. An example is the irrigation project that enables corn production in one area, thereby marginally lowers national corn prices, and possibly leads other farmers to go out of business. We saw in the previous section that this displacement effect can often be neglected.

*6.5.10 Effects from Other Effects— Multiplier Effects

The same irrigation project may enrich one farmer in one year by $10,000—a compensating variation in hard cash. Suppose that he uses the money to buy a new truck. The $10,000 price he pays is $500 more than the minimum break-even price for the dealer, who thus gets a positive CV of $500. The purchase also benefits the manufacturer of the truck and his suppliers, each of whom profit from the manufacture and sale. Their total benefits (CVs) amount to another $500. The truck dealer may then spend his entire gain on a television set. This in turn benefits the store, the salesman, the manufacturer, and his suppliers. At every stage of exchange some of the benefit is passed along—the effect at each stage being on average a constant fraction multiplied by the effect at the previous stage. These are *multiplier effects:* effects deriving from effects and causing, in turn, still smaller effects. If 10 percent of the benefit is passed on at each stage, the total benefit will be the geometric series

$$\$10,000 + \$1,000 + \$100 + \$10 + \$1. \ldots$$

$$= \$11,111.11. \qquad [6.22]$$

The multiplier, the number by which the direct effect must be multiplied to determine the full effect, is 1.11. (This definition is somewhat different from the standard macroeconomic concept of the multiplier as the number relating changes in investment to changes in total income [Samuelson, 1976]. Benefit-cost analysis requires a different multiplier because, unlike macroeconomics, it is not concerned with the gross change in income. It focuses instead on personal improvements [CVs] over the status quo.)

*6.5.11 Should Multiplier Effects be Calculated?

Various reasons are given for ignoring multiplier effects: (1) they are hard to calculate; (2) they are small (only 11.1 percent—one-ninth—of the main [$10,000] benefit in the example above); and (3) they may affect all monies equally. Insofar as the third point holds, the first is undercut: If all monies have equal multiplier effects, their rate of occurrence may be calculated once for all. Different types of money may, however, pass along these effects at different rates. Monetary gains for people who save their money will, for instance, have a different total effect from monetary gains for spenders.

One may wonder, however, whether the multiplier effect itself—let alone the difference between multiplier effects—is large enough for the analyst to bother calculating. This depends on the desired accuracy for the analysis. However, it is always more accurate to give the best estimate of an effect than to ignore the effect because the estimate is not precise.

If all monies have approximately equal multiplier effects, they can be' treated as an intrinsic aspect of money (that, when spent, its advantages are passed along) and therefore ignored. This view acknowledges that costs too have their multiplier effects: that, when a man is taxed, he loses not just the tax amount but a sequence of people lose the gains they would have realized had he spent the money. If this is true, ignoring the multiplier effect will not change the benefit-cost ratio since

$$\frac{b}{c} = \frac{b \cdot m}{c \cdot m},$$
[6.23]

where m is the multiplier. Unfortunately, this observation and simplification can hold only for monetary effects. The gain arising because a person enjoys breathing better air is not passed along and has no multiplier effect—thus invalidating 6.23. Most accurate benefit-cost analysis must therefore take the multiplier effect into account.

6.6 PRACTICALITY

We have discussed several program effects that are difficult to calculate as well as controversial in the sense that many benefit-cost analyses overlook them. To some extent, we have overlooked the question of practicality: The actual benefit-cost analyst does not have the time or resources to pursue all the theoretical refinements of his craft. Reverting to the example of the desert road, we now examine whether and how the notions discussed in this chapter should be included in actual benefit-cost analyses.

Opportunity costs. In a well-functioning market, the actual prices that must be paid for resources approximate the opportunity costs. With reasonable processes for awarding and administering contracts, the money actually paid a construction company to build the road should be an adequate estimate of the resources used. A number of signals generally should alert the analyst to the need to calculate opportunity costs instead of just using the prices actually paid. These signals include (1) any serious imperfections in the perfectly competitive market (often indicated by product lumpiness—a few big and indivisible influences), (2) slack factors, (3) unpaid time of program participants, (4) governmental ownership of resources, and (5) resource constraints (such as national limitations on convertible currencies). In building the road, attention might have to be given to opportunity costs under a variety of hypotheses. If the construction workers were trainees exempt from income tax, the tax they would have paid in alternative employment is an opportunity cost. If some workers would otherwise have been unemployed, their opportunity cost would be far less than their wage. Because the government owns the desert land used for the road, its value should be taken to be the net benefits the land could achieve under alternative use. These effects are somewhat difficult to calculate—but not prohibitively so—and should be considered in an accurate benefit-cost analysis. Two further kinds of opportunity costs are dealt with by other methods: The alternative uses of money in different years are handled via discounting and in different projects are handled via appropriate choice (see Chapter 5) among alternative projects.

Collection costs, invisible interest, effects on rates and prices, excess burden, excess unburden, and forgone private consumer surplus. These are important effects that benefit-cost analyses for individual projects should not be expected to address. Many of these effects determine how much private benefits must be forgone to gain public money. The government should determine this: a determination that can then be used in analysis and decision-making for all its activities and that, moreover, will indicate the appropriate way to raise additional money. Governments do not do this, but they should. We indicated in Section 6.5.8 when it is important to quantify effects on rates and prices. Some price effects have been dealt with in Chapter 4. Purchase of the various materials required for road construction will marginally increase many prices throughout the extended markets of the materials. These effects should probably be ignored: The purchases will be insignificant parts of the total market and the marginal distributional effects (millions of persons in many regions might each have to pay a few pennies more for their cement) do not seem critical. Forgone private consumer surplus due to governmental acquisition of money enters into the determination above of the trade-offs between public money and private benefits. Forgone private consumer surplus due to governmental acquisition of nonmonetary resources should be handled as an opportunity cost. This seems unlikely to be a factor in the road decision, but might be if large tracts of land had to be acquired from private developers.

Externalities. The pollution effects of the road have been included. Externality effects are often hard to identify (who knows what various effluents can do to different human organs and systems?) and to value (see Chapter 7).

Global effects. The road might be valued as contributing to the cherished ideal of multi-modal regional transportation. It might be thought unfair to the Indians: one more example of hurting the poor to help the rich and thus a blot on the region's aspirations toward social equity. These global effects would be hard to measure and seem best handled by not quantifying them but by alerting decisionmakers to their presence.

Displacements. If the road were to reduce toll revenues on other roads or to benefit drivers on those roads by reducing congestion, these effects should appear in the analysis.

Multiplier effects. The government should calculate the size of any multiplier effect, whereupon any benefit-cost analysis can apply the multiplier to all monetary effects. Benefit-cost analysts for individual projects should not have to estimate the multiplier themselves.

6.7 THIS CHAPTER AND OTHER WRITINGS

Although the themes are not original here, we have empha- sized more than other authors the importance of identifying the decisionmakers, the pertinent values, and the true alternatives.

A number of analyses go astray through misspecification of alternatives. Opportunity costs are a standard topic in many papers on benefit-cost analysis (for example, Haveman and Weisbrod, 1977, Rothenberg, 1975) and are treated here much as there. Haveman and Krutilla (1968) point out that opportunity costs may take on a wide range of values, depending on the level of resource use.

The notion of the invisible interest cost for public funds is occasionally dealt with in the theoretical literature of economics (Harberger, 1972) but has not been addressed by benefit-cost texts. Much the same can be said for excess burden—a familiar term in public finance economics (Musgrave, 1959) but a stranger to benefit-cost analysis. Excess unburden is a term introduced here, while the allied concept of the second-best situation has received extensive attention (Lipsey and Lancaster, 1956; Allingham and Archibald, 1974). Forgone private consumer surplus is a logical extension of standard microeconomic concepts—but again, rarely seen in the benefit-cost literature.

Externalities are well known and often written about. The concept of the global effect has been gradually recognized and spoken to by analysts over the past fifteen years—often using quite different terminology. Close to the notion here of global effects is that of Sugden and Williams (1978), who define "interpersonal external effects" as existing "when one person considers himself to be better off (or worse off) simply from knowing that someone else is consuming some good, even though this consumption has no physical effect on the first person." The standard tack taken by benefit-cost analysts (Harberger, 1971) has been that effects on rates and prices are of the second order and hence not worth including. The discussion above argues for the more frequent reflection of these effects (recognizing, however, that they often are not worth the trouble of measuring). A similar philosophical approach has been adopted by Maciariello (1975).

Displacement effects are well known in transportation economics (Friedlaender, 1965) and often mentioned in individual analyses (Hanke and Walker, 1974)—if not labeled with this name. The multiplier is a familiar and critical notion in macro-economics that has rarely been taken up in benefit-cost analysis. This may owe to the generally unjustified assumption of perfect competiticn. Under perfect competition, there are no bonuses (positive CVs) to successive sellers and, hence, no multiplier effect.

Most of this chapter will be novel even to persons familiar with actual benefit-cost analyses and with texts on the methodology. It should not be so. The effects considered here are, largely, logical extensions of well-known economic phenomena that should be accorded their due role in public decision-making.

7

Valuing Effects Monetarily, Discounting, and Catering to Distributional Effects

A penny saved is a penny earned [sic].

—Ben Franklin

7.1 CHAPTER OVERVIEW

Identified program effects must, before being included in benefit-cost analysis, be quantified in money terms. We saw in Chapter 3 that all program effects may be conceptualized as compensating variations. However, difficulties may arise because of difficulties in estimating CVs and because the value of the measurement units—dollars—may vary with circumstances. These general difficulties are the subject of Section 7.2, which reviews methods of monetary valuation, the inconsistent value of units of money, and how these inconsistencies may be dealt with.

The thorny subject of discounting is taken up in Section 7.3, where we first review the rationale for governmental discounting. These rationale differ from those for private discounting—as do the actual discount rates used in the two situations. Review of the difficulties, disagreements, and consensus on discounting leads to a somewhat surprising dual conclusion: Many economists agree that one should, in theory, reflect the opportunity costs of capital as a shadow price and should discount at the marginal rate of time preference, but that this is currently a practical impossibility. This makes a more simple methodology in which opportunity costs are reflected in the discount rate the preferred technique. We follow this method, examining the distinction between real and nominal discount rates when inflation is present and working through two examples of discounting in program evaluation. In choosing among projects, an alternative to maximizing net present value is to maximize the internal rate of return—a concept discussed in Sections 7.3.16 to 7.3.19.

In Section 7.4, we turn to distributional aspects of benefit-cost analysis: considering instances where the most efficient choices may not be socially preferred. One conceptually appealing approach is based on the notions of the social welfare function and the social value function—which can take distributional concerns into account. Another is to value distributional concerns as global effects. Both approaches are sound in theory but hard to apply. In light of this, a reasonable course for current benefit-cost analysts is to describe distributional effects but to leave their valuation to decisionmakers.

7.2 VALUING EFFECTS MONETARILY

7.2.1 Main Problems in Monetary Valuation

Costs and benefits may both be valued as compensating variations. Two main pitfalls, however, appear.

First, It is hard to place dollar figures on many kinds of effects. Such effects include virtually all benefits and disbenefits not traded in markets. The problem is exacerbated when moral issues are involved or when effects are spread diffusely over broad populations. Money measurement and market valuation are the simplest ways of valuing effects. When they will not work, valuations may be based on econometric estimations, on answers to hypothetical questions, and on observed political choices.

Second, The units of the CVs—dollars—may not have uniform value. A great attraction of benefit-cost analysis over other forms of analysis is its concreteness: It deals with dollars and everyone knows what a dollar is. Or do they? Pretax dollars are different from posttax dollars; this year's dollars are different from next year's; public dollars are different from private dollars. Benefit-cost analysis should reflect these differences.

7.2.2 Methods of Monetary Valuation

Valuing program effects as compensating variations requires determining how, in money terms, those affected rate the impacts. This may be done by money measurement, market valuation, econometric estimations, hypothetical questions, or observing political choices.

(1) Money measurement. The easiest program effects to value are gains or losses of money. When a new road saves a traveler gasoline and car depreciation, the gain is money in his pocket (plus time, which would be separately valued).

(2) Market valuation. This is related to money measurement. When cloud-seeding increases crop yields, the gains in bushels may be translated into money by valuing them at market prices. The value of a new and better school might be partly gauged as the price increases for homes nearby. When using market valuations, one should be aware of consumer surplus and of taxes or subsidies that may distort prices.

(3) Econometric estimations. Total consumer surplus can be estimated by demand curve analysis—at times (with risk of error) from the demand elasticity at the actual price. Assessment of effects on rates and prices, of displacements and opportunity disbenefits, and of multiplier effects is gained from sensitive understanding of supply and demand phenomena. Sophisticated techniques may often be applied, but these require a grasp of the market (for example, how many patients can shift from one clinic to another, how much of the market price is an effective net gain to the seller, how much gain an entrepreneur could realize elsewhere). Econometric techniques could be used in measuring the market-valued convenience gain of a proposed road. Linear regression analysis might first estimate the relationship between travel convenience and home value (with other factors taken into account). From this relationship and from the road's estimated contribution to travel convenience, the change in home values due to the road could be calculated.

(4) Hypothetical questions. For effects difficult to value by other means, the direct approach of asking people the values of the effects to them (their CVs) may be pursued. A fluoridation program, for instance, could be valued by asking families how much money they would be willing to pay to have their water fluoridated (or how much they would have to be paid to offset the harm they see in fluoridation). Features in airport design can be evaluated, for example, by asking travelers how much they would pay for greater convenience—or would have to be paid to reconcile them to greater inconvenience. Consumer surplus for travel on a new road might be estimated by asking travelers the maximum tolls they would pay without reducing their travel on the road. Such direct questioning has pitfalls: (1) Potentially affected persons may not have thought out their valuation of effects; (2) they may be reluctant to reveal their values; (3) they may have incentive (or think they have) to misreport their values; and (4) they may have systematic and unconscious biases (people usually understate their values if asked how much they would pay and overstate them if asked how much they should be paid).

(5) Observing political choices. Suppose that a downstream town votes to spend $150,000 to make a river fit for swimming, but reverses itself when the cost is raised to $160,000. A regional water purification project upstream would make river swimming possible for a number of localities, including this town. The approximate value of the project for the town could then be taken as $155,000—which could be added to benefits for other localities to determine the project value. To value human lives, one might note that a government approved a highway project estimated to save lives at $36,000 per life but not a disease control project thought to save one life per $40,000 spent. The two figures (assuming no other dimension of benefits for either project) would bracket the life value to the government. Problem 7.3 requires more complex inference of political values. Objections may be raised to valuation by observed political choices:

(a) the multiplicity of program effects—making it difficult to disentangle how different effects influenced decisions;

(b) evident inconsistencies—the government in the second example above might have implemented a meat inspection project saving lives at $55,000 per life;

(c) the randomness of political decisions—reflecting quirks of procedure, the limited opportunities to express intensity of preference (if half plus one of a legislature sees mild net benefit in a project and the rest of a legislature senses substantial net costs, it can be passed), personal idiosyncrasies, transitory public whims, interest group power, and the like; and

(d) the logical reversal in that analysis should be performed to guide public decisions and not the other way around.[1]

7.2.3 Differences Among Dollars

For many reasons, dollars are not all the same. Benefit-cost analysts should be alert to the differences between dollars and should take steps to make dollars of different types commensurable.

(1) Fluctuations in currency value. Due to inflation and to changes in international exchange rates, the buying powers of currencies vary. Either inflation or devaluation of the dollar may prevent next year's dollar from buying as many goods in real terms as this year's dollar. This may be partly handled by adjusting for anticipated inflation (see Section 7.3.10). Currency devaluations or revaluations are less predictable and cannot usually be adjusted for prospectively (analysts who can anticipate these should be making fortunes by currency speculation instead of doing benefit-cost studies).

(2) Varying marginal utility of money. For the average person—who is risk-adverse—the valued difference between losses of $10,000 and $9,000 exceeds the valued difference between the status quo and a gain of $1,000 which in turn exceeds the valued difference between gains of $10,000 and $11,000. This is a major theme in decision analysis (Hammond, 1967; Raiffa, 1968) where preference curves and valuation by hypothetical lotteries can capture these value differences.

---

[1]Mishan (1976: 65) is impatient with the idea of taking analytic guidance from political decisions: "Political decisions may be poor decisions for a large number of reasons too tedious to recount "

(3) Taxes, subsidies, price supports. People and firms know the difference between pretax and posttax dollars. The discrepancy makes it better to save than to earn equal amounts. Consider, for instance, the man in the 18 percent marginal tax bracket who needs work done on his home. He can hire professionals or take time off from his job and do the work himself. Suppose that the fee charged by the professionals would equal the wages lost in taking the necessary time off from work. The man then saves money by doing the work himself. Professionals are paid in his posttax dollars, whereas the missed wages are in pretax dollars. Ben Franklin erred in this case, for a penny saved (not paid to professionals) is actually equivalent to

$$1 \div (1 - .18) = 1.22 \qquad [7.1]$$

pennies earned (due to the certainty of taxes if not of death, which will be considered below). Dollars allocated to subsidized expenditures (perhaps charitable donations or capital investments eligible for tax deductions) go further than dollars for items not subsidized. To obtain the true market valuation of commodities, the effects of taxes, subsidies, and price supports must be separated out from the nominal prices. Firms and individuals should consider the pretax dollar equal to one minus the marginal tax rate of a posttax dollar.

(4) Differences between public and private monies. More than \$1 of private benefits must usually be forgone to obtain a public dollar (due to collection costs, unseen interest costs, excess burden, and lost private consumer surplus and despite excess unburden). Marginal dollars, moreover, can generally achieve more than \$1 of private benefits per \$1 of public outlay. This implies that a public dollar is worth more than a private dollar. While analysis can theoretically relate the values of private and public dollars, this is arduous and rarely done. A more feasible, if analytically imperfect, way to deal with these value differences is to focus on public-private benefit-cost ratios in choosing among programs—as in Sections 5.20 to 5.23 above. (Following the same lines of reasoning, some private dollars—for example, funds scraped together to add a needed new wing to a hospital—may be worth more than others—such as income

supplements for households. The former may have collection costs or excess burden associated with them and may have the capacity to yield more than $1 in benefits per dollar spent. The shadow price of investment—see Section 7.3.6—reflects the greater value [in a second-best world] of private dollars invested over the value of dollars spent on consumption. These differences, too, should be taken into account. Notwithstanding the high value of some private dollars, public dollars will, on average, tend to be worth more than private dollars.)

(5) Discounting. Even if there were no inflation, interest would be paid for savings and would have to be paid for loans. This means that present dollars are worth more than future dollars and less than past dollars. These differences can be taken into account by discounting.

(6) Distributional concerns. A $1 benefit to a person judged deserving is valued more highly by society than a $1 benefit to a person thought less deserving. Ways of dealing with such distributional concerns will be discussed in Section 7.4.

Whenever possible, the analyst should cater to the variable worths of monies by making them commensurable—using the methods mentioned above. This is better than leaving disaggregated the many categories of dollar-valued effects which is, however, in turn better than the too-common practice of treating all types of dollars as equivalent and recklessly consolidating them.

7.3 DISCOUNTING

7.3.1 Governmental Discounting

Individuals and firms can discount to make dollar values occurring at different times commensurable. Governments should discount for the same reason: Investment opportunities and societal preferences may make having one more dollar today just as good as having 1+d more dollars one year from today. Like individuals and firms, governments prefer (other things being equal) to get benefits sooner and pay costs later.

Formulae for present valuation of benefits and costs in the benefit-cost evaluation of a project are:

$$PV(B) = \sum_{i=0}^{n} \frac{b_i}{(1+d)^i} \text{ and} \qquad [7.2]$$

$$PV(C) = \sum_{i=0}^{n} \frac{c_i}{(1+d)^i}, \qquad [7.3]$$

where

$PV(B)$ represents the present value of benefits,
$PV(C)$ represents the present value of costs, and
b_i and c_i represent, respectively, benefits and costs occurring
    i years from the moment of valuation.

(We can see intuitively that these formulae make sense. Getting a benefit equal to b_i dollars i years from today is equivalent to getting a benefit of

$$\frac{b_i}{(1+d)^i} \qquad [7.4]$$

dollars today since that amount of dollars today can be invested to be worth b_i dollars in i years. Similarly, a cost of c_i dollars to be borne i years from today is equivalent to a cost of

$$\frac{c_i}{(1+d)^i} \qquad [7.5]$$

dollars today since, if that amount is put aside today, it will grow to c_i dollars in i years [when the cost must be paid].)

These arguments for governmental discounting might be resisted because governments, unlike individuals and firms, do not invest in savings accounts or stocks and bonds. One response to this is that not taking money out of the private sector to pay for government programs is equivalent to investing in the private sector. Money left in the private sector goes to increasing production, productive capacity, and private consumption—all of which governments value.

7.3.2 The Difference Between Public and Private Discount Rates

The main numerical difference between private and public discounting is that the latter is done at a higher discount rate. This is due largely to the tax structure. Suppose that a government in an economy without inflation defers an expenditure. The citizens put the money temporarily gained in savings accounts, the banks invest the money in corporate stocks, and the corporations use the money from stock sales to increase their plant size. Suppose that the corporations get a 14 percent annual return on their investment. This gain may be distributed as shown in Figure 7.1. The corporations pay corporate income tax amounting to, let us say, half of their pretax profit. The aftertax profits of seven percent benefit its shareholders. The bank, as a shareholder, gets a return of seven percent but has to pay its own overhead and therefore pays only six percent interest on its savings accounts. The difference—one percent—goes to bank overhead. The person getting six percent interest on his savings may be in the 25 percent marginal income tax bracket. He will then annually pay 1.5 percent of his investment as personal income tax. This person would discount his money at 4.5 percent—the rate at which he could personally shift money from year to year (as long as he has a surplus to put in the bank; if he becomes a borrower, his discount rate will be based on the rates at which he could borrow).

The government, on the other hand, sees a 14 percent return to its investment decision (of leaving the money in the private sector). It gains the corporate and individual income taxes directly and is pleased that its banks and citizens are also gaining. The entire gain in its eyes is 14 percent—the rate at which it will discount its monies.

7.3.3 Disagreements over Discounting

For a long time, the U.S. government had a different perspective and focused only on the interest rates paid on its borrowing. Tax advantages of owning government bonds and other factors (for instance, patriotic buying) kept these rates low. In recent years, emphasis on all the benefits that can be

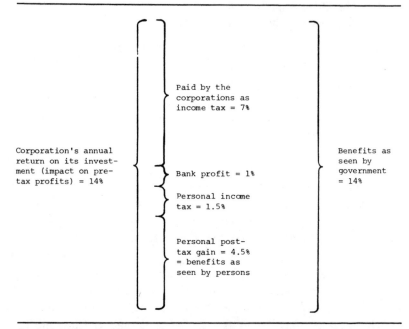

Figure 7.1: Why Persons and Governments Discount at Different Rates: How the Gains from a Personal Investment May be Distributed

achieved by leaving money in the private sector has led to much higher discount rates for analyzing public programs. Determining the most appropriate discount rate for public analysis remains a murky issue. Reasons for disagreement include: (1) Monies put or left in different parts of the private sector have different overall effects; and (2) in valuing gains realized by persons, it is not fully satisfactory to apply the governmental discount rate when the people will value them using their own, much lower rates. (This is one aspect of a larger problem of suboptimal allocation due to the tax structures: Persons deciding whether to postpone some consumption have no incentive to take into account all the good their savings might do in terms of increasing government tax revenues and bank profits.) We examine this issue further in Sections 7.3.5 to 7.3.7.

7.3.4 Agreements on Discounting

These difficult issues have prevented agreement among experts on the best rate for public discounting. Experts do agree that discounting is necessary, and most feel that benefit-cost analyses should both discount by the rate thought best in the particular case and investigate how slightly different assumptions about that discount rate would affect the overall results. (Although some analyses have chosen not to discount at all due to the disagreement on the best rate, this is equivalent to discounting at a rate of zero percent—like deciding a person has zero height because you cannot tell whether he is 5'6" or 5'7"—and is clearly wrong.)

7.3.5 Cases for Different Discount Rates

Example: Determining the Discount Rate

Suppose that capital invested in the private sector earns a six percent return in an economy without inflation (or, equivalently, a six percent real return in an economy with inflation). Half of the return on investment is taxed annually—meaning that individuals obtain a three percent return on investment. Assume that all persons are net savers—and, hence, can transfer consumption funds over time at a discount rate of three percent. Marginal governmental revenues are spent on programs with public-private benefit-cost ratios of 1.0. Consider a project requiring that all persons pay $100 now to gain benefits of $125 in five years. Should this project be enacted? What should be taken as the discount rate if program funding comes from private investment or from private consumption?

Opportunity-cost-of-capital approach. We assume first that the $100 is taken from private investment. The opportunity cost of capital is six percent. Leaving the money in the private sector, it will grow to

$$(\$100)(1.03)^5 = \$115.93 \qquad [7.6]$$

for each person. Meanwhile, the government by reinvesting its taxes at six percent has after five years

$$(\$100)(1.06)^5 - (\$100)(1.03)^5 = \$17.89 \qquad [7.7]$$

per person—which can be returned to the people as program

benefits. For leaving the money in their investments, each person at the end of five years can get a total of

$$\$115.93 + \$17.89 = \$133.82 = (\$100)\,(1.06)^5 \qquad [7.8]$$

in benefits. This is more than the $125 in benefits received through the program, indicating that the program should not be enacted.

When program funds come from private investment, the appropriate discount rate to use is the opportunity cost of capital: here, six percent. Projects will be net beneficial if and only if they have a positive net present value when discounted at this rate.

Marginal-rate-of-time-preference approach. Assume now that project funding comes from private consumption. Persons can transfer consumption monies across years at a three percent discount rate. This implies that the amount of gain realized for the marginal dollar this year should equal the amount of gain realized for the marginal $1.03 next year. If this were not so, money could be transferred between the years to improve the person's position. This relationship holds between all consecutive years, implying that the value of $100 consumed now should be equal to the value of

$$(\$100)\,(1.03)^5 = \$115.93 \qquad [7.9]$$

consumed in five years. To forgo present consumption of $100 and to put the money into the project yields benefits of $125 five years later. This is valued by the person as equivalent to

$$(\$125) \div (1.03)^5 = \$107.83 \qquad [7.10]$$

in money available for present consumption which is more than the $100 required by the project. The person gets a positive compensating variation of $7.83 if the project is enacted. It should therefore be enacted.

When program funds come from private consumption, the appropriate discount rate to use is the marginal rate of time preference: here, three percent. Projects will be net beneficial if and only if they have a positive net present value when discounted at this rate.

The discrepancies between the discount rates based on the opportunity cost of capital and the marginal rate of time preference arise because of taxation: Without taxes on investment, people would realize the opportunity cost of capital on their savings and this would also be the marginal rate of time preference.

*7.3.6 Reconciling Two Approaches to Discounting

The theoretically correct way to reconcile the two approaches—the opportunity cost of capital and the marginal rate of time preference—is laid out by Feldstein (1972). This solution focuses on changes in the welfare of persons: positive and negative compensating variations—often resulting from increases or decreases of money individually spent on consumption. People value these changes by discounting at the marginal rate of time preference and make decisions on consumption and investment accordingly. The opportunity cost of capital is not relevant to the individual who can only invest at the social rate of time preference. It is, however, relevant to society which realizes that investments yield benefits not just to the individual investor but also to the government as taxes. (These are the main effects of investment—which also benefits financial institutions and may affect the productivity of other investments.) The total rate of occurrence of all benefits deriving from investment is the opportunity cost of capital.

Feldstein handles the opportunity cost of capital by defining S, the shadow price of capital as all the good done the investor plus the good done others through the use of the tax money arising from the investment. These benefits are present-valued in calculating S by using the social rate of time preference (the rate at which those benefited value their gains).

Suppose now that a specific project is to be evaluated with benefits b_t and costs c_t in year t of the project and with a total lifetime of T years. Suppose further that any governmental deficit resulting from the project is financed by taxation. Part of the tax, a proportion p, comes from investment (that is, would otherwise have been invested) and the rest, a proportion

1-p, from consumption. We assume the benefits b_t to be non-monetary (an assumption not made by Feldstein). We assume also for the moment that there are no further costs (such as collection costs or behavioral distortions) in the taxation itself. We let d be the marginal rate of time preference.

The net gain of the project is now

$$\sum_{t=0}^{T} \frac{b_t - [pS + (1\text{-}p)]\ c_t}{(1 + d)^t} \qquad [7.11]$$

This is the valuation of the project made by all affected people on the basis of the nonmonetary benefits they receive and their changes in consumption. In the numerator of the formula:

b_t are the nonmonetary benefits;
pSc_t are the effects of taking an amount of money
     pc_t out of investment in year t; and
$(1\text{-}p)c_t$ is lost consumption in year t.

The opportunity cost of capital figures in this expression only in S, the shadow price of capital.

*7.3.7 Reflecting Further Concerns in a Formula for Discounting

Using concepts developed in previous chapters, expression 7.11 can be further refined to reflect both the nonequivalence of public and private money and the multiplier effect. Feldstein's shadow price of capital, S, is the multiplier for investment. Call M_c the multiplier for consumption in the sense that one dollar spent now on consumption yields total benefits of M_c dollars to all affected by the consumption. (S may be analogously perceived.) Net private effects (as seen above) are PRG-PRL. Call the monetary part of this PRIME (private monetary effects) and the nonmonetary part PRINE. The nonmonetary effects have no further repercussions. The monetary effects (whether positive or negative) affect investment and consumption in the proportions p and 1-p. This means that the full effects of the private monetary gains and losses are

$$\text{PRIME} \cdot [pS + M_c (1\text{-}p)] \qquad [7.12]$$

as valued by all affected. The second factor,

$$pS + M_c (1-p) \qquad [7.13]$$

we label S_{prime} , the shadow price of private monetary effects.
Net public effects are PUG-PUL. Call this PUE. Label as S_{pue}
the shadow price of public effects—reflecting the fact that
marginal public money can go toward net beneficial projects or
to reduce the burden and excess burden of taxes and will have
further repercussions as persons invest or consume these monetary gains. (A further effect that should be reflected in the
shadow prices occurs through influence on rates and prices—as
seen in Sections 6.4.10 through 6.4.18. Public borrowing, for
instance, not only bids resources away from the private sector
but also increases the interest paid on other public and private
borrowing: a transfer to lenders.) Labeling the year as t, the net
effects of any project may be expressed as

$$\sum_{t=0}^{t=T} \frac{PRINE(t) + PRIME(t) \cdot S_{prime} + PUE(t) \cdot S_{pue}}{(1 + d)^t}. \qquad [7.14]$$

This expression caters to the opportunity cost of capital, the
marginal rate of time preference, the shadow price of capital,
the multiplier on consumption, and the nonequivalence of
public and private money. All the arguments advanced for
considering each of these concerns are reasons for taking expression 7.14 as the best formulation of project value.

Perhaps, some day, expression 7.14 (or related formulae) will
become the yardstick for valuation. At present and for the near
future, it will not be. The shadow prices and multipliers are not
known and would be troublesome to calculate. Simpler procedures are essential.

7.3.8 Practical Considerations

Even Feldstein's simpler expression 7.11 is unwieldy to use
and is generally ignored in applied benefit-cost analysis. Its
theoretical correctness must be weighed against the practical
difficulties it entails. Instead of using a shadow price for capital,

analysts (see, for instance, Harberger, 1969; Ramsey, 1969; Usher, 1969) most often pick some discount rate (generally as a weighted average) between the opportunity cost of capital and the marginal rate of time preference. Some (Joint Economic Committee, U.S. Congress, 1968; Harberger, 1969; Ramsey, 1969) have suggested that the appropriate discount rate be obtained as a weighted average of different rates of return depending on where the money comes from. Feldstein (1972), however, has shown that any such weighted rate leads to analytic errors.

Expressions 7.11 and 7.14 avoid such errors, but at some cost. To incorporate all the refinements implicit in these formulae and to perform their requisite calculations is presently judged to be an excess burden on the benefit-cost analyst. As a practical measure, it seems best to follow current practice: to choose one reasonable discount rate and to apply it consistently to all benefits and costs. If there is disagreement about which rate is most reasonable to use, the analysis can be performed again using other rates. We examine further this standard approach.

7.3.9 Discounting in the Presence of Inflation

Inflation complicates discounting.

Example: Personal Investments During Inflation

Suppose that a person invests in tax-free municipal bonds which give a seven percent return and that inflation runs steadily at five percent. Two years from today, the person will make a $1,000 payment on his home mortgage and will buy a car equivalent to one costing $4,000 today. What is the person's present valuation of these future payments?

Solution. For the mortgage payment, the person knows the actual money amount to be paid; for the car, the person knows its real value in present money. If

$$\frac{\$1,000}{1.07^2} = \$873 \qquad [7.15]$$

is set aside today, it will grow to $1,000 when the mortgage payment is due. The present value of the mortgage payment is $873, found using the discount rate of seven percent. This is the

nominal discount rate: the rate at which the decisionmaker trades off sums of money at different times.

The car cost may also be present-valued using the nominal rate. We first calculate the dollar cost of the car in two years. This cost, along with other prices, inflates at an annual rate of five percent and is

$$(\$4,000)\,(1.05)^2 = \$4,410 \qquad [7.16]$$

after two years. The present value of this is

$$\frac{\$4,410}{(1.07)^2} = \$3,852. \qquad [7.17]$$

The car cost may be alternatively valued using the

real discount rate: the rate at which the decision actor trades off real-valued quantities at different times.

In real terms, the person's money is only growing at a rate of

$$\frac{1.07}{1.05} = 1.0190, \qquad [7.18]$$

or 1.9 percent. While the nominal dollar value of his investment grows at seven percent, inflation is eating up the investment at an annual rate of five percent, leading to a real growth rate of only 1.9 percent. The cost of the car in real terms does not change: It remains priced at $4,000 in two years in terms of today's money. (Only the diminishing value of the dollar increases the cost in dollar terms.) To pay in two years an amount real-valued at $4,000 in present dollars requires that

$$\frac{\$4,000}{(1.019)^2} = \$3,852 \qquad [7.19]$$

present dollars be set aside today. This is the present value of the car cost and agrees with our previous calculation. To present-value a real-valued quantity we have used the real discount rate.

7.3.10 Real and Nominal Discount Rates

(1) To present-value nominal values, one uses nominal discount rates. Nominal values are actual dollar amounts—for instance, payments to be paid or received—that, once decided on, are not affected by inflation.

(2) To present-value real values, one may either (a) inflate them to obtain their nominal values and then discount these using the nominal discount rate, or (b) value them directly using the real discount rate. The second way is usually easier. Real values include benefits and costs—for example, consumer surplus, the worth of increased crop yields, hospital equipment costs, teacher salaries, road construction expenses—that are expressed in the money terms of one time but that appreciate over time (in money terms but not in real terms) due to inflation. Resource costs occurring i years in the future may be present-valued by dividing present costs (how much the resources would cost if purchased today) by

$$(1 + rd)^i, \qquad\qquad [7.20]$$

where rd is the real discount rate.

(3) The real discount rate, rd, is given by

$$1 + rd = \frac{1 + nd}{1+p} \qquad\qquad [7.21]$$

where nd is the nominal discount rate and p is the rate of price inflation. Different real discount rates may be applied to different resources if the rates of their price inflation vary.

(4) Reasonable real discount rates for the U.S. government to use based on the opportunity cost of capital are between five and seven percent. These numbers are based on the real rate of return—pretax profits divided by assets of nonfinancial institutions over the long run. (The rate of return was slightly

higher than seven percent in the 1960s and has declined below seven percent in the 1970s.) Real discount rates based on marginal rates of time preference would be somewhat lower.

Adjusting for inflation while discounting is arithmetically straightforward. Unfortunately, it represents one more consideration to be kept in mind during the analysis and has therefore often led to mistakes.

7.3.11 Discounting in Project Evaluation

Example: Comparing Public and Private Effects

A contemplated project has costs and other effects in thousands of dollars according to Table 7.1. The nominal discount rate for the government is 12 percent. What is the public-private benefit-cost ratio for the project?

Solution. We see that the first three years of the project are the start-up phase requiring substantial government investment and some private disbenefits. In the third year, program benefits commence and are accompanied by public fund gains (fees or tolls collected). These reach a steady-state level in the fourth year and remain there through the sixth year. Public costs in the fourth through sixth years drop to a maintenance level, while program operation increases private disbenefits.

The public-private benefit-cost ratio compares net public costs (NPUC) to net private benefits (NPRB). The former are calculated by subtracting public fund gains from public costs; the latter, by subtracting private disbenefits from private benefits. Performing these subtractions for each year condenses costs and effects to those shown in Table 7.2. Each of these streams of effects is now present-valued (PV) to the perspective of the first year:

$$\text{PV(NPUC)} = 100 + \frac{100}{1.12} + \frac{60}{(1.12)^2} - \frac{75}{(1.12)^3} - \frac{75}{(1.12)^4} - \frac{75}{(1.12)^5}$$

$$= 93.51;$$

$$PV(NPRB) = -10 - \frac{10}{1.12} + \frac{35}{(1.12)^2} + \frac{85}{(1.12)^3} + \frac{85}{(1.12)^4} + \frac{85}{(1.12)^5}$$

$$= 171.72 \hspace{3cm} [7.22]$$

From the vantage point of the first year, the net private costs amount to an equivalent of 93.51 thousand first-year dollars and net private benefits to 171.72 thousand first-year dollars. The public-private benefit-cost ratio is

$$B/C = 171.72/93.51 = 1.84. \hspace{2cm} [7.23]$$

This ratio is independent of the year taken as the basis for present valuation. If, for instance, the present valuation were set in terms of second-year dollars, all terms on the righthand sides of equations 7.22 would be multiplied by 1.12. This yields:

$$PV_{second\ year}\ (NPUC) = 104.73,$$
$$PV_{second\ year}\ (NPRB) = 192.33, and$$
$$B/C = 1.84. \hspace{3cm} [7.24]$$

7.3.12 Discounting for the Public-Private Benefit-Cost Ratio

The general rule for calculating the public-private benefit-cost ratio is to divide present-valued net public costs into present-valued net private benefits:

$$public\text{-}private\ B/C = \frac{PV(NPRB)}{PV(NPUC)}. \hspace{1cm} [7.25]$$

The two expressions on the right-hand side are calculated by

$$PV(NPUC) = \sum_{i=0}^{n} \frac{PUL(i) - PUG(i)}{(1+d)^i}, \hspace{1cm} [7.26]$$

where n is the number of years over which project effects are felt, PUL(i) is public loss i years in the future, PUG(i) is public gain i years in the future, and d is the discount rate (the

TABLE 7.1   Costs and Effects of a Project Over a Six-Year Period as
            Nominal Dollar Amounts

Year	1	2	3	4	5	6
Public Costs	100	100	100	5	5	5
Public Fund Gains	0	0	40	80	80	80
Private Gains	0	0	50	110	110	110
Private Disbenefits	10	10	15	25	25	25

nominal rate if PUL(i) and PUG(i) are in actual dollar terms, the
real rate if they are in real terms); and

$$PV(NPRB) = \sum_{i=0}^{n} \frac{PRG(i) - PRL(i)}{(1 + d)^i} ,$$

[7.27]

where PRG(i) and PRL(i) are private gains and losses i years in
the future.

7.3.13   The Influence of Discount Rate Choice

Increasingly sensed by decisionmakers is the importance of
the discount rate chosen as the basis for present valuation.
Suppose that the discount rate of 12 percent used above is
thought to be two percent too high. (The debate over the
appropriate rate ranges far beyond this two percent difference.)
What effect will lowering the discount rate by two percent have
on the benefit-cost ratio?

At first glance, the difference seems minor: First-year effects
will not be altered and second-year effects will be altered by less
than two percent. Sixth-year figures will be 9.4 percent higher
when discounted to first-year present value. Present valuation to
first-year terms at 10 percent gives

$$PV(NPUC) = 100 + \frac{100}{1.1} + \frac{60}{(1.1)^2} - \frac{75}{(1.1)^3} - \frac{75}{(1.1)^4} - \frac{75}{(1.1)^5}$$

$$= 86.35,$$

TABLE 7.2   Project Impacts Consolidated to Public and Private Status

Year	1	2	3	4	5	6
Net Public Costs (NPUC)	100	100	60	−75	−75	−75
Net Private Benefits (NPRB)	−10	−10	35	85	85	85

$$PV(NPRB) = -10 - \frac{10}{1.1} + \frac{35}{(1.1)^2} + \frac{85}{(1.1)^3} + \frac{85}{(1.1)^4} + \frac{85}{(1.1)^5}$$

$$= 184.53, \text{ and}$$

$$B/C = 2.14 \qquad\qquad [7.28]$$

Lowering the discount rate by two percent thus raises the benefit-cost ratio from 1.84 to 2.14—an increase of 16 percent. For programs with longer time horizons—for example, long-range research and development—the sensitivity of the benefit-cost ratio to slight changes in the discount rate is even more pronounced.

7.3.14 Consistent Discounting

Example: Supplemental Education

A government is pondering long-run approaches to programs of supplemental education. One alternative is to provide a program to second graders at a cost of $50 per pupil. A second alternative is to implement a program for seventh graders at a cost of $155 per pupil. The third alternative is to put both programs into effect. Program benefits are measured at grade 12 when the students enter the labor market. The second-grade program is found to produce per-pupil cognitive and affective combined gains of 7.4 rating points measured 10 years later For present twelfth graders, the present value of this gain is $195. The seventh-grade program gains 15.9 rating points—a current twelfth grade value of $420. The two programs combined gain 21.8 rating points, a twelfth-grade value of $575.

Funds not spent on these programs will go instead to special one-year programs with a public-private benefit-cost ratio of 1.4. The government's nominal discount rate is 12 percent and the rate of inflation is five percent. Which program should be implemented?

Solution. We consider what should be done for present second graders and lay out the alternatives in Table 7.3 on a per-pupil basis. We note that all benefits and costs are set in real dollar terms: They will grow from year to year at the inflation rate. We discount them at the real discount rate of

$$\frac{1.12}{1.05} = 1.0667 \qquad [7.29]$$

or 6.67 percent. The present-valued benefits and costs shown in Table 7.3 have been calculated using this discount rate.

We see that all three alternatives are better than no program of supplemental education: Their benefit-cost ratios exceed 1.4, which is the ratio of benefits to costs for alternative uses of the money (the special one-year programs). Comparing Alternatives 1 and 3 shows that the only difference between them is the seventh-grade program included in Alternative 3 but not in Alternative 1. The additional costs of the seventh-grade program have a present value of $112 and the additional benefits of

$$\$575 - \$195 = \$380 \qquad [7.30]$$

have a present value of

$$\frac{\$380}{1.0667^{10}} = \$200. \qquad [7.31]$$

The ratio of present-valued benefits to costs for adding the seventh-grade program to the second-grade program is

$$\frac{\$200}{\$112} = 1.79. \qquad [7.32]$$

It is better to spend this money to add the seventh-grade program to Alternative 1—getting a benefit-cost ratio of 1.79 from this addition—than to spend it instead on the special one-year programs. This establishes that Alternative 3 is better than Alternative 1.

We next compare Alternatives 2 and 3, the only difference between them being that the second-grade program is added to Alternative 2 to transform it into Alternative 3. This addition has present-valued costs of $50 and present-valued benefits of

$$\frac{\$575 - \$420}{1.0667^{10}} = \$81. \qquad [7.33]$$

The benefit-cost ratio is

$$\frac{\$81}{\$50} = 1.63. \qquad [7.34]$$

This is also higher than 1.4—establishing that it is better to spend $50 per pupil to change Alternative 2 into Alternative 3 than to spend this money instead on the special one-year programs. Alternative 3—programs of supplemental education in the second and seventh grades—is thus the best policy.

7.3.15 A Pitfall

Before leaving this example, we should note a common trap. With programs spending money in different years, it may seem reasonable to discount the costs and benefits for each program to the year in which program spending begins. However, this is wrong: Programs can only be accurately compared by discounting them consistently—present-valuing them to the same year.

Suppose in this example that we had present-valued all benefits and costs to the year in which the monies are first spent for each alternative. This would have meant that Alternative 2 would have been present-valued to a moment five years in the future. At that time, all prices would be higher by a factor of

$$1.05^5 = 1.28 \qquad [7.35]$$

and both benefits and costs would be discounted by five years

TABLE 7.3 Display of Costs and Benefits for Alternative Programs of
Supplemental Education (000)

Alternative	Money Spent Now	Real Value (in terms of present money) of		Present-Valued Costs	Present-Valued Benefits	Present-Valued B-C	B ÷ C
		Money Spent In Five Years	Benefits In Ten Years				
1	$50	$ 0	$195	$ 50	$102	$ 52	2.05
2		$155	$420	$112	$220	$108	1.96
3	$50	$155	$575	$162	$302	$140	1.86

less—meaning that their present values would increase by a
factor of

$$1.0667^5 = 1.38. \qquad [7.36]$$

These two differences imply that present-valuing Alternative 2
to five years in the future would multiply both the present-
valued benefits and costs shown in Table 7.3 by

$$(1.28)(1.38) = 1.76. \qquad [7.37]$$

Net benefits for Alternative 2 then work out to be $190—which
are higher than those for Alternative 3. The benefit-cost ratio
(not affected by the decision on how to calculate present
values) for Alternative 2 is higher than that for Alternative 3.
With higher net benefits and a higher benefit-cost ratio, Alternative 2 may seem clearly better than Alternative 3. This
erroneous conclusion has arisen because the alternatives were
inconsistently discounted—present-valued to different years.

An incorrect answer would also be obtained if the alternatives were compared in a different way: by assuming that each
program begins immediately and present-valuing all costs to the
present. This means that Alternatives 1 and 3 would be evaluated for present second graders but Alternative 2 would be

evaluated for present seventh graders. This would have the
effect of multiplying benefits and costs by

$$1.0667^5 = 1.38 \qquad [7.38]$$

for Alternative 2 and would find its net benefits to be $149.
This again makes Alternative 2—with higher net benefits and a
better benefit-cost ratio—look better than Alternative 3. This is
wrong because the alternatives have not been consistently compared: The choice is not between implementing Alternative 2
for present seventh graders and implementing Alternative 3 for
present second graders, but between implementing either policy
over the long run for the same pupils. Consistent discounting—
as performed in Section 7.3.14—shows Alternative 3 to be the
best.

7.3.16 Internal Rate of Return

In choosing among projects with benefits and costs dispersed
over time, we have urged that present valuation be relied on. An
alternative to present valuation is the *internal rate of return*:

the discount rate at which the net present value of a
project is zero.

A project that consists of investing $100,000 today and getting
$108,000 in benefits a year from today would thus have an
internal rate of return of eight percent. To deposit your money
in a savings account paying six percent annual interest is a
project for you with an internal rate of return of six percent. In
general, the greater the internal rate of return for a project, the
greater its attractiveness as an investment. This suggests that
public decisionmakers might choose among projects by selecting
those with highest internal rate of return. This intuitive principle turns out not to work.

7.3.17 Calculating and Using
the Internal Rate of Return

We revert to the example of Section 7.3.14 and attempt to
choose among alternatives using the internal rate of return. For

simplicity, we now assume that public and private dollars are equivalent. For Alternative 1, the internal rate of return is a discount rate of d_1 such that

$$PV = 0 = -\$50 + \frac{\$195}{(1 + d_1)^{10}}. \qquad [7.39]$$

This is solved to find that

$$d_1 = 14.58 \text{ percent}, \qquad [7.40]$$

the internal rate of return. Similarly, the internal rate of return for the second alternative is calculated to be 22.06 percent. For the third alternative, calculation is more difficult: requiring calculation of a discount rate, d_3, such that

$$PV = 0 = -\$50 - \frac{\$155}{(1 + d_3)^5} + \frac{\$575}{(1 + d_3)^{10}}. \qquad [7.41]$$

A process of trial and error reveals that

$$d_3 = 16.85 \text{ percent}. \qquad [7.42]$$

If we were to select projects on the basis of internal rates of return, Alternative 2 would be selected, while, as we saw in Section 7.3.14, Alternative 3 is truly best.

7.3.18 Problems with the Internal Rate of Return

There are many reasons why heeding the internal rate of return may lead to errors.

(1) Improper comparison of alternatives. We saw in Section 5.3 that benefit-cost ratios are a poor basis for choosing among mutually exclusive alternatives. More relevant are marginal benefit-cost ratios. In the problem above, the relevant marginal internal rate of return is that between Alternatives 2 and 3, d_{23}, yielding between the two:

$$PV = 0 = -\$50 + \frac{\$575 - \$420}{(1 + d_{23})^{10}}. \qquad [7.43]$$

This gives

$$d_{23} = 11.98 \text{ percent.} \qquad [7.44]$$

This shows that the internal rate of return for expanding Alternative 2 to Alternative 3 (11.98 percent) is greater than the real discount rate (6.67 percent) and hence that Alternative 3 should be preferred. Setting out the appropriate comparison of alternatives thus enables us to determine the best alternative using the internal rate of return. However, specifying just what alternative is to be considered in comparison to which other can be unwieldy—more so than the similar comparisons required using present valuation.

(2) Irrelevance. Consider two alternative projects, A and B, as shown in Table 7.4 in an economy without inflation. Assume the appropriate discount rate to be 10 percent. The projects require the same outlay but require different waits until different benefit amounts are received. Present valuations of benefits at 10 percent and the internal rates of return have been calculated and are shown. Present valuation indicates that B is better; rate of return, that A is better. Which should be preferred?

The arguments given in Chapter 2 showed that the project with higher present value—here, Project B—is better. If this valuation is for a private firm, after 10 years it will have

$$(\$249)\,(1.10)^{10} = \$645 \qquad [7.45]$$

more for undertaking Project A rather than no project; and

$$(\$429)\,(1.10)^{10} = \$1113 \qquad [7.46]$$

more for undertaking Project B rather than no project.

The internal rates of return show that only Project A would be profitable (have net positive present value) if the discount rate were between 14 and 15 percent. But this is irrelevant: The discount rate is 10 percent, not between 14 and 15 percent.

One way of explaining these results is by noting that Project A obtains a better return over the first five years but only a 10 percent return (when reinvested in other projects) over the second five years. Project B—returning 14 percent per year over 10 years—turns out better. If the profits from Project A could be reinvested for the second five years at 15 percent (or a bit less), then A would be better. (If many such investment opportunities existed, then the discount rate (the opportunity cost of funds) would not be 10 but rather 15 percent.)

(3) Multiple internal rates of return. One project may have more than one internal rate of return. Consider a project that requires $1 million initial investment, pays off $2.19 million one year later, but causes further costs of $1.1984 million two years later. It is left to the reader to show that both seven and 12 percent could be taken as internal rates of return.

7.3.19 The Choice Between Project Criteria

For all these reasons, reliance on present valuation instead of internal rate of return seems superior in benefit-cost analysis. The primary worth of internal rate of return occurs for the private firm or individual faced with a broad variety of opportunities—so broad and various that the marginal opportunity cost of money (the discount rate) is not immediately known. By calculating the various internal rates of return, the marginal opportunity cost of capital can be determined—and subsequently used as a discount rate for present valuation.

7.4 TAKING DISTRIBUTIONAL EFFECTS INTO ACCOUNT

7.4.1 When Testing for a Potential Pareto Improvement is Insufficient

The major shortcoming of benefit-cost analysis as based on the notion of the potential Pareto improvement is the neglect of distributional concerns. Consider two different situations:

(1) A program has the effect of taking $100 from each of 1,000 poor people and of benefiting each of 1,000 rich people by $105. A society might well decide that this program—a potential Pareto improvement—is bad because the harm done to the poor outweighs the good done to the rich. This conclusion is partly based on the impossibility of adequately compensating

TABLE 7.4   Situation in which Present Valuation and Internal Rate of
Return Give Contradictory Guidance for Project Selection

Project	Money Spent Now	Years Until Benefits Realized	Benefits	Present Valuation of Benefits Discounting at Ten Percent	Internal Rate of Return
A	$1,000	5	2,011	$1,249	.15
B	$1,000	10	3,707	$1,429	.14

the poor. With appropriate redistributions from the benefiting
rich to the losing poor, there would be no losers (a Pareto
improvement) and no objection to the program. Appropriate
redistributions, however, are practically difficult to bring
about—a difficulty that forces decisionmakers to look beyond
the net benefits of a program to their distributional effects.

(2) A program has the effect of taking $105 from each of
1,000 rich people and benefiting each of 1,000 poor people by
$100. Society might well consider this a good program even
though it is not a potential Pareto improvement. This judgment
would be based on a feeling that the good done the poor
outweighs the harm done the rich. The program would lose
appeal if there were more efficient ways of transferring money
or benefits from the rich to the poor (for example, benefiting
the poor in the same amount while costing the rich less).
Without better ways to aid the poor, this program may be a
wise choice for society.

In the first example, a potential Pareto improvement (net
benefits) is considered bad; in the second, a program that is not
a potential Pareto improvement (having net costs) is thought
good. Distributional concerns underlie each judgment. We wonder, though how these considerations might best be incorpor-
ated into or linked with benefit-cost analysis. Three strategies
are considered: (1) fashioning a social value function, (2) valuing distributional effects as global effects, and (3) describing but
not valuing distributional effects.

7.4.2 Social Value Functions

A *social welfare function* is

a function of all aspects of a society—both economic and noneconomic—that reflects the choices the society would make (by some accepted decision criterion) when faced with a decision among many different possible situations.

A *social value function*

values all aspects of a possible program or change in such a way that programs or changes assigned higher values by the social value function are preferred to others assigned lower values.

A social value function is thus an objective function for valuing programs and changes. It may be derived from a social welfare function by applying the latter to the state of society that a program or change would bring about.

7.4.3 Valuing a Program with Differentially Weighted Impacts on People

Example: Variable Valuation

Suppose that a society considers a person the more deserving of governmental program benefits the less money he has. A civic improvements program might benefit or harm lawyers with salaries of $50,000, postmen with annual earnings of $15,000, and laborers with annual wages of $7,000. One version of the program would provide a gain of $10,000 to lawyers; another version would, for the same cost, benefit postmen in the same amount. This society clearly prefers the latter. However, what if the second version of the program would, at equal cost, benefit the postmen by only $8,000? Is this better or worse than the original version benefiting lawyers by $10,000?

Toward a solution. The answer depends on the values of society. The society could determine that a benefit of $1.00 to lawyers is equivalent to (just as good as in the eyes of society) a benefit of $0.60 to postmen or a benefit of $0.50 to laborers. Losses might be similarly weighted. With a scale setting the social importance of gains and losses as a function of individual income (or other attributes), a social value function (SVF) can be constructed: the social value is obtained by summing over all individuals their compensating variations for the action multiplied by the importance of each individual. In mathematical formulation:

$$SVF(a) = \sum_{i=1}^{n} CV_i \cdot I_i, \qquad [7.47]$$

where

    $SVF(a)$ is the social value of action a,
    n is the number of persons affected by the action,
    CV_i is the compensating variation (either positive or negative) for individual i, and
    I_i is the importance to the society of a dollar's gain or loss accruing to individual i.

This social value function is just the standard formulation for calculating net benefits, modified by weighting the effects for each individual by his importance. (Conversely, standard net benefit calculation is this social value function with all individuals weighted equally (all I_i equal to 1.0).) With the societal determinations given above, we would have

$$
\begin{aligned}
I_{lawyer} &= 1.00,\\
I_{postman} &= 1.67, \text{ and}\\
I_{laborer} &= 2.00. \qquad [7.48]
\end{aligned}
$$

7.4.4 Interpreting Social Value Functions

Such a social value function confirms that a potential Pareto improvement may be a bad thing. A program that benefits lawyers by $15,000 while hurting laborers by a negative CV of

$10,000 is a pPi but has negative social value:

$$SV(\text{program}) = (\$15,000)(1.00) - (\$10,000)(2.00)$$
$$= -\$5,000. \qquad [7.49]$$

The rationale for the pPi—that the winners *could* more than compensate all losers—is, in this view, irrelevant until such compensation takes place. Conversely, a program that is not a pPi may have positive social value. A program version that yields a benefit of $8,000 to postmen at a cost of $10,000 to lawyers is not a pPi (because costs exceed benefits) but has positive social value

$$SV(\text{program}) = (\$8,000)(1.67) - (\$10,000)(1.00)$$
$$= \$3,333. \qquad [7.50]$$

In the example of the contemplated road, we noted that a regional government might disregard all effects on noncitizens of the region and that politicians might overlook all effects on persons outside their constituencies. This is equivalent to assigning zero weight ($I_i = 0$) to those people. A social value function with varying weights is a more sensitive form of this. Instead of merely differentiating between one group to be ignored and another to be weighted equally, gradations of value may be reflected.

7.4.5 The Pros and Cons of Social Value Functions

Do such social value functions exist? Yes—if implicitly and in modified form. Income redistributions, varying marginal income tax rates, and special service programs for segments of the population indicate that societies weight (value) gains and losses for some people more highly than for others. Could the implicit weightings of a society be discovered? In theory, yes; in practice, maybe not. Marginal tax rates provide a rough gauge of weights but also reflect such other considerations as incentives. Program decisions could be retrospectively analyzed to see what value trade-offs were involved and how they were resolved (why families with incomes between $4,000 and $5,000 annually were given one level of support and families between $5,000 and $6,000 another). While a general notion of weightings might be derived, these would not be exact or unambiguous or even completely consistent. Legislative decisionmakers avoid determining too precisely their value structures. The ambiguity they allow both shields their actions from too-close scrutiny and prevents analysts armed with such quantified values from making their decisions for them.

True, implicit functions for social valuation are more complex than the formulation of 7.47. Actual decisions may be guided by:

(1) population characteristics other than income—number of dependents, age, ability to work, past history all bear on the social weights accorded individuals;

(2) program attributes—CVs for health program benefits may, for example, be valued more highly than CVs for transportation programs;

(3) weighting losses more heavily than gains; and

(4) declining marginal weights for individuals—the difference between positive CVs of $1,000 and $2,000 is likely to be valued lower for the same person than a positive CV of $1,000 (with the reverse true for negative CVs). This may be due to the declining marginal utility of money.

7.4.6 Valuing Distributional Considerations as Global Effects

An alternative approach to reflecting distributional concerns is to value them as global effects. Suppose that a society judges a program that takes $105,000 from the rich in order to give $100,000 to the poor to be good. This implies that the society values transferring the money from the rich to the poor more than it regrets the economic inefficiency (the loss of $5,000). Perhaps the individual members of society get personal global benefits in knowing that the poor are adequately cared for. These global benefits could be measured as compensating variations: how much each person would be willing to pay to know that money or other benefits are being delivered to the poor. If 10,000 people would each pay $1 (their positive CV) to have

$105,000 taken from the rich and $100,000 given to the poor, then that program becomes a potential Pareto improvement. If such global effects could be measured, then including them in standard benefit-cost calculations might eliminate the need for special weighting of benefits and costs received by different groups as in a social value function. (The weighting is not really eliminated but takes place in each person's head as he decides how much he would pay for the global effects.) Unfortunately, estimating the CVs for global effects is difficult (see Section 6.5.5) and means that this methodology is impractical for most program evaluations.

7.4.7 Describing But Not Valuing Distributional Effects

Given the difficulties in formulating social value functions or in measuring global effects, a more modest strategy for dealing with distributional effects suggests itself. Instead of trying to include distributional effects mathematically in the benefit-cost calculations, it may be best for the analyst to just keep track of groups and individuals who bear costs and realize gains and to provide information (for instance, on income, dependents, histories) affecting the way that society would value benefits and costs received by different people.

Until a satisfactory methodology for capturing distributional concerns is developed, this more limited approach seems best. It essentially asks the analyst to remain alert to the distributional issues but not to try too zealously to boil them down into numbers. It leaves the decisionmakers the delicate problem of making policy choices in the light of benefit-cost calculations and further information on the incidence of benefits and costs.

7.5 THIS CHAPTER AND OTHER WRITINGS

Most works on benefit-cost analysis address the question of how program effects should be measured and valued. Valuation is generally by estimation of actual monetary transfers or of changes in consumer or producer surplus. Each of these estimates may require intricate econometric work. Interesting econometric applications include the measurement of demand for mass transit use as a function of service level (Kain, 1964), the estimation of the harm done by airport noise seen in its effect on property values (Morrall, 1979), the estimated harm done by automobile emissions based on market valuations (U.S. Senate Committee on Public Works, 1974), and the valuation of housing externalities through the measured variation in home prices (United States Department of Housing and Urban Development, 1974). Hypothetical questions—asking people their compensating variations—have been tried (see Mishan, 1970; Acton. 1973b) but have met so far with limited success, as many answers obtained are demonstrably inconsistent. One reasonably successful application of hypothetical questions (asking workers how they would commute if not by their current mode) is described by Beesley (1965), who used econometric methods to sort through the evident inconsistencies. A well-known attempt to infer societal values from actual governmental decisions is that of Weisbrod (1968).

The texts on benefit-cost analysis in developing countries (Little and Mirrlees, 1974; Roemer and Stern, 1975; Squire and van der Tak, 1975) address problems of some goods being priced in local, nonconvertible money and others in convertible currency. This requires the shadow pricing of currencies rather than relying on official exchange rates. The declining marginal utility of money for individuals is a standard topic in economics (see Friedman and Savage, 1948) and in decision analysis (see Raiffa, 1968). In benefit-cost analysis, these concepts seem never to have been applied and would be relevant, in any case, only for programs dealing with large changes in personal assets (for example, disaster insurance).

Discounting has traditionally been among the murkiest areas of benefit-cost analysis. Important theoretical articles on discounting are by Feldstein (1964) and Diamond (1968). Baumol (1968) gives a wide-ranging and somewhat pessimistic discussion of the conceptual and operational difficulties involved in discounting. An enlightening view of the tremendously different ways that discounting has been performed in the U.S. government is provided by Staats (1968). For detailed explanations of why and how the opportunity cost of capital should be handled as a shadow price (instead of a weighted part of the discount rate), Marglin (1963) and Feldstein (1972) are recommended. A good introductory discussion of discounting is found is Stokey and Zeckhauser (1978). Their treatment of the internal rate of return is typical of most current literature: They explain what it is (because the student may someday encounter it); they show its problems; and they urge focusing instead on net present value. Bierman and Smidt (1975), in the capital budgeting literature, take a similar tack. A noteworthy empirical piece relying heavily on the notion of the internal rate of return is by Weisbord (1971). Squire and van der Tak (1975) consider using the discount rate as a rationing device; adjusting it to the point where the total outlay on projects with net present value equals the budget money available. This is generally equivalent to choosing according to the internal rate of return—entailing many problems described in Section 7.3.18 (which are recognized by Squire and van der Tak).

Social welfare functions can be traced back to Bergson (1938) and are critically reviewed by Zeckhauser and Schaefer (1968). Harberger (1971) urges that distributional adjustments not be allowed to intrude in the relatively clear-cut calculations of project efficiency. Sugden and Williams (1978) describe the use of "distributional weights" allied to the social value functions presented above. Squire and van der Tak (1975) present their own parameterized version of a social welfare function. Feldstein et al. (1972) apply a similar parametric form to the problem of evaluating plans for national health insurance. Five intriguing papers considering different aspects of distributional efficiency and equity are found in Section II-B of Zeckhauser (1975a). Harrison and Rubinfeld (1978) estimate the distributional impact of benefits from air quality improvements using econometric estimations based on housing market values.

8

Valuing Human Lives

8.1 CHAPTER OVERVIEW

To associate a monetary value with a human life is, as argued in Sections 8.2 to 8.4, difficult and distasteful, but inevitable. If we are to value lives, a number of complexities (seen in Section 8.5) must be dealt with and an appropriate philosophy for calculating money values must be determined. By looking, in Sections 8.6 and 8.7, at different funds that might be spent to extend lives, four alternative life values can be formulated. Of these, the most important is the Pareto life value—based on the notion of a potential Pareto improvement. Drawbacks to this value are the narrowness of its view and its amorality—the latter a common aspect of analysis.

In Sections 8.10 through 8.12, we examine three related life values, of which one—the earnings life value—is by far the most commonly used of all life values. All three of these values have justifications but also telling defects. In Sections 8.13 through 8.15, we consider a methodology—the willingness-to-pay life value—that can reflect the willingness of people to save or to buy insurance to be able to cover the costs of life extensions. An extension of this—the social life value seen in Sections 8.16 through 8.18—meets many of the objections raised to other life values. Its theoretical appeal is tarnished by the practical difficulties in its estimation.

A numerical example shows in Section 8.19 the dependence of the willingness-to-pay life value on circumstances. Alternative life values are reviewed and commented on in Section 8.20. This overview brings out the importance of the continuing improvement of these methodologies.

8.2 WHY WE NEED TO VALUE HUMAN LIVES

Many programs affect the lengths of human lives. For such programs as disease control and highway safety, life-saving is a primary goal. For other policy decisions, such as the choice of primary energy sources, differential impacts on lives (coal miner deaths weighed against lives shortened by radiation exposure) are important peripheral effects. Somehow the importance of shortening or extending lives must be reflected in the analysis of programs with such effects.

We consider for the sake of concreteness a specific program effect: extending a person's life from age 55 to age 75. Several hypothetical decisions may require valuing this effect:

(1) A publicly supported health intervention program might be able to extend an estimated 10 lives (from 55 to 75) at a total cost of $1,500,000. To decide whether to implement this program, decisionmakers must determine whether, given the other demands on public resources, society can afford to mount this program and in effect to extend lives at a cost of $150,000 per life extension.

(2) A high-speed highway would bring estimated net economic benefits of $2,000,000 per year but would increase traffic fatalities by an estimated five per year—over the age range from zero to 80. Somehow, in deciding whether to build the highway, the value of these lost lives has to be weighed against the economic benefits.

(3) A government contemplates requiring more stringent emissions standards for factories. These standards would cost

the factories $1,700,000 but would extend an estimated 10 lives from 55 to 75. In making this decision, the decision maker will reveal whether he considers the average value of each life extension to be worth more or less than $170,000.

8.3 WHY WE SHOULD NOT PLACE MONEY VALUES ON LIVES

The most direct way for the analyst to help resolve these policy decisions is to place dollar values on specific types of life extensions. The benefit-cost analyst may attempt to set these figures by asking what the compensating variations of the life extensions are: how much the persons whose lives would be extended and others affected by the extensions would pay for them.

This approach has many shortcomings. Even if a decision-maker values swimming pools and roads by what people are willing to pay to use them, it does not follow that life-saving should be similarly valued. In many ways to many people, the life-saving effects of programs are different from other effects.

(1) Morality. For no other program effect are moral questions as important as for life-extending effects. To many people, it is not a question of what people are willing to pay for life extensions but whether it is simply right for any government to take any life-extending or life-shortening actions. (To be technical, we could interpret this sentiment as implying that life-saving policies have global effects, that people would be willing to pay to have their governments adopt policies that they consider moral. But this approach misses the point: that this is, above all, a moral not a technical issue.)

(2) Magnitude. When a program costs a person money or degrades his environment, benefit-cost analysis measures this harm as the amount of money that would have to be given to the person to make him as well off as if the program were not implemented. For a program that figures to cost some people their lives, this approach may not work because, in general, no amount of money will make dead persons as well off as if they were alive. Conversely, when a program would save lives, the

positive compensating variations (what people would pay for the life extensions) will reflect not so much the value of the lives to the people but rather how much money they can put their hands on. (Measuring other benefits as positive CVs works because the amounts of money people would pay for them—for instance, for the convenience of a new road—lie well within the financial capacities of most people and therefore will not just reflect how much money they have, although this will have some influence).

(3) Symbolism. To put a dollar value on a human life is to say that dollars and lives are commensurable when our moral feelings may tell us that they are basically incommensurable. The symbolic effect of this may lead policymakers to equate lives to numbers of dollars and, in a callous way, to lose sight of their human dimensions.

8.4 WHY WE SHOULD PLACE MONEY VALUES ON LIVES

Notwithstanding the arguments above, values are implicitly and inevitably placed on lives every day: by governments deciding that only certain measures can be taken to control environmental hazards; by individuals buying or not buying cars with certain safety devices or deciding whether or not to accept hazardous employment. Modern technological dangers and possibilities enable policymakers to extend lives in many ways and at many costs. The entire gross national product could be devoted to life-saving which implies that a line must be drawn somewhere to limit public life-saving. Such a line might be drawn by deciding, for instance, to obtain certain kinds of life extensions if they cost less than $185,000 but not if they cost more than that. If such a line is not drawn and if life-saving decisions are made more randomly, then however much public money is spent on life-saving will not save as many lives as it could. The limits for spending on life-saving could be taken as life values. (Persons worried about symbolism might, however, say that using such limits as guides to increase life-saving is permissible, but it is best not to publicize the limits; that these limits should not be described or thought of as values; and that it might even be better to have suboptimal life-saving policies than to start thinking of lives as commensurable with dollars.)

Another way of looking at these limits for spending on life-saving is in terms of risks for individuals. For them, money can go toward enhancing the quality of their lives (better food, better housing, better leisure) or toward extending them by reducing risks. In either case, money enhances the value they expect to get from life. If they can in their own judgment get more value by putting money toward consumption rather than by reducing risks, they should do so. Such individual decisions should guide public decisions: Governments should devote money to life-saving if and only if this will enhance life values more than alternative spending. As the costs of reducing risks rise, there comes a point at which people are better off if money that could go toward reducing risks is instead spent on enhancing lives (for instance, through private consumption or through other public programs). The most expensive life extensions society is willing to pay for (calculated by dividing dollar costs by the expected number of lives saved) might be taken as the value of the extended life. But we have to be careful: This is not the value of a life in any intrinsic sense; it is instead the most that a given society with its limited resources and its perceptions of its own tastes and values is willing to pay to extend lives.

8.5 COMPLICATIONS

If we are going to measure program effects on life-saving by placing dollar values on certain types of life extensions, several analytic complexities must be dealt with.

(1) Double counting voluntarily incurred risks. When a new road increases travel, the risk of death from accident may rise. Each traveler, however, should take this risk into account in deciding how much to use the road. Consumer surplus—the most a traveler would pay to use the road less the actual cost—should reflect this risk: The greater the risk, the less the traveler would pay to use the road. To value the road as its

consumer surplus less the dollar value of its fatalities is to double count the risk.

(2) Public and private monies. The usual distinction should be maintained between public and private monies. Dollars a government might spend on a health program are not the same as dollars people might spend for hang-gliding lessons.

(3) Discounting. In an economy without inflation but with a real discount rate of seven percent, the value of extending a life from age 55 to age 75 may be constant in dollar terms—for example, $185,000. To extend such a life next year is valued then at $185,000, but $185,000 next year is equivalent to

$$\frac{\$185,000}{1.07} = \$172,897 \qquad [8.1]$$

this year. We can therefore infer that the most the society would pay this year to save a life next year is $172,897. Alternatively, one can discount lives: Take the value of saving a life i years in the future to equal

(the value of saving the same kind of life today) $\div 1.07^i$. $\qquad$ [8.2]

Saving n lives i years in the future is just as good (in terms of the most money society would be willing to pay today for these gains) as saving

$$\frac{n}{(1.07)^i} \qquad [8.3]$$

lives today.

(4) Distributional equity. Rich people can spend more than poor people to extend their lives. A society may wish for equity's sake to treat rich and poor lives equally. To do this, it need only determine how much it would spend to extend the life of the person of average means, then apply the same policy to rich and poor alike.

(5) Aspects of lives. Societal decisions often reflect whether the lives affected are identified rather than statistical and

whether the risks incurred are voluntary rather than involuntary. The policy debate is likely to be more charged for the identified life (for example, a person needing a heart transplant) than for the statistical life (such as a marginal reduction in lung cancer mortality). Society tends to be more concerned (per life endangered) about risks involuntarily incurred (such as through siting of toxic waste disposal) than about voluntarily accepted risks (for example, smoking). Like other global effects in decision-making, the analyst probably does best to describe them, but not to quantify them—leaving the value judgments to decisionmakers.

8.6 AMOUNTS THAT MIGHT BE SPENT TO EXTEND LIVES

Example: Medical Treatment

A government can subsidize treatment for a medical condition that strikes people at age 55. Without such treatment, the condition kills; with the program, the people would survive on average until 75. What is the most the government should pay, per life extended for this program? To answer this question, we will consider a variety of ways in which the government might assign a dollar value to a life.

We consider first a 55-year-old person who has developed the condition and ask how much money various people including himself would be willing to pay for his treatment. There are several money amounts that could go toward the treatment:

Savings (S). The diseased person may spend his accumulated savings on the therapy.

Earnings less consumption (E-C). All future earnings of the person less the amount of them he would consume (present-valued) could be used to pay for the therapy.

Life (L). A friend or relative might be willing to spend money to keep the person alive. This might be paid for the benefits of friendship or merely for the satisfaction of knowing that the person lives. Schelling (1968) termed such direct nonmonetary benefits to others the benefits of *life* which he distinguished from the benefits of *livelihood*.

Livelihood (LL). Dependents and heirs may receive greater financial support from the diseased person if his life is extended and hence be willing to pay up to the present value of the support for the treatment. A youth will typically associate with the life extension of his father both a value of life ("I want him to live because I love him and his companionship") and a value of livelihood ("I also want him to live to earn money to pay my tuition").

Indirect effects (IE). The person's death will affect many who may never have known him in a variety of ways. If the person creates a greater economic product than he receives in wages, the difference may be split up among such people as the stockholders of the corporation in which he works. This difference disappears when he dies, as do the multiplier effects of his consumption. Society as a whole loses these indirect effects when he dies and should therefore be willing to contribute at least this much to keeping him alive. Some people may sense a global benefit just in knowing that their society is humane enough to provide certain types of life extensions to all needing them. This global benefit does not require actually knowing those whose lives are extended. These are positive indirect effects. Negative indirect effects are contributions to environmental pollution. The effects of a person's continued life on wages, prices, and other rates are also indirect effects. While difficult to calculate, indirect effects may be sizable and should be included in conceptualizing the value of a life.

8.7 THE PARETO LIFE VALUE

The affected person can afford to pay only

$$E - C + S \qquad [8.4]$$

toward the cost of his treatment. This is his own life value (OLV): his own positive compensating variation for the treatment. His heirs, dependents, and friends can pay a total of

$$L + LL \qquad [8.5]$$

for his treatment and still be just as well off as if the person is allowed to die. This is the *acquaintanceship life value* (ALV):

the positive CV of these acquaintances for the treatment. Other persons indirectly affected by the person's possible death would be willing to pay

$$IE \qquad\qquad [8.6]$$

to keep the person alive. This is the *indirect life value* (ILV)— the positive CV for people benefiting indirectly from the life extension.

The net benefits of treatment (the sum of the compensating variations) are

$$E - C + L + IE. \qquad\qquad [8.7]$$

Livelihood (LL) and savings (S) do not appear in this formulation. Benefits of livelihood stem from E - C so that to count LL in addition to E - C is double counting: If all of E - C were to be paid for treatment, there would be no LL. Savings are not included in net benefits because every dollar of savings spent on treatment deprives an heir of an equal amount—effects that cancel in computing net benefits. These net benefits (E - C + L + IE) must exceed costs if the treatment is to be a potential Pareto improvement. For this reason,

$$E - C + L + IE \qquad\qquad [8.8]$$

is the *Pareto life value* (PLV). A government that only takes actions that are pPi's (many economists have urged that this be the guiding principle of governments) would only pay for treatments that cost no more than the PLV. To such governments, the PLV is the value of the life extension.

8.8 PROBLEMS WITH THE PLV

But is this sensible? The government valuing lives as their PLVs will not pay any money to extend the life of a person who is no longer working (meaning that the E - C is negative), who has few friends (and low L), and small indirect effects. There is no way that the government could spend one penny to extend that life and make everyone else at least as well off as if the person were allowed to die. To most of us this is repugnant: If we were in such a position, we would hope that society would not cold-heartedly perform the analysis above, conclude that the rest of society would be better off if we die, and leave it at that.

This analysis is unsatisfying in part because it is amoral: not moral or immoral, but devoid of moral sense. In a way, this is inevitable: Analysis itself does not create a conscience; it only reflects the consciences of those who use it. This analysis also is inadequate because it takes too narrow a view. It asks, in essence, "What do we, the healthy, get out of treating them, the sick?" Not surprisingly, the answer in economic terms is often: "Very little." A broader view of the situation asks, "What arrangement would we like to have made for the healthy to subsidize the treatment of the sick, recognizing that each of us has some chance of remaining healthy and some chance of becoming sick?"

We will look further at the amorality of analysis, examine other simple strategies for accounting the value of a life, and finally derive a life value based on a broader perspective.

8.9 THE AMORALITY OF ANALYSIS

Determining whether a life-saving action is a potential Pareto improvement does not indicate whether the action is right in the sense of being moral. Neither benefit-cost nor cost-effectiveness analysis can ever establish absolute rightness or wrongness. Each is used instead to learn whether an action is in the best interests of persons with the power to take action. Insofar as the values of those persons are moral (perhaps inevitably a subjective determination)—they might, for instance, place a high premium on all lives—analysis can be used to help them choose actions consistent with those values and, hence, moral. Analysis may, however, be used by the selfish to determine what best serves themselves.

A poor dying man in need of treatment may have spent his life in charitable works. His society may cold-heartedly find little benefit (low L and low IE) in extending his life. If so, they may judge his treatment not to be in their interests (not a pPi) and not pay for it. While we can detest their attitude, their analysis may be flawless. Benefit-cost and cost-effectiveness analysis can only establish what actions are best according to set value structures; they can neither justify those values (beyond attesting to their consistency) nor expose defects in them.

8.10 THE SIMPLIFIED PARETO LIFE VALUE

The two terms in the Pareto life value of

$$PLV = E - C + L + IE \qquad [8.9]$$

most difficult to estimate are the benefits of life and indirect effects. Analysts often choose to omit these terms from the PLV (as much from being difficult to quantify as from their alleged insignificance) to arrive at the *simplified Pareto life value* (SPLV) which is just discounted future earnings less discounted future consumption:

$$SPLV = E - C. \qquad [8.10]$$

Difficulties with taking the SPLV as the value of extending a life are: (1) that, since consumption often represents what people want from life (the home, the vacation, the meal), it hardly seems right to subtract it from earnings in determining the life value; and (2) that persons who consume without earning or who for periods consume more than they earn have, by inference, negative SPLV. The problem is that the SPLV ($E - C$) represents the value of the life to others while consumption is part of the life value to the person concerned.

8.11 CONSUMPTION AS THE VALUE OF A LIFE

This problem may be avoided by explicitly recognizing that consumption creates life value: We cannot live without consuming and, in most circumstances, we can enjoy our lives a little more if we can spend a little more on consumption. To the person who saves 11 months for a trip in the twelfth, it makes more sense to measure life value as consumption than as earnings less consumption. The most extreme position taken in line with this reasoning is to take discounted future consumption as the value of a life. This is the *consumption life value* (CLV):

$$CLV = C. \qquad [8.11]$$

The main problem with taking the CLV even as the value people place on their own lives is that, while people prefer more consumption to less, consumption is a poor measure of life value.

(1) Consumption is not linearly related to life value. To consume twice as much is not to value your life twice as highly. Most people have declining marginal utility of money and would never consider accepting a gamble that offered them a .5 chance of immediate death and a .5 chance of the rest of their normal life at a doubled consumption level.

(2) Interpersonal comparisons of value are hazardous. He who earns and consumes $50,000 annually can hardly be assumed to achieve five times the life value of one who earns and consumes $10,000 (who might indeed have had the opportunity for the more expensive lifestyle and rejected it).

(3) Earnings may impel consumption. Higher paying positions may require a better lifestyle—a better home, better clothes.

(4) Higher pay—which enables more money to be spent on consumption—may reflect the premium necessary to attract persons to less desirable work.

(5) The more time one spends earning—making possible more expensive consumption—the less time is left for consumption.

(6) The type of consumption matters. It may be better not to include in the CLV the consumption of health care services necessary to keep a person alive. The life value of a person spending $10,000 per year on kidney dialysis and $10,000 on other consumption seems closer to that of a healthy person spending $10,000 on consumption than to one spending $20,000.

8.12 EARNINGS AS THE VALUE OF LIFE

Notwithstanding these problems, one might, in a rough way, maintain that earnings less consumption (the SPLV) measure the value of a life to others and consumption (the CLV) its value to the person in question. If so, the value of the life to all persons combined is the sum of the two. This is the *earnings life value* (ELV):

$$ELV = SPLV + CLV$$
$$= E - C + C$$
$$= E. \qquad [8.12]$$

Taking the ELV as the life value is the *human capital* approach to life valuation: A person's worth is seen as his discounted future earnings just as the value of a machine is the discounted future profits it can be used to obtain. Evaluators have more frequently used the ELV to measure the worth of lives saved (through disease control programs, or safety programs, for example) than any other life value.

Conceptual shortcomings of the ELV are that (1) earnings are not linearly related to the satisfaction we get from life; (2) interpersonal comparisons are dangerous; and (3) periods without earnings—leisure and retirement—are positively valued. Measuremental difficulties of the ELV include (1) estimating future earnings—extrapolating from the present and somehow incorporating expected rises in productivity; (2) taking into account the possibility of unemployment; and (3) valuing unpaid labor—a long-running debate (see, for instance, Cooper and Rice, 1976) concerns whether housespouse labor should be valued at the wage levels of domestic servants, or as opportunity costs (what the person could earn), or in other ways.

8.13 TAKING SAVINGS INTO ACCOUNT

The SPLV and the ELV neglect savings. Two arguments for this are that spending savings on treatment deprives heirs of that amount and that the government, in calculating how much it should pay for treatment, does not need to include savings since the affected person can pay that much himself.

But neglecting savings goes against the grain of common sense and fairness. If people want to put aside money that eventually can be used to pay for their expensive medical treatments, they should be allowed to do so. Rich people can save more to pay for their medical treatment than can poor people. A society believing that medical treatment should not depend too much on means might decide to cover for all of its people the costs of all treatments that the average person would himself pay for. Much of his payment would come from savings. The value of the life extension implied by this approach is the most that the average person would pay for a treatment that would result in the life extension. This is the *willingness-to-pay life value* (WTPLV).

8.14 THE WILLINGNESS-TO-PAY LIFE VALUE

Any person suddenly developing a life-threatening condition and having no insurance against it can only himself pay his own life value (OLV), consisting of his savings plus his discounted future earnings minus his discounted future consumption. The OLV in these circumstances—and whenever there is no insurance—is thus also the willingness-to-pay life value.

The average person will, however, be willing and able to pay more than the OLV for treatment if he knows in advance about the possibility of developing the condition and if he can purchase insurance that would cover the treatment costs. The definition of the WTPLV recognizes this possibility:

The willingness-to-pay life value (WTPLV), for a given person and a given life extension that might someday be needed, is the maximum cost of the life extension that the person would be willing to buy actuarially fair life insurance to cover.

Suppose, for example, that a person has a .001 chance of needing a life-extending treatment that would cost $100,000. Suppose further that the person would be willing to pay $100

(=(.001)($100,000), hence the actuarially fair premium) for an insurance policy that would cover the treatment costs if needed. The WTPLV is therefore at least $100,000: The person would be willing to arrange to pay for treatment costing this much.

A governmental policy of paying for the $100,000 treatment for all who need it serves the purpose of the insurance. For the person considered above, such a policy essentially eliminates the .001 risk of needing the treatment and of not being able to pay for it. The person would be willing to pay at least $100 to eliminate this risk while $100 per such person is the expected cost to the government of the policy.

For populations homogeneous in risk and their attitudes toward risk, government policies of paying for life-extending treatments whose WTPLVs exceed their costs will generally be potential Pareto improvements. In these cases, the positive compensating variations of people (how much they would be willing to pay for the risk reductions) exceed the expected costs to the government.

8.15 DETERMINING THE WTPLV

The WTPLV can be determined by considering decision trees of the type shown in Figure 8.1. There, the decision for any given treatment cost is whether the person thinks he would be better off (in his own valuation of his own future) if he were to buy that treatment insurance than if he used this money instead for extra consumption (a nicer house or one more trip to Bermuda). If we assume evenly spread risks and negligible indirect effects and effects on acquaintances, the WTPLV can be alternatively formulated as the maximum treatment costs that they would like to have the government pay for. If the treatment costs more than this amount, if the government therefore decides not to pay for the treatment, and if a person gets the condition and dies without treatment, he cannot reasonably complain. He knew his chance of getting the condition and thought that he would be better off with additional consumption than in paying extra taxes (that would have been equal to his insurance premiums) so that the government would pay for treatment of the condition. He valued his extra con-

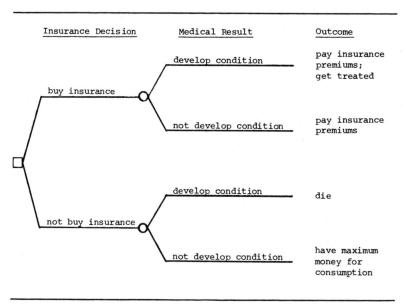

| Insurance Decision | Medical Result | Outcome |

buy insurance
- develop condition → pay insurance premiums; get treated
- not develop condition → pay insurance premiums

not buy insurance
- develop condition → die
- not develop condition → have maximum money for consumption

Figure 8.1: Decision Tree for Individual Determining His Own WTPLV*
*The largest treatment cost the individual would be willing to buy insurance to cover.

sumption more highly than eliminating this risk of an early death, he got a higher expected life value when the government decided not to cover treatment costs, and in dying with the condition he only suffers an outcome of whose possibility he had been aware.

8.16 THE SOCIAL LIFE VALUE

However, the willingness-to-pay life value does not fully capture the benefits of a government policy of paying for treatment. It does not take into account the benefits of life (L) and the indirect effects (IE) that occur when a life is extended. A better social decision on whether to cover the costs of treatment will be made if framed in the following way:

Consider a newborn baby with the small normal chance of developing a life-threatening condition. The government may adopt a policy of covering treatment for the condition. What is the largest treatment cost that a thinking baby would like the government to have a policy of paying for?

This maximum treatment cost is the *social life value* (SLV)—the most that a society trying to maximize the expected life value for the average person would pay for the life extension.

8.17 DETERMINING THE SLV

The social life value can be determined by referring to decision trees of the type shown in Figure 8.2. Each person—with the average chance of developing the life-threatening condition—considers whether he would like the government to have a policy of paying for treatment: whether he would be better off on average with the government coverage or without it. The difference between the individual decision on purchasing insurance (Figure 8.1) and the individual decision on setting government policy (Figure 8.2) is that the latter decision takes into account the benefits of life (L) and the indirect effects (IE) arising because the lives of other people with the condition are extended. The decision is thus made as the average citizen balances off (1) the benefits of the additional consumption or of other governmental programs made possible if the government does not pay for treatment, and (2) the benefits of having the government pay the treatment costs for him and for others who might develop the condition.

If the average person feels better off with a governmental policy of paying for treatment, then the society maximizing the expected life values of its average citizens should have such a policy. If the average person prefers not to have the policy, this society should not have it. This implies that this government should pay for precisely those life-extending treatments whose SLVs exceed their costs. This perspective makes the SLV a more reasonable basis than the other life values discussed for resolving the original question of the most the government should pay for the life-extending treatments.

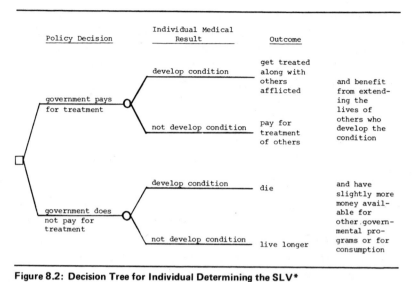

Figure 8.2: Decision Tree for Individual Determining the SLV*

*The largest treatment cost the individual would like the government to adopt a standard policy of paying.

8.18 ASPECTS OF THE SLV

We now examine various aspects of the social life value, including problems associated with basing social decisions on it.

(1) Indicator of a potential Pareto improvement. When a specific person develops the life-threatening condition at age 55, treating him will be a potential Pareto improvement only if the treatment costs less than the Pareto life value. Taking the broader perspective of persons in their 20s, the policy of paying for their eventual treatment costs will be a potential Pareto improvement if and only if the treatment costs less than the SLV. The SLV is thus the indicator of a pPi taking a broader perspective in time.

(2) Magnitude. The SLV is typically larger than the PLV— indicating that a life valued in the longer perspective is worth more than a life valued at the moment of possible death. This occurs because the SLV allows for saving and risk-pooling to pay for treatment.

(3) Inadequate compensation. Even though the SLV exceeds the PLV, it is not a compensating variation for death—as, in general, no money amount can be.

(4) Equity. The WTPLV and the SLV are fairer than alternative life values in asking not "How much would you pay to save another's life?" but "How much would you be willing to take out of your own consumption to reduce your own risk of premature death?" There is, however, a major problem: People typically do not have the same risk of life-threatening conditions. Those at high risk are naturally more willing than those at lower risk to have the government adopt a policy of paying for treatment. This problem of interpersonal equity must somehow be resolved.

(5) Moral hazard. Complicating the issue of equity and the calculation of the WTPLV and SLV is the factor of *moral hazard:* the tendency of people to incur greater risks of outcomes against which they are insured. With a public policy of paying the treatment costs of a disease, personal health precautions against the disease may erode. People at low risk for the disease may be less willing to subsidize the treatment of high-risk persons who took poor care of themselves. In determining how much would have to be taken out of consumption to provide insurance against treatment costs, the moral hazard effect must be figured in. It is possible that best social policy would fine private behavior that increases the risks of life-threatening conditions.

(6) Anxiety. The WTPLV and SLV reflect anxiety. When a policy of publicly supporting life-saving treatments is adopted, people gain not only through their life extensions but also by being freed from worry about a possible early death. Schelling (1968) provides a sharp, hypothetical example of anxiety:

> Let me conjecture that if one among forty men had been injected with a substance that would kill him at the end of five years, and the forty were known to the doctor who didn't know which among them had the fatal injection, and if the men didn't know it yet, the doctor would do more harm by telling them what he had done than he had already done with the injection.

(7) Focus on risks. The WTPLV and SLV avoid the problems of valuing lives by focusing on risks as part of lives. Money is rarely able to compensate for sure death (a person willing to die

to secure a fortune for his heirs being an exception). Limited risks are routinely incurred: in driving, climbing mountains, smoking, or washing the windows of tall buildings. Such small risks of death may be treated like other aspects of these activities against which they are traded off (people do accept slightly higher risks to take a quicker road or to earn more money). In such contexts, it is reasonable to value risks as compensating variations.

(8) Measurability. The WTPLV and SLV are difficult to measure. Present life insurance policies are purchased not to protect a life but to preserve livelihood—to provide for dependents. People would pay more if they could protect their own lives in addition to providing for heirs. Finding out how much people would be willing to pay for various reductions in risk of death is thwarted by incentives to give other than true responses and by the difficulties people face in determining the largest premiums they would pay. Moreover, tastes change. (At 20 a person may pay a minimal premium to be spared a heart attack at 55; at 30, a sizable premium for the same gain; and at 40, again but a minimal premium. All things considered, preferences at age 25 seem a reasonable empirical basis for determining the SLV.)

*8.19 CALCULATING WTPLVs UNDER DIFFERENT CONDITIONS

An array of life values can be calculated for any given life-extension. To give concrete examples of each value and to get a notion of the likely numerical differences among the values, we perform the various calculations for a hypothetical situation. Our focus will not be on the numerical methodology for deriving these values but on formulating them conceptually and on interpreting the results. We first examine the dependence of the willingness-to-pay life value on the circumstances of the life.

Example: Alternate Life Values

Several 25-year-olds without savings have each one chance in 20 of contracting a life-threatening condition at age 55. With the condition, only immediate expensive treatment will ensure their survival. The treatment extends their lives to 75, the age at which those without the condition die.

The persons earn $15,000 annually through age 65. Consumption monies can be shifted between years at an annual discount rate of seven percent. For simplicity, assume no inflation (or, alternatively, that all money amounts are given in real terms). These people do not have to provide for heirs, and should convert all their savings to consumption by the end of their lives.

We wish to know the willingness-to-pay life value (the most a person would himself pay for treatment of the condition) if:

(a) he does not learn about it until he contracts it at age 55;
(b) he learns at age 55 that he has one chance in 20 of developing the disease momentarily, but may immediately buy insurance to provide money for treatment;
(c) he knows at age 25 that he will get it at age 55;
(d) he knows at age 25 that he has one chance in 20 of getting the condition, but there is no way to buy insurance to provide money for the treatment;
(e) he knows at 25 his chance of the condition and can purchase actuarially fair insurance against it; or
(f) the conditions of (e) hold and he moreover can purchase actuarially fair annuities.

These life values should be calculated by making reasonable assumptions about the utility structures of the people.

Results. The technical details of the solution are given in the appendix to the chapter; the numerical answers to (a) through (e) are shown in Table 8.1.

The important lessons to be drawn from the table are the ways in which the WTPLV varies with circumstances. Notice first the impact of the age at which the decision is made: all entries for the age-25 decision are larger than those for the age 55 decision. The greatest increase occurs in the certainty case in which the person will cut back in his consumption so that an additional $173,379 (= $280,956 - $107,577) can be spent 30 years later on treatment.

TABLE 8.1   WTPLVs for a Treatment that Would Extend a Life From
Age 55 to 75 Under Different Conditions

		Age at which Decision on Allocating Money for Insurance or Treatment is Made			
		Age 25		Age 55	
	Sure (1.0)	c$280,956		a$107,577	
Chance of Developing Condition	Probabilistic (0.05)	d$149,120	e$363,829	a$107,577	b$342,238
		Insurance not Available	Insurance Available	Insurance not Available	Insurance Available

Letters "a," "b," "c," "d," and "e" indicate sections of problem solution where figure is discussed.

Second, the importance of the availability of insurance should be noticed. The differences here are more dramatic. Insurance possibilities increase the WTPLV by $214,709 (= $363,829 – $149,120) or by $234,661 (= $342,238 – $107,577) depending on the age at which the decision is made. Both values are large because the resources of all those at risk for the condition can be pooled to make it possible to pay for more expensive treatment.

Third, knowing that the condition is certain to develop instead of probable increases the WTPLV only for the age 25 decision when insurance is unavailable. When insurance is available, the certainty of developing the condition means that the money of the 19 people in 20 who will not develop the condition cannot be drawn on to pay for the treatment. This effect outweighs the additional money that the person who will develop the condition will put aside to pay for it.

Actuarially fair annuities enhance the attractiveness of not arranging to pay for treatment. The WTPLV in this case is $315,727. Governmental policies of income support and of paying for treatment can act as actuarially fair annuities and insurance. Suppose that the government had a choice between prohibiting the treatment because of its expense and paying for the treatment of all who need it through a tax on the consumption of every person. The government would maximize the utility of these people by paying for the treatment so long as its cost did not exceed $315,727. For this reason, this life value is the one implied by Schelling (1968) and Mishan (1971a)— although they do not concern themselves with the computational details.

This example, in summary, shows the dependence of the WTPLV on individual knowledge and on the adequacy of the insurance market. In a society where people do not plan ahead or have insurance available, the WTPLV is only $107,577. Telling them their chances of getting the condition and making actuarially fair insurance available increases the WTPLV to $363,829—a drastic difference for a society using the WTPLV to decide on the maximum treatment cost its government should pay for. To avoid the ambiguity arising because the WTPLV depends on circumstances, it is best to standardize the circumstances assumed for the WTPLV. Because governmental policies can, theoretically, be based on foreknowledge of risk and act as actuarially fair insurance and annuities, these conditions should—unless others are specified—be assumed. This is in line with the conceptual work of Schelling and Mishan.

8.20 COMPARISON OF ALTERNATIVE LIFE VALUES

Table 8.2 summarizes the various life values mentioned here. The first column gives the name and abbreviation of the value and the second column gives a simple formulation of it. For the first seven values listed, the algebraic formulations for calculating them are given. All symbols used are defined at the end of the table. For the last five values, verbal formulations are provided.

In the third column are illustrative sizes of the various values. All derive from the example worked out in Section 8.19 where the life extension being valued was from ages 55 to age 75. Further assumptions have been introduced here about the levels of indirect effects and nonmonetary benefits to others. These values are purely illustrative—to show what numbers would be derived as life values—and have no meaning beyond that.

The fourth column recapitulates reasons why governments might take the different life values to be the amounts they

(text continues p. 212)

TABLE 8.2 Comparison of the Different Values a Government Might Take to Be the Worth of Obtaining a Specific Life Extension

Life Value	Formulation	Illustrative Size	Arguments for Governments Focusing on it	Arguments Against Governments Focusing on it	Prominent Pieces Mentioning Describing or Using This Value
Own Life Value (OLV)	$E-C_m+S$	$107,577	This is the amount the average person himself can pay for treatment. Having governments pay for treatments of this amount enables the poor to have the treatments the average man can afford.	Neglects the value of life to others. Is only what the average person could pay with poor anticipation of the condition.	Schelling (1968)
Acquaintanceship Life Value (ALV)	$L+LL$	$75,000	This is the most the acquaintances of the average person can pay to extend his life without making themselves worse off. Having governments pay for treatments of this amount enables poor acquaintances to have the treatments that the acquaintances of the average person might pay for.	Neglects the value of the life to the person and to nonacquaintances. Difficult to measure.	Schelling (1968)

TABLE 8.2 Comparison of the Different Values a Government Might Take to Be the Worth of Obtaining a Specific Life Extension (Cont)

Life Value	Formulation	Illustrative Size	Arguments for Governments Focusing on it	Arguments Against Governments Focusing on it	Prominent Pieces Mentioning Describing or Using This Value
Indirect Life Value (ILV)	IE	$17,000	A government might decide that it should take into account the indirect benefits of life since those getting direct benefits can themselves get together and arrange to pay for treatment.	Neglects the value of life to the person and his acquaintances. Assumes private sector can arrange for appropriate insurance. Leaves the poor to fend for themselves	Schelling (1968) Mishan (1971)
Pareto Life Value (PLV)	$E - C_n + L + IE$	$40,474	This is the most that can be paid for treatment so that, with suitable redistributions, no one is worse off. It is in this sense the value of the life extension to others.	Neglects the value of life to the person who might save to pay for his own treatment.	Schelling (1968) Mishan (1971)
Simplified Pareto Life Value (SPLV)	$E - C_n$	-$51,526	This is an approximation to the PLV that is easier to calculate.	Implies that a life that consumes more than it earns has negative value.	Weisbrod (1961) Klarman (1965)

TABLE 8.2 Comparison of the Different Values a Government Might Take to Be the Worth of Obtaining a Specific Life Extension (Cont)

Life Value	Formulation	Illustrative Size	Arguments for Governments Focusing on it	Arguments Against Governments Focusing on it	Prominent Pieces Mentioning Describing or Using This Value
Consumption Life Value (CLV)	C_n	$164,255	To some extent, the value of a life to a person depends on the money he can spend to enjoy it. This is a far better approximation than the SPLV to the value of a life to the person himself.	Consumption is too poorly correlated with even the value that a person places on his own life.	Fischer and Vaupel (1976)
Earnings Life Value (ELV)	E	$112,728	Combines the SPLV and the CLV to approximate the value of the life extension to others and to the person.	Earnings fail to reflect many aspects of life value. The value of a life of a person not earning is not necessarily zero.	Weisbrod (1961) Rice and Cooper (1967)
Willingness-to-Pay Life Value (WTPLV) (assuming probabalistic foresight and available insurance and annuities) private, implicit	The maximum treatment cost a person is willing to pay through his own resources and insurance.	$315,727	The rational average person will pay for treatment costing this much. For equity, the government might decide to pay this much for anyone's treatment.	Neglects the value of the life to others. Difficult to measure.	Schelling (1968) Mishan (1971)

TABLE 8.2 Comparison of the Different Values a Government Might Take to Be the Worth of Obtaining a Specific Life Extension (Cont)

Life Value	Formulation	Illustrative Size	Arguments for Governments Focusing on it	Arguments Against Governments Focusing on it	Prominent Pieces Mentioning Describing or Using This Value
Willingness-to-Pay Life Value (WTPLV) private, revealed	The amounts of money people actually are paying to reduce their risks of death.		The government should arrange to pay for all people the costs of life-extending actions that average people are paying for themselves.	There is little reason or consistency in the private decisions on life-extending actions.	Thaler and Rosen (1974)
Willingness-to-Pay Life Value (WTPLV) private, explicit	The amounts of money people say they would be willing to pay for life-extending programs.		The government should pay for life-extending programs that its citizens individually say they are willing to pay for.	People have not thought through this difficult determination.	Acton (1973)
Willingness-to-Pay Life Value (WTPLV) public, revealed	The amounts of money governments actually are paying to reduce risks of death.		The government should be consistent in its attitudes toward life-extending programs.	Until more analysis leads to more consistent and rational governmental decisions, this value will largely reflect the random determinants of public decision-making.	Starr (1969)

TABLE 8.2 Comparison of the Different Values a Government Might Take to Be the Worth of Obtaining a Specific Life Extension (Cont)

Life Value	Formulation	Illustrative Size	Arguments for Governments Focusing on it	Arguments Against Governments Focusing on it	Prominent Pieces Mentioning Describing or Using This Value
Social Life Value (SLV)	The greatest cost of treatment that a group of average people would feel that it would be in the best interest of each to have the government pay for (before it is learned precisely who would need treatment).	$475,000	A social policy of always paying for treatments costing up to this much maximizes the expected utility of the average person.	Difficult to measure; assumes that the government should take into account every consideration that might lead private persons to pay for treatment.	Schelling (1968) Mishan (1971)

$C_m \equiv$ discounted future consumption at a minimum level = $56,678.
$C_n \equiv$ discounted future consumption at a normal level = $164,255.
$L \equiv$ life = direct nonmonetary benefits to others = $75,000.
$E \equiv$ discounted future earnings = $112,728.
$IE \equiv$ indirect effects = $17,000.
$LL \equiv$ livelihood = $0. (The person was not planning to do anything with his earnings but spend them on his own consumption.)
$S \equiv$ savings = $51,526.

should pay for life extensions. The fifth column gives counter-arguments. The sixth column lists important references that have formulated, mentioned, or used the life values or have considered the concepts on which the values are based. Each of these values or concepts related to them has been discussed elsewhere—although often with different names.

The first entry, the own life value, is what the person surprised by the life-threatening condition could pay for his own treatment. The next two entries, the acquaintanceship life value and the indirect life value, represent what the acquaintances of the person and other people could pay for the treatment without feeling any worse off themselves.

The Pareto life value is next given, using a different figure for discounted future consumption than does the OLV. We have seen in the previous section that the willingness-to-pay life value can vary tremendously, depending on the conditions. The same is true of all the other life values and parameters given here. We calculate the OLV by asking to what level the person could reduce his own consumption to pay for his treatment. The PLV, on the other hand, is here calculated assuming that the government steps in to pay for the treatment and that life goes on for the person just as if he never had the condition. Consumption in this case is much higher. The same assumptions hold in calculating the simplified Pareto life value, the consumption life value, and the earnings life value.

The willingness-to-pay life value has been discussed in the previous section. We here take the recommended standard version—assuming foreknowledge of risk and the availability of actuarially fair annuities and insurance. Because this is so difficult to calculate, other versions of the WTPLV have surfaced. Three of these are shown next in the table. The private, revealed WTPLV estimates the life value by seeing how much people actually pay to reduce their risks of death—to have a safer job or car or airplane, for example. The private, explicit WTPLV gauges the life value by asking people hypothetical questions on how much they would pay for possible life-extending programs. The public, revealed WTPLV is found by examining how much the government actually does pay for reductions in risk in various programs.

The estimate for the social life value given in the last row is a conjecture. We know that the SLV should exceed the WTPLV by the worths of nonmonetary benefits to others and of indirect effects; however, these are extremely hard to value.

8.21 WHAT LIFE VALUES SHOULD WE USE?

Example: Swine Flu

An analysis of the 1976 swine flu inoculation decision is given by Schoenbaum (1976). The value of the estimated 50,000 lives that could have been saved via inoculation had an epidemic truly been imminent was calculated to be $3.2 billion—based on ELVs. Suppose that the excess deaths prevented by inoculation were exclusively those of 55-year-olds (close to the median age of the lives saved as estimated by Schoenbaum). What life value should be used in estimating program benefits? What effect would use of this life value have?

Solution. As argued above, the SLV seems to be the appropriate life value. It is based on all the compensating variations people obtain through implementation of the program: how much people would be willing to pay to reduce their own marginal risk of death from swine flu and to reduce the chances of other people dying.

The example given in Section 8.19 indicates that the SLV is many times larger than the ELV: there roughly 4.2 times larger. Although this proportion has never been empirically determined, this value seems reasonable and could even be a sizable underestimate. If this proportion holds for the 1976 population of the United States, the total benefit of preventing an epidemic would be not $3.2 billion (as estimated by Schoenbaum using the currently most widely accepted techniques) but $13.5 billion. That is, U.S. citizens could agree to pay a total of $13.5 billion for the inoculation program and, just after making this agreement, every person in the country could (assuming the required payments to be suitably distributed over the population) feel at least as well off as if there were to be no program.

While the precise numbers are in doubt, the overall conclusion to be drawn from this example and that in Section 8.19 is clear: Current methods of life valuation based on the human capital approach are substantial underestimates of what people are truly willing to pay to reduce marginally the chances of premature death.

8.22 IMPRECISION IN ESTIMATING LIFE VALUES

Perhaps the most important lesson to be drawn from Tables 8.1 and 8.2 is one of uncertainty. While the fourth column in Table 8.2 gives reasons for looking to each of the life values, the next column casts doubt on each. This uncertainty seems belied by the third column, which calculates to the nearest dollar many of the values. But this nearest-dollar precision is misleading as can be seen by examining all the numbers in that column. These range from minus $51,526 for the SPLV to $475,000 for the SLV. Table 8.1 showed, moreover, how much a single one of these life values could vary with the circumstances. The single value most commonly used in benefit-cost calculations as the worth of a life—the ELV—is less than one-quarter of the SLV.

This huge range of uncertainty in the numbers, coupled with the many arguments for and against each life value, shows just how unsure and imprecise estimations of life values are. Perhaps, indeed, the estimations are so intrinsically difficult that analysts should refrain from forcing out numbers that are not nearly so precise as they seem. Instead, they might prefer methods that let them leave unquantified anything as difficult to value numerically as a human life. We consider such an analytic strategy in the following chapter.

8.23 THIS CHAPTER AND OTHER WRITINGS

As indicated by the references in Table 8.2, little in this chapter is altogether new. Much early work on life valuation derived from the health field, where such authors as Fein (1958), Mushkin and Collings (1959), and Weisbrod (1961) explored ways for assigning dollar values to morbidity and mortality. The arguments for focusing on the SLV have been well presented by Schelling (1968) and Mishan (1971a). The names for the alternative life values are somewhat original here. We have also emphasized more than have most other sources the disparity among the various life values.

Good general reviews and critiques of methods for measuring life value are by Acton (1976), Linnerooth (1975), and Zeckhauser (1975b). A methodology for measuring the WTPLV allied to that of Section 8.19 is given by Jones-Lee (1969). Empirical works that have used the earnings life value are by Berry and Boland (1977), Conley and Milunsky (1975), Cooper and Rice (1976), and Ridker (1967).

Refinements not reflected here have been described by Holtmann and Ridker (1965) and Weinstein et al. (1980). Holtmann and Ridker take into account the greater present value of burial costs due to premature death. This could be considered part of the consumption stream in calculating the PLV or SPLV. Weinstein et al. note that willingness to pay for risk reduction depends on the overall amount of risk: The more risk, the more people will pay per unit of risk reduction. When the risks in question are small, this factor is not important. (Suppose in the example of Section 8.19 that a governmental program could only reduce the chance of death at age 55 from .10 to .05. The WTPLV is then $316,522—slightly more than the WTPLV of $315,727, in reducing the risk from .05 to zero.)

Appendix to Chapter 8

Solution to Valuation of
Life as Willingness to Pay
Under Different Circumstances

To solve this problem, we must make assumptions about the life values perceived by the people and the relationship of these values to length of life and to consumption levels. A plausible relationship to assume is that utility, U, is a function of consumption:

$$U(\text{life}) = \sum_{n=26}^{n=75} \frac{1-e^{-c_n}}{(1 + d)^n} ,$$ [8.13]

where

n labels the year (n equal to 26 being the twenty-sixth year of life and so on),
e is 2.71828, the base of natural logarithms,
c_n is consumption in tens of thousands of dollars occurring in the nth year, and
d is the discount rate of seven percent annually.

This utility function is reasonable in that it exhibits declining marginal utility of money—as is normally the case. Survival is assumed not possible at a consumption level of less than $5,000 per year. The utility of being dead is zero.

(a) Without foreknowledge. Under conditions of certainty, a risk-averse individual whose individual rate of discounting future utility is the same as the rate at which he can transfer consumption monies across years should consume the same amount each year. (With unequal consumption across years, total utility would be increased by evening it out.) This fact facilitates the solution.

The age 25 present value of 40 years of earning is

$$\sum_{n=26}^{n=65} \frac{\$15,000}{1.07^{n-26}} = \$213,974.$$ [8.14]

The person who does not know that he may contract the condition should consume a constant amount, c, each decade that would by age 75 exactly exhaust his savings. The present value of this consumption must equal the present value of the earnings:

$$\sum_{n=26}^{n-75} \frac{c}{1.07^{n-26}} = \$213,974. \tag{8.15}$$

This can be solved to find that c is $14,490.

After 30 years of earning $15,000 and consuming $14,490, a person suddenly learns that he has the life-threatening condition. He will pay all that he can for treatment: his own life value of E - C + S. His discounted (to present value at age 55) future earnings for the next decade total $112,728 out of which he must spend $5,000 per year to live. The (age 55) present value of this future consumption is $56,678. He will have saved $51,527—which was to cover consumption after age 65. Putting these components together, we find that the person can muster his future earnings (E) less future consumption (C) plus his savings (S), or

$$\$112,728 - \$56,678 + \$51,527 = \$107,577, \tag{8.16}$$

to pay for treatment. This is not only his OLV but also his WTPLV in these circumstances. (Another $19,102—the age 55 present value of minimal consumption between 65 and 75—could be raised if the person chooses to end his life at 65.)

(b) With insurance after learning late of risk. The 55-year-old who learns that he has one chance in twenty of developing the condition momentarily may not do anything about it. Should the condition strike and its treatment cost more than E - C + S, he will die. Under these conditions, his expected utility for his remaining life is

$$(.95) \sum_{n=56}^{n=75} \frac{1 - e^{-1.4490}}{1.07^{n-56}} + (.05)(0) = 8.2402956. \tag{8.17}$$

The two terms on the lefthand side represent utility should the condition not develop (likelihood of .95) and should it develop (.05 chance). The exponent n-56 indicates that utility is present-valued to age 55.

To secure this utility by consuming equal amounts in the next 20 years would require consumption of $12,981 each year. (The reader may take this on faith or fill in the missing analytic steps.) This implies that a person maximizing his expected utility would be willing to pay any premium for insurance covering treatment costs up to an amount that would leave $12,981 to be consumed in each of the next 20 years. That amount is $17,111.91. Twenty people would pay this amount (on average) for every one who collects insurance. This means that an actuarially fair insurance policy charging this premium could cover treatment costing 20 times the premium, or $342,238. With actuarially fair insurance opportunities, persons would arrange to pay for treatment costing up to this much: the WTPLV.

(c) With sure foreknowledge. The person who knows at age 25 that he will get the condition can plan either to live only 30 more years or to put aside enough money to pay for treatment and thus live 50 years more. In the first case, he would consume $15,000 each year and would realize a utility of

$$\sum_{n=26}^{n=55} \frac{1-e^{-1.5}}{1.07^{n-26}} = 10.315024. \tag{8.18}$$

To secure this utility by consuming over 50 years would require consumption of $11,991 each year. The present value (at age 55) of 40 years of earning $15,000 is $1,628,824 and of 50 years of consuming $11,991 is $1,347,868. The difference between these figures is the WTPLV for these circumstances of $280,956. A person could pay up to that amount for treatment and be at least as well off as without treatment. He could not pay more than that without lowering his total utility below what it would be without treatment.

(d) With probabilistic foreknowledge but without insurance. The 25-year-old knowing that, with probability .05, he will develop the condition can plan to accumulate enough money to pay for treatment or plan not to. We consider first the latter case, in which developing the condition leads to death. The (age-25) expected utility is

$$\sum_{n=26}^{n=55} \frac{1-e^{-c_e}}{1.07^{n-26}} + .95 \sum_{n=56}^{n=75} \frac{1-e^{-c_\ell}}{1.07^{n-26}}, \tag{8.19}$$

where

c_e represents the consumption level (in $10,000/year) until 55 (early consumption), and
c_ℓ is the consumption level after 55 (late consumption).

The second summation is multiplied by .95 reflecting the probability that the condition will not be contracted. For the .05 chance that it is contracted, death occurs and utility after 55 is zero. The consumption figures are constrained, in that earnings must be sufficient to provide for them. Under a strategy of consumption that would maximize expected utility, early consumption, c_e, is higher than later consumption, c_ϱ, because of the one-twentieth chance that death will come at 55. (The greater is the chance of death at 55, the lower is the incentive at earlier years to put aside money for retirement.) Expected utility is maximized by consuming \$14,542 each year from 25 to 55 and consuming \$14,029 in later years. Expected utility under this strategy is 11.242983.

Setting money aside for treatment will be worthwhile only if it leads to expected utility equal at least to 11.242983. Expected utility now is

$$\sum_{n=26}^{n=55} \frac{1-e^{-c_{\acute{e}}}}{1.07^{n-26}} + .95 \sum_{n=56}^{n=75} \frac{1-e^{-c_{\acute{\varrho} nc}}}{1.07^{n-26}} + .05 \sum_{n=56}^{n=75} \frac{1-e^{-c_{\acute{\varrho} c}}}{1.07^{n-26}} , \quad [8.20]$$

where

$c_{\acute{e}}$ is consumption each year until 55,

$c_{\acute{\varrho} nc}$ consumption after 55 in the case that the condition does not develop, and

$c_{\acute{\varrho} c}$ is consumption after 55 having paid for the treatment.

These consumption amounts are subject to the constraints that

$$PV(c_{\acute{e}}) + PV(c_{\acute{\varrho} nc}) = PV(c_{\acute{e}}) + PV(c_{\acute{\varrho} c}) + PV \text{ (treatment cost)} \quad [8.21]$$

$$= PV \text{ (earnings)},$$

where

PV   indicates present valuation (to any year as long as con-sistency is maintained),

$PV(c_{\acute{e}})$ is the present value of all consumption before 55, and

$PV(c_{\acute{\varrho} nc})$ and $PV(c_{\acute{\varrho} c})$ are the present values of all consumption after 55 under the conditions, respectively, that the condition is not and is acquired.

We want to know the maximum treatment cost such that equation 8.21 will hold and that expected utility will be at least equal to 11.242983.

This is found to be a cost of $149,120–the WTPLV as well as the OLV in these conditions. Consumption is $14,079 ($\dot{c}_e$) per year until age 55, $5,000 ($c\dot{\varrho}_c$) per year after treatment, and $18,155 ($c\varrho_{nc}$) per later year if treatment is not needed.

(e) With probabilistic foreknowledge and insurance. The 25-year-old with one chance in twenty of developing the condition is now assumed able to purchase actuarially fair insurance to provide the costs of treatment. Without purchasing such insurance, he will–as in (c) above– consume $14,542 each year until 55 and $14,029 thereafter if still alive. Expected utility is 11.242983.

With insurance, the person should consume an equal amount each year. It is found that consuming $14,328 annually until 75 yields total utility of 11.242983. The age 55 present value of this is $1,610,633. We know from (c) that the present value of earnings over four decades is $1,628,824. The difference between these figures of $18,191 is the age 55 present value of all premiums that could be paid to the insurance company to cover treatment costs and achieve total utility of 11.242983. Since the company would receive this amount of premiums 20 times for each time the condition is contracted, actuarially fair insurance could pay off 363,829 (20 times the more exact difference of $18,191.45) to each 55-year-old who gets the condition. The WTPLV is $363,829.

(f) With probabilistic foreknowledge, insurance, and annuities. If the person decides not to pay for the treatment cost if needed, he then does best to buy an annuity to help support himself should he not develop the condition. This will save him the waste–from his point of view–of dying with unspent savings. With such an annuity, higher expected utility is possible.

The optimal actuarially fair annuity arrangement is for the person to turn over all his paychecks in return for a promised payment of $14,513 for every year of his life. This enables the person to achieve an age 25 expected utility of 11.250515–slightly higher than that in (c) and (d). To achieve this utility over a sure lifetime ending at 75 would require spending $14,350 annually on consumption. The age 55 present value of this consumption is $1,613,038. This is $15,786 less than the age 55 present value of the earnings–implying as in (e) that 20 times this amount, or $315,727, is the maximum treatment cost that could be covered and leave the person no worse off than if he were not to receive treatment.

9

Cost-Effectiveness Analysis

9.1 CHAPTER OVERVIEW

Program effects may be made extremely hard to value by such factors as global effects, the inability to compensate losses, taking goals as constraints, and excessive uncertainty. When effects are difficult to value, the analyst may best adopt the strategy of cost-effectiveness: leaving at least one dimension of effect to be valued by decisionmakers. Cost-effectiveness analysis (C/E) so defined can be used to determine whether any objective is worth achieving, which among alternative objectives should be achieved, and the best way to achieve any set objective.

We look in Sections 9.7 to 9.11 at considerations in applying cost-effectiveness analysis: the choice of the unvalued output unit, using C/E in decision-making, dealing with multiple effects, and determining the best version of a program. The variability of the unvalued output unit can be troublesome—a problem particularly evident for programs affecting lengths of human lives. Possible life extensions will vary in length and in the quality of the years gained. This variability suggests that more basic units than just lives saved or lost should be used in measuring these effects. One more basic unit is the quality-adjusted life year: a unit that requires sensitive measurement of health quality. We conclude by comparing the operational methodologies of B/C and C/E.

9.2 DIFFICULT VALUATIONS

The previous chapter has shown the extreme difficulty of placing dollar values on actions that extend human lives. Other program effects most difficult to value include

(1) endangering lives—for instance, exposing people to carcinogens;
(2) altruistic effects—for instance, helping poor farmers in Central America to increase their crop yields;
(3) preserving ideals—for example, ensuring the equality of vocational opportunity; and
(4) increasing military capability—for example, building one more missile-equipped nuclear submarine.

With program effects this difficult to value, an appealing analytic approach is not to value them: to work through all other parts of the program evaluation; to organize and present information that will aid valuation of these effects; but to leave the actual value judgments on them to the decisionmakers (and not to the analysts). This is the strategy of *cost-effectiveness analysis*: the subject of this chapter.

9.3 SOURCES OF VALUE DIFFICULTIES

Several factors may make program effects difficult to value.

(1) Global nature. Many program effects are global and do not have impact, even indirectly, on people who care about them. Helping a Central American farmer may not make the taxpayer better off except in the satisfaction of knowing that such farmers are helped. Theoretically, this benefit might be measured as a positive compensating variation—how much the

taxpayer would be willing to pay to have a policy of helping poor farmers. Practically, valuing these effects as CVs is hard because of their dependence on salience, identifiability, and the imperfect knowledge of the valuers.

(2) The inability to compensate losses. When a program kills or maims, there may be no amount of money that can make the victims as well off as without the program. (Limited risks usually may be adequately compensated; large risks often cannot be.) These effects cannot, therefore, be measured as negative CVs. (While one might find out how much people would pay not to be killed or maimed, these are not compensating variations but equivalent variations.)

(3) Goals taken as constraints. The advocate of equal vocational opportunity may feel that any situation with such equality is better than any without it and, moreover, that any situation with more equality is better than one with less. To this person, it is impossible to value programs that marginally enhance or marginally impair equality of vocational opportunity: There is no amount of money that would compensate for the loss of any amount of this equality. Measurement by compensating variations is based on trade-offs, but insistence on any condition rules out trade-offs. The attitude of this advocate is: "Do not talk about valuing gradations of equal vocational opportunity. Accept as a constraint that we must achieve absolute equality, then we may talk about valuing other effects of our policies."

(4) An excess of imponderables. Decision analysis and benefit-cost analysis focus on making difficult valuations in uncertain situations. Sometimes, however, imponderable factors overwhelm even the methods addressed to them. In deciding whether to build another nuclear submarine, one must weigh the chances of using it, the marginal harm it would be capable of, its likely contribution to deterrence, and the value of life after a holocaust. No existing method can be confident of appropriately valuing all these uncertain events.

9.4 IS MONEY VALUATION INEVITABLE?

In a sense, the valuation of all program effects not considered as absolute constraints is inevitable. As a government decides whether it wants more or less of certain program outputs, it is weighing the value of the output against the value of other effects that could be achieved with the same resources. To decide to build one more submarine costing $10 million is to say that the submarine is, first, worth at least $10 million and second, worth at least the program benefits that would have been achieved by spending the money on other programs.

Yet we must be cautious in making such value inferences. Decisionmakers may be no better than analysts in dealing with the conceptual difficulties. Actual public choices may therefore reflect random factors as much as the consistent application of value judgments.

9.5 ORIGINS OF COST-EFFECTIVENESS ANALYSIS

Where program effects are difficult to value, benefit-cost analysis has the unenviable task of assigning monetary values to the effects so that they may be compared with costs. The benefit-cost approach is more direct and appealing when there are sound rationales for assigning monetary values to program benefits. In most social program areas, however, valuation of all benefits and costs is so difficult and controversial that methods avoiding these valuations are prized. Such a method was first developed in military analysis which was experiencing similar difficulty in valuing its objectives—determining, for instance, the worth of one more aircraft carrier. The solution for military analysis was the cost-effectiveness principle which says that "even if we do not know the value of achieving an objective, we do know that we wish to achieve the objective in a way that minimizes costs." The converse holds that any set amount of resources should be spent so as to gain the greatest number of benefit or output units—commonly paraphrased as the "biggest bang for the buck." The less the cost of any means to achieve a given goal, the more cost-effective is that means. Analysts saw that these principles were useful in all areas where outputs were difficult to value and soon applied cost-effectiveness techniques to education, health, transportation, and other social programs—often in preference to benefit-cost analysis.

Analysis based on cost-effectiveness principles was styled "cost-effectiveness analysis." The specific origin and author of the term are not known. Grosse (1967) reports that "indeed there seems to be no record of the first use of the term 'cost-effectiveness.' " The ambiguity with which the technique has been subsequently understood parallels the haziness of its beginnings.

9.6 ALTERNATIVE DEFINITIONS

Quade (1967) offered two definitions for cost-effectiveness analysis, one broad—"any analytic study designed to assist a decision maker identify a preferred choice among many possible alternatives"—and the other more narrow—"a comparison of alternative courses of action in terms of their costs and their effectiveness in attaining some specific objective."

Cost-effectiveness has also been frequently defined (Good, 1971; Williams, 1973) as benefit-cost analysis without monetary valuation of program outputs. In this view, the difference between B/C and C/E is that B/C is more aggressive in quantifying program effects. To value program outputs is, in this light, to change C/E into B/C. The main shortcoming of this view is its too sharply drawn distinction between monetary inputs and nonmonetary, difficult-to-value outputs. In practice, many programs have some outputs that can be readily valued in money terms and some inputs that cannot be.

The least formal perception of C/E—almost colloquial usage—holds that whenever both costs and program effects are considered in a decision, it is cost-effectiveness analysis. Because costs are too often wholly disregarded, this viewpoint has some merit.

While these definitions describe important aspects of cost-effectiveness analysis, they do not reflect well its experience in social program applications. The growing use of cost-effectiveness analysis has led to a modified perception of it, the preferred definition used here:

Cost-effectiveness analysis evaluates a decision alternative (1) by making all effects commensurable in terms either of money or of one unvalued output unit and (2) by comparing these dimensions of impact.

A less common and less convenient version of cost-effectiveness analysis allows effects to be stated in terms of more than one unvalued output unit (as in Example 3a below). The preferred definition above is not universally honored. It represents only one formulation of a growing consensus among cost-effectiveness practitioners (inter alia, Barsby, 1972; Cohn, 1972; Wildavsky, 1975; Weinstein and Stason, 1977).

Quade's often-cited prescription given above states that cost-effectiveness analysis should find the best way to attain "some specific objective" assumed to be worth achieving. This indicates that cost-effectiveness analysis is primarily a tool of formative evaluation—determining the best way to achieve a program objective. Benefit-cost analysis, on the other hand, is seen as largely summative—determining whether or not a program is justified.

For social program evaluation, this viewpoint is too confining. Analysts have shown, at variance with Quade's formula but within the framework of our preferred definition, that cost-effectiveness analysis may be used to (1) determine whether any specific objective is indeed worth achieving (see Examples 2, 3, 3a, and 4 below), and (2) compare alternative specific objectives (Examples 5, 7, and 8 below). Both B/C (as has been shown in previous chapters) and C/E (as will soon be shown) may contribute to either formative or summative evaluation.

9.7 JUDGING WHETHER PROGRAMS
ARE WORTHWHILE: SUMMATIVE EVALUATION

*Example 1: Choice of
the Unvalued Output Unit*

Suppose that a cancer screening program discovers 10 cancers at a cost of $180,000—a figure that includes treatment expense. Six of the 10 cancers are cured and in two cases (considered to be lives saved) limited remissions are achieved. In these eight cases, a total of 30 (present-valued) years of life extensions are gained.

We compare the monetary and nonmonetary dimensions of impact by dividing the latter into the former and thus obtaining the *cost-effectiveness ratio (C/E)*. For health programs, the nonmonetary impacts represent net health effects, making the cost-effectiveness ratio:

$$C/E = \frac{\text{net monetary effects}}{\text{net health effects}}. \qquad [9.1]$$

Depending on the choice of unvalued output unit, four different cost-effectiveness ratios might be calculated for this program:

$$C/E = \frac{\$180,000}{10 \text{ cases discovered and treated}} = \$18,000 \text{ per case discovered and treated;}$$

$$C/E = \frac{\$180,000}{6 \text{ cures}} = \$30,000 \text{ per cure;}$$

$$C/E = \frac{\$180,000}{8 \text{ lives saved}} = \$22,500 \text{ per life saved; or}$$

$$C/E = \frac{\$180,000}{30 \text{ life years gained}} = \$6,000 \text{ per life year gained.} \qquad [9.2]$$

Choice of the units in which to couch the analysis should reflect the availability of data and the concerns of decisionmakers.

Example 2: Using Cost-Effectiveness Analysis for Decision-Making

McNeil, et al. (1975) used cost-effectiveness analysis to evaluate diagnosis and treatment of hypertensive renovascular disease. We consider here a simplified version of that study.

Suppose (1) that a decision must be made whether to implement a diagnostic strategy for detecting hypertensive renovascular disease among the hypertensive population; (2) that only one version of the program is possible (that is, we need not be concerned with identifying the optimal version); and (3) that diagnosis, per 100 hypertensives screened, costs $14,940 and finds 7.8 cases of hypertensive renovascular disease. Dividing the net monetary effects by the net health effects we obtain the cost-effectiveness ratio:

$14,940 ÷ 7.8 cases found = $1,915 per case found.

This indicates that it costs $1,915 on average to use the program to find one case of the disease.

The cost-effectiveness ratio may now be used by decisionmakers. If they consider themselves able to afford paying $1,915 per case found, they should favor enacting the program; if not, they should not.

There is here a subtle but critical distinction between benefit-cost analysis and cost-effectiveness analysis. Under B/C, it is the analyst who must value a case finding—perhaps guided by a personal best notion of decisionmaker values. If a case is valued at more than $1,915, the benefits of the program will exceed the costs of $14,940 per hundred tested and will indicate that the program should be implemented. Under C/E, the same determination—whether finding a case is worth more or less than $1,915—also resolves the program decision. The difference, however, is that this judgment is not included within the analysis (as in B/C), but is made separately by the decisionmakers to whom the analysis is transmitted. In many situations, it is inappropriate for analysts to presuppose the crucial value judgments; these are left to decision makers. This is especially true where value judgments depend on economic, political, or social considerations that can fluctuate after the analysis is completed. In such cases, C/E is more suitable than B/C.

In summary, cost-effectiveness analysis eludes the task of valuing some effects only by passing it along to decisionmakers. It may sometimes look as though C/E has magically caused a problem of valuation to disappear. This is an illusion: The problem has only been passed through the trap door on the magician's stage to the decisionmakers.

9.8 COST-EFFECTIVENESS FOR LIFE-SAVING PROGRAMS

For health programs that postpone death, it is natural to express the cost-effectiveness ratio as the average number of dollars that must be spent to save a life. It then can be argued that the program should be implemented if and only if the average life saved is valued at more than this number of dollars. Many people, as Chapter 8 indicated, find this line of reasoning distasteful and object to thinking of life values in money terms.

These objections are partly answered by adopting a modified perspective on cost-effectiveness analysis. Since the resources that can be devoted to health problems are limited, it is important to allocate them effectively. Suppose that there are sufficient resources to fund only one of two preventive health programs: One program has a cost-effectiveness ratio of $35,000 per death averted; the other has a ratio of $40,000 per death averted. Other things being equal, it is better to fund the former program, the more cost-effective of the two, as indicated by the ratios. This decision need not imply that a life is worth at least $35,000 but less than $40,000. It instead reflects only the common-sense principle that limited resources should be spent to get more rather than fewer benefit units (here, to save the most lives). The benefit-cost approach requires that all program costs and benefits included in the analysis be quantified (although B/C analyses often evade problems of quantification by simply excluding certain elements on the basis of their alleged unquantifiability). Cost-effectiveness analysis, on the other hand, requires only the premise that we want our limited resources to do as much good as possible (in terms of units to which we may not wish to attach dollar values).

9.9 DECISION RULES FOLLOWING COST-EFFECTIVENESS ANALYSIS

The most common finding of a cost-effectiveness study is that net program benefits are gained at net monetary costs. The cost-effectiveness ratio makes explicit this trade-off between program gains and money losses. If the value of the benefit unit exceeds the cost of obtaining it, the program should be enacted. When resources are limited, the decision rule is to allocate them to programs in the priority order of their cost-effectiveness (and marginal) ratios. (Decision-making with C/E is analogous to that for B/C described in Sections 5.20 to 5.23.)

Less commonly, cost-effectiveness analysis finds (1) net program benefits and net monetary gains, (2) net program losses and net monetary losses, and (3) net program losses and net monetary gains. The former two are trivial decision cases: Actions in the first category are clearly desirable and in the second category clearly undesirable. The third case could arise when an economic innovation saves money but degrades the environment. Retrenchments in program expenditures might have similar effects. This case is the reverse of the common case in which benefits are gained and money lost and, like it, requires difficult trade-off judgments.

9.10 SUMMATIVE EVALUATION OF PROGRAMS WITH MULTIPLE EFFECTS

Example 3: Program Evaluation with Monetary and Mortality Effects

Suppose that a hypothetical influenza inoculation program would avert six deaths per 100,000 persons inoculated. One person in 100,000 would suffer a fatal reaction to the shot. The program costs $4 per inoculation but makes it possible to close emergency flu treatment units that cost $80,000 per 100,000 people. Considering only the deaths and the money effects, the problem is to decide whether the program should be enacted.

In the benefit-cost approach to this problem, dollar values would be attached to the deaths averted and caused, whereupon all program effects would be in monetary terms and the positive effects (benefits) could be compared with the negative effects (costs). If analysts find deaths too hard to value, the cost-effectiveness approach may be adopted. The net health effects are six deaths averted less one caused, or five deaths averted. The net monetary effects are $400,000 less $80,000, or $320,000. The cost-effectiveness ratio is

$$C/E = \frac{\text{net monetary effects}}{\text{net health effects}}$$

$$= \frac{\$320,000}{5 \text{ deaths averted}}$$

$$= \$64,000 \text{ per death averted.} \qquad [9.3]$$

This ratio indicates that the inoculation program should be implemented if and only if averting a death is worth at least $64,000 (that is, if and only if the society is able to spend at least $64,000 per life saved).

Risk-benefit analysis. A leading branch of cost-effectiveness analysis is risk-benefit analysis—of which there are two main variants. In the first variant, effects on lives are compared with effects on money. In this view, an economic development program bringing $1 million in net benefits but causing five premature deaths has a risk-benefit ratio of one life lost per $200,000 in net benefits.

The second variant considers program effects to fall into three categories: (1) money effects (both positive and negative), (2) benefits (positive nonmonetary effects), and (3) risks (negative nonmonetary effects). In this perspective, cost-effectiveness analysis consists of two parts: (1) a monetary or cost analysis determining the numerator of the cost-effectiveness ratio; and (2) a risk-benefit analysis determining the denominator.

Example 3 may be put into this format. The cost analysis involves subtracting the $80,000 in gains from $400,000 in costs to obtain net costs of $320,000. The benefits are six deaths averted; the risks, one death caused. The cost-effectiveness ratio is

$$C/E \ = \frac{\text{net monetary effects}}{\text{net health effects}}$$

$$= \frac{\text{results of monetary or cost analysis}}{\text{results of risk-benefit analysis}}$$

$$= \frac{\text{money losses minus money gains}}{\text{benefits minus risks}}$$

$$= \frac{\$400,000 - \$80,000}{6 \text{ deaths averted minus 1 death caused}}$$

$$= \$64,000 \text{ per death averted.} \qquad\qquad [9.4]$$

Example 3a: Program Evaluation with Diverse Effects

Suppose that the same program would prevent 2,000 non-fatal cases of flu per 100,000 inoculations and that decision-makers also want to take this effect into account. This situation poses a frequent dilemma in cost-effectiveness analysis: For clarity, both analysts and decisionmakers prefer a simple two-term ratio comparing what is spent with what is gained ($64,000 to gain one life in the original example). With more than two dimensions of effect—here, money, mortality, and morbidity—the two-term ratio is not immediately obtainable.

Two different approaches may be adopted: (1) a multi-term cost-effectiveness ratio may be calculated; or (2) the various dimensions of effect may, by assumptions about their commensurability, be reduced to two. With the former strategy, all effects could be divided by five to obtain the multi-term ratio of

$64,000 spent per one death averted and 400 non-fatal flu cases averted.

This ratio indicates that the program is worthwhile only if the combined value of averting one death and 400 nonfatal cases is considered to be at least $64,000. While this is somewhat unwieldy information for decisionmakers to use, this strategy has the advantage of not prejudging for the decision makers the relative values of the different effects.

A two-term cost-effectiveness ratio can be obtained in three ways: by making flu deaths commensurable with nonfatal cases, by making the deaths commensurable with money (that is, by placing a dollar value on averting a death), or by making nonfatal cases commensurable with money. Suppose, for example, that deaths are commensurable with nonfatal flu cases in the sense that averting one death is considered just as good as averting 200 nonfatal cases. The 2,000 nonfatal cases of flu prevented per 100,000 inoculations are therefore valued as 10 deaths prevented. Combining this figure with the six deaths actually prevented and the one death caused gives net health effects valued as 15 deaths prevented per 100,000 inoculated. The cost-effectiveness ratio for the program is therefore

$$\frac{\$320,000}{15 \text{ deaths averted}} = \$21,333 \text{ per death averted.} \qquad [9.5]$$

*Example 4: Comparing Effects on Private and Public Monies and Program Effects

A manpower training and placement program costs $6 million and places 1,000 otherwise unemployed persons in jobs. Employers receive bonuses for hiring program graduates that amount for them to present-valued positive compensating variations of $1.5 million. Analysts wish to present this information in condensed form to assist decision-making on the possible expansion of the program. Because valuing job training and placement is difficult, a cost-effectiveness analysis is undertaken.

Like the benefit-cost ratio, the cost-effectiveness ratio seeks to compare concisely what is gained with what is spent. The ratios in Example 1 showed how much money had to be spent to discover and treat a case, to achieve a cure, to save a life, and to gain a life year. The ratio in Example 2 showed that $1,915 sufficed to find a case of hypertensive renovascular disease; in Example 3 that $64,000 averted a death. In each case, dollars were compared with difficult-to-value output units. In the public-private benefit-cost ratio, public dollars are contrasted with private dollars. The present problem involves both comparisons: money to the output unit of the job placement and public money to private money. A three-term ratio—public costs to private benefits to job placements—would maintain the two distinctions but would lose the crisp two-term comparison between what is gained and what is spent.

Analysts and decisionmakers prefer the briefer and clearer two-term ratio and accordingly tend to adopt either of two approaches. In the benefit-cost approach, the job placement is valued as its impact in terms of public and private money. The public-private benefit-cost ratio can then be calculated. In the cost-effectiveness approach, public and private monies must be made commensurable. The money effects can then be compared, in a cost-effectiveness ratio, with the number of job placements achieved. (This is usually done by assuming the equivalence of public and private dollars.) The choice of analytic approach should reflect the concerns of the decision actor: If the decision depends on the relationship between money-valued and other effects, cost-effectiveness analysis is the more appropriate; if the contrasting of public and private effects is more important, benefit-cost analysis should be employed.

9.11 DETERMINING THE BEST VERSION OF A PROGRAM: FORMATIVE EVALUATION

We turn now to four examples—three hypothetical, one actual—of ways in which cost-effectiveness analysis can be used to determine the optimal program version: (1) the best level of intensiveness for an educational program; (2) the best way to generate a set amount of electricity; (3) the best strategy for finding cases of child abuse; and (4) the best number of cancer-screening tests. The key concept in each example is the cost-effectiveness ratio based not on comparing each program version with no program, but instead on that comparing alternative versions directly—weighing the difference in costs between two alternatives against the difference in benefits.

Example 5: Determining the Optimal Intensiveness
for an Educational Program

A remedial education program achieves an average increase in cognitive skills of 4.5 months at a cost of $70 per pupil. It has been suggested that the program be made more intensive— increasing the per-pupil cost to $80 and the growth in cognitive skills to 4.9 months of gain.

The benefit-cost analyst must value monetarily progress in cognitive skills. However, if this is thought too difficult, a cost-effectiveness approach might be taken. This would calculate a cost-effectiveness ratio based on the differences between the present and the modified programs:

$$(\$80 - \$70) \div (4.9 - 4.5 \text{ months of cognitive gain})$$

$$= \$10 \div (0.4 \text{ months})$$

$$= \$25 \text{ per month of gain.} \qquad [9.6]$$

If decisionmakers consider themselves able to spend at least $25 per month of gain, they should make the program more intensive; if not, they should not.

Example 6: Choosing Among Alternative
Means for Achieving a Set Objective

A region has identified three basic strategies—A, B, and C—for achieving the electrical capacity it desires. The costs of each strategy are shown in Table 9.1. How should the choice of strategy reflect valuation of the lives lost?

Solution. To identify the best strategy, we compare the competing alternatives directly. Strategy B, in contrast to Strategy A, saves 40 more lives but costs an additional $8 million. The cost-effectiveness ratio of these differences is

$$(\$26 \text{ million} - \$18 \text{ million}) \div (120 \text{ lives} - 80 \text{ lives})$$

$$= \$8 \text{ million} \div 40 \text{ lives}$$

$$= \$200,000 \text{ per life.} \qquad [9.7]$$

TABLE 9.1   Costs of Alternative Energy Strategies in
                       Terms of Money and Lives

Energy Strategy	Present-Valued Dollar Cost	Present-Valued Lives Lost
A	$18 million	120 lives
B	$26 million	80 lives
C	$32 million	60 lives

If the regional decisionmakers consider lives to be worth more than $200,000 apiece (that is, if they think they can pay at least $200,000 per life saved), they should prefer Strategy B to Strategy A; if lives are valued at less than $200,000 apiece, A is preferred to B.

Strategy C saves 20 more lives than does B at an additional cost of $6 million. The cost-effectiveness ratio is

$$(\$6 \text{ million}) \div (20 \text{ lives})$$

$$= \$300,000 \text{ per life.} \qquad [9.8]$$

This indicates that ascribed life values of less than $300,000 per life should lead the region to prefer B to C; that valuing lives at more than $300,000 should lead it to prefer C to B.

Putting these results together indicates that (1) for all life values under $200,000, Strategy A should be followed; (2) for life values between $200,000 and $300,000, Strategy B should be followed; and (3) for life values over $300,000, Strategy C should be followed.

The possibility of implementing none of the three strategies has not been considered and was, in effect, ruled out in the statement of the problem which assumed that one of the three strategies had to be adopted. This form of cost-effectiveness analysis has thus avoided determining two important values: the worth of the electrical capacity and the life values.

Example 7: Choosing Among Alternative Program Versions Offering Different Levels of Benefit

A city may adopt any or none of three alternative strategies, D, E, and F, for discovering cases of child abuse. Their respective costs and results in terms of numbers of confirmed cases discovered are shown in Table 9.2. Decisionmakers have not yet made up their minds on the value of the average case finding but ask the analysts to calculate how that value would affect the choice of strategy.

Table 9.2 shows that D finds cases at an average cost of $1,000 (= $400,000 ÷ 400); E at an average cost of $1,100; and F at $1,227. This implies that, if cases found are valued at less than $1,000, none of the strategies would be implemented. Only at a cost of $1,000 does it become sensible to implement Strategy D.

If Strategy D were implemented, additional cases of abuse could be found by switching to Strategies E or F. The problem is to determine the level at which E or F would become preferred to D. Strategy E would discover 100 (500-400) additional cases at a further cost of $150,000 (= $550,000 - $400,000). This is a cost-effectiveness ratio of

$$\$150,000 \div 100 \text{ cases}$$

$$= \$1,500 \text{ per case} \qquad [9.9]$$

for the 100 additional cases that would be found by substituting Strategy E for Strategy D. If the city is willing to pay at least $1,500 per case to find 100 more cases under Strategy E than under D, then it should implement E.

A common analytic mistake in this and similar situations is to be guided by the average costs of case-finding as given above. That is, Strategy E's average cost of $1,100 per case found would be taken as a reason for shifting from D to E if the cases

TABLE 9.2   Costs and Results of Alternative
             Strategies for Discovering Child
             Abuse

Case-finding Strategy	Cost	Confirmed Cases Found
D	$400,000	400
E	$550,000	500
F	$675,000	550

were valued at $1,100 or more. Indeed, if Strategy D did not exist and if cases found were valued at just more than $1,100, then E should be implemented. But the existence of D changes the focus from asking whether it is worth $550,000 to discover 500 cases to asking whether it is worth spending $150,000 to discover 100 more cases. To decide appropriately between D and E, the critical question is whether it is better to find an additional 100 cases at $1,500 per case or better instead to use the $150,000 in some other way.

The decision to shift from Strategy E to Strategy F is made similarly. F costs $125,000 more than E and finds 50 more cases. The cost-effectiveness ratio is

$$\frac{\$125,000}{50 \text{ cases}} = \$2,500 \text{ per additional case found.} \qquad [9.10]$$

The city should decide among the strategies as shown in Table 9.3.

Example 8: Marginal Program Evaluation in Cancer Screening

Physicians ordering diagnostic tests often face the trade-off question of whether the greater accuracy of a more expensive test justifies its greater expense: is a CT-scan worth getting instead of an x-ray?; Are the extra case findings achieved by repeating screening tests worth the added costs?

Solution. An empirical study of this issue is that of Neuhauser and Lewicki (1976), who estimate the gains of

TABLE 9.3   Ranges of Values for Finding
Cases of Child Abuse within
which Different Strategies are
Preferred

Values of a Case Finding	Preferred Strategy
under $1000	none
$1000 to $1500	D
$1500 to $2500	E
over $2500	F

successive stool guaiac tests for colon cancer. Their results are
shown in Table 9.4. They found that single tests detected 65.9
cancers per 10,000 screened at a cost of $77,511. This gives a
cost-effectiveness ratio of

$$\frac{\$77,511}{65.9 \text{ cancers found}} = \$1,175 \text{ per cancer found.} \qquad [9.11]$$

Many screening protocols specify six stool guaiac tests in the
interest of greater diagnostic accuracy. Neuhauser and Lewicki
found that the sixth tests cost less—$13,190 for the original
10,000 population. These tests also found fewer cancers—an
estimated 0.0003 cases. The cost-effectiveness ratio for the
sixth test is thus

$$\frac{\$13,190}{0.0003 \text{ cancers found}} = \$47,100,000 \text{ per additional cancer found.} \qquad [9.12]$$

This ratio indicates that the sixth tests do not use societal
resources in a cost-effective way.

It is likely that the formulators of the screening protocols
were misled by the average cost figures. The average cost per
case detected with six tests is $2,451, which is not unreason-
able. However, it is not relevant. The critical question for the
sixth guaiac is whether there are better ways to spend money
than at a rate of over $47 million per cancer found. Since there
are, this money should not go toward sixth stool guaiacs.

TABLE 9.4   Cancer Detection and Screening Costs with Sequential
            Guaiac Tests

No. of Tests	Cancer Detection		Screening Costs ($)		
	no. of cases	incremental gain	total[*]	incremental	average[†]
1	65.9469	65.9469	77,511	77,511	1,175
2	71.4424	5.4956	107,690	30,179	1,507
3	71.9004	0.4580	130,199	22,509	1,810
4	71.9385	0.0382	148,116	17,917	2,059
5	71.9417	0.0032	163,141	15,024	2,268
6	71.9420	0.0003	176,331	13,190	2,451

[*]Calculated by addition of cost of guaiac stool testing on 10,000 people and cost of
barium-enema examination with positive tests.
[†]Calculated by division of total cost by number of true-positive results detected.
SOURCE: Neuhauser and Lewicki, 1976.

9.12 VARIABLE VALUES OF OUTPUT UNITS

A major problem of benefit-cost analysis is that different
dollars (public or private, present or future, pretax or posttax)
have different values (see Section 7.2.3). While cost-effectiveness analysis shares this problem, it has a further one of its own:
The worths of the unvalued units of effect may also vary. The
deaths caused by flu inoculations, for example, might be
mainly those of young, mostly healthy persons and the lives
saved might be those of a generally older group (suggesting
perhaps that the inoculations should be restricted to the old—
but that is not the issue here). To estimate net health effects by
subtracting deaths caused from lives saved is misleading because
the lives lost are, overall, quite different from the lives saved.
The death of an elderly bedridden person may well be considered not so much of a calamity as the death of a healthy
young person. Similarly, the cases of child abuse found in
Example 7 by Strategy E, but not by Strategy D, might be
different from those found by Strategy D. They might be more
or less serious, or more or less remediable. If so, society will
value them differently, and lumping them all together in a
cost-effectiveness analysis will misrepresent social values.

In the instance of flu epidemics, the marginal cases contracted at low levels of disease may simply tax the health care

system a bit more. At higher levels of disease, marginal cases of flu may shut down whole institutions (for example, schools) or impair their efficiency (as with fire or police departments). The health care system might be so overburdened that the quality of care would decline. In such situations, the value of preventing a first case of flu will differ from the value of preventing a thousandth or a ten thousandth case. There is undeniable analytic convenience in assuming that marginal units of input or output have constant value. This assumption, unfortunately, is sometimes unjustified. Variations in value must be recognized and appropriately reflected in the analysis.

There are two primary ways to approach output units with variable values. The first is to describe as well as possible the differences in the units and to let decisionmakers make suitable adjustments based on their own values. The second way is to seek more basic units, less subject to variability in value. We examine this latter method further in the context of governmental decision-making on life-saving programs.

9.13 ADJUSTING FOR VARIABLE OUTPUT UNITS

Example 9: Decision-Making For
Life-Saving Programs

Suppose that a society must decide between putting more money into increased highway patrolling or into mobile coronary care units (MCCUs). The decision is to be based only on a determination of which program demonstrates the greatest value of life extension per dollar spent. This assumes that the marginal gains of the two programs are close to their average gains and that morbidity effects are not an important point of difference between the programs.

Suppose that the past program of increased highway patrolling saved an estimated two lives per year at a cost of $200,000 and that MCCUs saved an estimated four lives annually at a cost of $240,000. The cost-effectiveness ratio for highway patrolling is

$200,000 ÷ (2 lives saved)

= $100,000 per life saved.   [9.13]

That for the MCCUs is

$240,000 ÷ (4 lives saved)

= $60,000 per life saved.   [9.14]

These cost-effectiveness figures argue for expanding the MCCU program at the expense of increased highway patrolling.

A closer look at the lives involved, however, may indicate differences. Suppose that the average life saved by increased patrolling gains 40 years and that the average life saved by the MCCUs is extended six years. Suppose further that the discount rate is seven percent.

These additional facts suggest that measuring output merely as numbers of lives saved is not adequate. Perhaps a better unit would be years of life added. Using this unit, we should discount years added in the future and thus should think in terms of present-valued life years. The present value of the 40 years of life saved by averting a traffic fatality is thus

$$\sum_{n=1}^{40} \frac{1}{(1.07)^{n-1}} = 14.26 \text{ life years.} \qquad [9.15]$$

Similarly, the present value of six years gained with an MCCU is

$$\sum_{n=1}^{6} \frac{1}{(1.07)^{n-1}} = 5.10 \text{ life years.} \qquad [9.16]$$

The cost-effectiveness ratios are now expressed in terms of dollars per present-valued life year. The cost-effectiveness ratio for patrolling is

$200,000 ÷ [(2 lives) · (14.26 present-valued life years saved per life)]

= $7,010 per present-valued life year.   [9.17]

The ratio for MCCUs is

$240,000 ÷ [(4 lives) · (5.10 present-valued life years saved per life)]

$$= \$11,764 \text{ per present-valued life year.} \qquad [9.18]$$

These figures indicate that budget monies are more effectively spent on patrolling than on MCCUs.

Taking account of life quality. Suppose now that departmental decisionmakers perceive differences in the qualities of lives extended by patrolling and by MCCUs and want to take these into account. Specifically, they might feel that those not killed in road accidents have a normal degree of illness and thus have an average life quality equal to 0.95 of that of a completely healthy person. Heart attack survivors due to MCCUs might, because of pain and activity restrictions, have average life quality equal to 0.65 of that of a completely healthy person.

From this perspective, cost-effectiveness ratios are calculated as dollars per fully healthy, present-valued life year—commonly labeled "quality-adjusted life year" and abbreviated QALY. Survival this year at a life quality thought equal to 0.65 of a completely healthy life year is counted as 0.65 QALYs. The cost-effectiveness ratio for the increased patrolling is now

$200,000 ÷ [(2 lives) · (14.26 present-valued life years per life)

$$\cdot \text{ (average life quality of 0.95)]} \qquad [9.19]$$

$$= \$7,379 \text{ per QALY.}$$

The ratio for the MCCUs is now

$240,000 ÷ [(4 lives) · (5.10 present-valued life years per life)

$$\cdot \text{ (average life quality of 0.65)]}$$

$$= \$18,099 \text{ per QALY.} \qquad [9.20]$$

With this quality adjustment, the advantage of the patrolling program over MCCUs has increased further. Results for the three different types of cost-effectiveness calculations are shown in Table 9.5. The fourth row in the table shows that the program of increased patrolling appears to be only 0.60 as good as MCCUs in the analysis based on lives, but better by a factor of 1.68 in the analysis based on life years, and better by a factor of 2.45 in the analysis based on quality-adjusted life years.

9.14 EXTENDING AND ENHANCING LIVES

A further advantage of taking life quality into account is that life-saving interventions can be compared with life-enhancing actions.

Example 9a: Comparing Life Extensions
with Health Enhancements

Another program comprises subsidized surgery to relieve the pain of angina pectoris without extending lives. At a cost of $30,000, persons with angina pain can be raised from a condition felt to be equivalent to 0.33 of a fully healthy status to 0.68 of a fully healthy status. Such persons have a life expectancy of eight years. We wish to compare the value of this enhancement in life quality with the value of life-saving with MCCUs.

The present value of eight consecutive life years is 6.39 life years. A quality enhancement of 0.35 (0.68 minus 0.33) is experienced for each of those eight years. We calculate that one surgical operation thus gains an increment in life quality of 2.24 (6.39 times 0.35) present-valued perfectly healthy years. One QALY is thus gained for $13,415 ($30,000 ÷ 2.24). This is less than .the cost of a perfectly healthy life year purchased through the MCCU program—indicating that subsidized surgery for angina pain is more cost-effective (obtains more life value per unit of cost) than are the MCCUs.

9.15 MEASURING LIFE QUALITY

The methodology above presupposes a means of measuring life quality. Such measurement might be made by reference to a

TABLE 9.5   Comparison of Cost-Effectiveness Calculations Based on
            Alternative Output Units

	Cost-Effectiveness Calculations Based on		
	Lives (L)	Life Years (LY)	Quality-Adjusted Life Years (QALY)
1. C/E ratio for increased patrolling	$100,000 per life	$7,010 per life year	$7,379 per QALY
2. C/E ratio for MCCUs	$60,000 per life	$11,764 per life year	$18,099 per QALY
3. The program appearing to be better	MCCUs	Patrolling	Patrolling
4. Cost-effectiveness of patrolling as proportion of that of MCCUs (Row 2 entries ÷ Row 1 entries)	0.60	1.68	2.45

hypothetical lottery. The person whose life quality is being gauged is asked to choose between living his life that day and undergoing a lottery that, with probability p, would give him perfect health for the day and, with probability 1-p, would render him unconscious for the day. The choice is depicted in Figure 9.1. The unconsciousness is here purely hypothetical and does not imply any worsening of condition or subsequent effects.

For some p, the person will be exactly indifferent between the actual day and the lottery. That value of p is the measure of life quality. The perfectly healthy person is indifferent between the actual day of life and the lottery only when p = 1.0. A person so ill as to be indifferent between living the actual day and being unconscious for that day has a life quality of zero. The person with life quality of 0.5 is indifferent between any actual day and submitting to a lottery offering half a chance of perfect health for the day and half a chance of unconsciousness. Alternatively, this person may be visualized as indifferent between his actual life and the alternative of living every other day in perfect health and the intervening days in unconsciousness. Negative life qualities occur whenever pain is so great that a person would rather be unconscious. Life qualities higher than

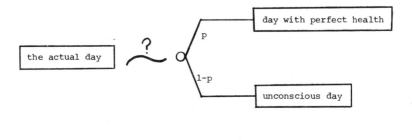

Figure 9.1: Hypothetical Lottery for Determining Life Quality

1.0 are, by definition, precluded (but might be achieved with interventions bringing persons to health levels better than those previously deemed perfect). (Because probabilities range from zero to 1.0, the methodology pictured in Figure 9.1 must be modified to measure life qualities that are negative or greater than 1.0.)

9.16 UNDERSTANDINGS IN MEASURING LIFE QUALITY

Cost-effectiveness ratios comparing money with quality-adjusted life years (QALYs) require certain assumptions:

(1) that a unit of gain is independent of health status level. A gain from life quality of 0.1 to one of 0.4 is thus presumed equivalent to improving quality from 0.7 to perfect health.

(2) that a unit of gain is independent of the size of gain. For example, the gain associated with enhancing life quality from 0.4 to 0.6 for each of five persons for one year is taken as equivalent to extending the life of a perfectly healthy person by one year.

(3) that interpersonal comparisons of life qualities are impossible. Cases could be made for valuing the perfectly healthy day of a 20-year-old more highly than that of an 80-year-old; or the perfectly healthy day of a happy person more highly than that of a suicidally depressed person. Current analytic methods do not allow such distinctions. Life quality is scaled only in relation to the hypothetically perfect health of the person in

question (at present not reflecting phychological dimensions of health except as they affect such other factors as mobility or activity).

9.17 THE BENEFIT-COST AND COST-EFFECTIVENESS PROCESSES COMPARED

The examples above are based on a common numerical methodology for cost-effectiveness analysis that is similar to the eight-step approach for benefit-cost analysis. We compare the benefit-cost methodology with that for cost-effectiveness.

Step 1. Identifying the decisionmaker and his values. This is virtually the same in B/C and C/E, the only difference being that the C/E analyst need not go quite as far. He can leave unvalued one dimension of effect while the B/C analyst must somehow value all dimensions.

Step 2. Identifying alternatives. This is the same for B/C and C/E. The examples above show that the actual numerical operations vary somewhat depending on the nature of the decision alternatives—whether, for instance, the evaluation is summative or formative. The form of the final numerical result in C/E, however, is the same for all these cases: a cost-effectiveness trade-off ratio relating money effects to unvalued effects.

Steps 3 and 4. Identifying costs and benefits. These are the same in B/C and C/E.

Step 5. Valuing effects. This is easier in C/E than in B/C since the most difficult dimension of program effects may be left unvalued in C/E.

Step 6. Discounting. Money discounting is the same in B/C and C/E. The unvalued effects must also be discounted in C/E.

Step 7. Catering to distributional effects. Essentially the same in B/C and C/E.

Step 8. Aggregating and interpreting the valued effects. Benefit-cost analysis ends up with either a measure of net benefits or the benefit-cost ratio considered most suitable; C/E presents the cost-effectiveness ratio. Sensitivity analysis is useful in both B/C and C/E.

In summary, cost-effectiveness is most appealing when exactly one dimension of program effects is hard to value monetarily. Without such a dimension, B/C is at least as good as C/E. With more than one such dimension, difficulties in achieving commensurability and in presentation lessen the attractiveness of performing C/E.

9.18 THIS CHAPTER AND OTHER WRITINGS

For a broader perspective on cost-effectiveness analysis, a number of historical references mentioned in this chapter—for example, Quade (1967) and Williams (1973)—are useful. A good overview on the application of cost-effectiveness analysis in health with special attention to the use of quality-adjusted life years is provided by Weinstein and Stason (1977). Levin (1975) gives a more general exposition of the technique. Good illustrative application are by Zeckhauser and Shepard (1976) and Swint and Nelson (1977).

Measurement of health quality is receiving increased attention from analysts. One extended group of collaborators has applied alternative questioning techniques toward developing health indices (Patrick et al., 1973a, 1973b), has applied them to a disease prevention program (Bush et al., 1973), and has examined the reliability and validity of the indices (Kaplan et al., 1976, 1978). Ware et al. (1979) have authored a series of articles addressing conceptual issues in measuring health quality.

10

Valuation in Context

10.1 CHAPTER OVERVIEW

Evaluators have long recognized that contextual adjustments may be required to compare alternatives appropriately. However, because these adjustments are sometimes overlooked, a limited formalization of them is presented. Backward adjustments take into account the different circumstances under which past performances may have occurred; forward adjustments take into account the different circumstances in which future performances will occur and the different standards against which they will be judged. When future context and values are known, it is useful to reduce many attributes to one dimension of value. When the future context and values are doubtful, information on the separate attributes is best not aggregated. Value adjustments open depend—as is seen in Sections 10.9 through 10.11—on the ways in which events or factors complement each other. We finally examine cases in which accurate evaluation requires maintaining a broad contextual perspective.

10.2 THE BACKWARD ADJUSTMENT

Example: Teacher Choice

There are two third-grade teachers, A and B, in a school system. You will rehire one for the coming year and will release the other. Your criterion for the decision is the candidates' ability to achieve cognitive gains. The students of Teacher A last year made greater cognitive gains than those of Teacher B. Teacher A, however, had the advantages of teaching earlier in the day—when student restlessness is lower—and of having classes with fewer disruptive elements. How should you choose between the teachers?

Suppose first that you are uniquely interested in one teacher quality: the ability to produce cognitive gains in the specific situation for which one is to be hired. Based on experience of teachers in similar situations, you might judge that last year's classroom situation of Teacher A is similar to the prospective situation. You therefore expect that Teacher A, if hired, would bring about cognitive gains comparable to those of the previous year. Suppose that other teachers who have taught in classrooms like those of both A and B realized on average 2.2 months more of cognitive gains per pupil in Teacher-A-type classrooms than in Teacher-B-type classrooms. You should, in this case, add 2.2 months to the cognitive gains made by B's students before comparing them with those of A's students. If B's cognitive gains so adjusted exceed those of A, B should be preferred; if not, A should be preferred.

This type of interpretation is a *backward adjustment:*

modification in the estimate of one quality by taking into account the circumstances under which that quality appeared.

10.3 CIRCUMSTANCES REQUIRING BACKWARD ADJUSTMENTS

Backward adjustments may be indicated in various evaluative situations.

Example: Construction Costs

Alternative design strategies for constructing public housing are being compared. One dimension of comparison is that of cost. Suppose that Strategy C was implemented in areas where costs for labor, land, and materials exceed those of other areas by 20 percent. A backward adjustment, calculated by dividing the costs of C by 1.2, is in order before comparing the strategies.

Example: Smoking Reduction

A smoking reduction program (call it D) has been tried in a rural high school and has brought about a 43 percent reduction in smoking. One wonders how effective it would be in an urban high school. A more intensive program, E, has been found to achieve average smoking reductions of 48 percent in rural schools and of 22 percent in urban schools. A less intensive program, F, reduced smoking by 18 percent in rural schools and by 10 percent in urban schools. With no further information, one must estimate the ability of Program D to reduce smoking through a backward adjustment. This may reasonably be done by noting that D had results five-sixths of the way from F to E in rural schools. Assuming this same relationship to hold in the urban setting, D would reduce smoking by 20 percent there. Other reasonable assumptions leading to other answers are also possible.

10.4 THE FORWARD ADJUSTMENT

Example: Teacher Choice and Different Qualities

Suppose that the choice between Teachers A and B is now altered by the perception that there is no unitary teacher quality of ability to produce cognitive gains. Instead, an array of teacher attributes differentially affects slow, intermediate, and fast learners. Separate tests gauge the abilities to teach each type of student in a standardized situation similar to that in which the rehired teacher will perform next year. Teacher A, on the basis of the tests, is expected in one year to achieve 5.9 months of cognitive gains with slow learners, 10.2 months of gains with intermediate learners, and 13.7 months with fast learners. Teacher B achieves 7.8, 9.7, and 11.0 months of gains with the same three groups. Next year's class will be composed of seventeen slow, nine intermediate, and four fast learners. Assuming that the objective is to maximize average cognitive gains over the whole class, which teacher should be hired?

Solution. We calculate that the average cognitive gain achieved by Teacher A is

$$\frac{(17)(5.9) + (9)(10.2) + (4)(13.7)}{30} = 8.23 \qquad [10.1]$$

months. B's average gain is

$$\frac{(17)(7.8) + (9)(9.7) + (4)(11.0)}{30} = 8.80 \qquad [10.2]$$

months. B would be preferred.

If the class had consisted instead of twelve slow, eleven intermediate, and seven fast learners, A's average gain would have been

$$\frac{(12)(5.9) + (11)(10.2) + (7)(13.7)}{30} = 9.30 \qquad [10.3]$$

months. B's average gain would have been

$$\frac{(12)(7.8) + (11)(9.7) + (7)(11.0)}{30} = 9.24 \qquad [10.4]]$$

months. In this case, Teacher A would have a slight advantage over Teacher B.

The calculations performed above are examples of the *forward adjustment:*

> weighting or valuing the attributes of different options by taking future context into account.

10.5 VALUES IN FORWARD ADJUSTMENTS

Forward adjustments reflect both context and judgmental valuation. In the present example, we have so far made only contextual adjustments—taking into account how many of each student type would be in the class (which guided the calculations in equations 10.1 through 10.4).

Example: Teacher Choice and Values

To complicate the problem further, one might value differently the gains of the different student types. A society might, for instance, care especially about the progress of its better and poorer students. A month of cognitive gain by a slow learner might thus be considered as good as 1.3 months of gain by an intermediate student and a month of gain by a fast learner thought as good as 1.4 months of intermediate learner gain. This information enables commensurability of all gains by couching them as equivalent gains for intermediate learners. The sum of these is the objective function. We now compute—as a forward adjustment—that Teacher A will achieve a total of

$$(1.3)(17)(5.9) + (1)(9)(10.2) + (1.4)(4)(13.7) = 298.9 \quad [10.5]$$

equivalent months of intermediate learner gain and Teacher B

$$(1.3)(17)(7.8) + (1)(9)(9.7) + (1.4)(4)(11.0) = 321.3 \quad [10.6]$$

equivalent months of intermediate learner gain. Teacher B would be preferred.

10.6 A SITUATION REQUIRING BACKWARD AND FORWARD ADJUSTMENTS

Example: Snowplows

City G contemplates the purchase of snowplows—either Type K or Type L. The types are equally costly. Neighboring City H—comparable in size to City G—has tried the two types and has found that Type K handles the smaller snowfalls better and Type L handles the larger snowfalls better, as indicated by Table 10.1. City G tends to have moister and heavier snow than City H. This difference is thought to add five percent to the plowing time for small snowfalls and 30 percent to the plowing time for larger snowfalls. City G averages ten small and three large snowfalls each winter and wishes to minimize total plowing time. Which snowplow type should it acquire?

Solution. This problem requires both backward and forward adjustments: the former to account for snow differences between the cities; the latter to determine the relative worths of the plows in City G. For the backward adjustment, we simply multiply the first row of Table 10.1 by 1.05 and the second row by 1.30, obtaining Table 10.2. This shows the expected times to handle the two snowfall types in City G. Using these figures, we can now forward adjust to calculate the total average times for plowing in City G over an entire winter. For Type K, this is

$$(10)(3.57) + (3)(19.89) = 95.37 \text{ hours} \qquad [10.7]$$

and, for Type L,

$$(10)(5.15) + (3)(14.43) = 94.74 \text{ hours.} \qquad [10.8]$$

Type L is preferred. Without the backward adjustment for snow heaviness, the forward adjustments would have been

$$(10)(3.4) + (3)(15.3) = 79.9 \text{ hours} \qquad [10.9]$$

for Type K and

$$(10)(4.9) + (3)(11.1) = 83.2 \text{ hours} \qquad [10.10]$$

for Type L—making K appear better.

TABLE 10.1   Snowplow Efficiency in City
H Measured as the Time Required
to Plow City After Small and Large
Snowfalls

	Type K Snowplow	Type L Snowplow
Small snowfall	3.4 hours	4.9 hours
Large snowfall	15.3 hours	11.1 hours

Example: Snowplows and Waiting

The citizens may value differently their hours of waiting for the two sizes of snowfall. For the larger snowfalls, their restlessness and impatience may mount over time, making it an appropriate objective of the city to minimize the plowing hours for small snowfalls plus 1.2 times the plowing hours for large snowfalls. Taking this as an objective function, we find

O.F. (Type K) = (10)(3.57)+(1.2)(3)(19.89)

$$= 107.30, \text{ and} \qquad [10.11]$$

O.F. (Type L) = (10)(5.15)+(1.2)(3)(14.43)

$$= 103.40. \qquad [10.12]$$

Type L is now seen to have a more distinct advantage over Type K than in equations 10.7 and 10.8.

10.7 ARGUMENTS FOR COLLAPSING VECTORS OF ATTRIBUTES

Example: Personnel

The personnel division of a firm employs an evaluative analyst to help it decide which job applicants to hire. Through interviews, psychological testing, and reference contacts, the

TABLE 10.2   Adjusted Snowplow Efficiency in
City G Measured as the Estimated
Time Required to Plow City After
Small and Large Snowfalls

	Type K Snowplow	Type L Snowplow
Small snowfall	3.57 hours	5.15 hours
Large snowfall	19.89 hours	14.43 hours

division obtains ratings of all applicants along a number of attribute dimensions. These are

q_d — diligence;

q_e — experience;

q_i — intelligence; and

q_p — a measure of personality and the ability to get along with others.

Ratings range from zero (bad) to 10 (outstanding) along each dimension. An issue for the division is whether to report the whole vector of attributes—the rating of each candidate along each dimension—or, by appropriately weighting the qualities, to reduce the four dimensions to the single attribute of desirability for employment.

The argument for collapsing the vector of attributes to a single scale runs as follows: By careful solicitation of supervisor preferences, the importance of various qualities for specific positions can be determined; the evaluative analyst could greatly aid the decision actor on employment if he would calculate as a single number for each applicant their assessed prospective value for the firm.

For the position of computer programmer it has been determined, for example, that intelligence (q_i) is highly important— to the extent that intelligence levels below 5 (out of 10) are thought incompatible with the position. Intelligence is only useful, however, if combined with diligence (q_d). Experience (q_e) is moderately useful, but intelligence and diligence may, if experience is lacking, compensate for it. Personality (q_p) is even less important to success as a programmer. The firm has, however, a policy of weeding out abrasive persons and will hire no one with a personality rating below 2. The analyst fashions an objective function for computer programmer applicants:

$$OF_p(\text{applicant}) = (q_i - 5)(q_d) + 2q_e + q_p; \qquad [10.13]$$

subject to

$$q_i \geqslant 5, \text{ and}$$

$$q_p \geqslant 2. \qquad [10.14]$$

The subscript p to OF indicates that valuation is for the job of programmer. All may agree that this is a satisfactory formulation of qualities sought in programmers. It shows, in effect, how forward adjustments ought to be made for programmer qualities.

Three applicants to the firm are M, N, and P, whose qualities are shown in Table 10.3. Each column in the table is a vector of job candidate qualities. Having worked out the objective function of (10.13), the analyst can obtain summative ratings of the applicants by plugging their qualities into this formula and finding that

$$OF_p(M) = 30,$$

$$OF_p(N) = 26, \text{ and}$$

$$OF_p(P) = 20. \qquad [10.15]$$

If precisely one programmer is to be hired, it should be M; if two, M and N. If the firm is not sure whether it will hire anyone until looking at the rest of the applicant pool, it is sufficient for the personnel department and analyst to report the applicant scores.

TABLE 10.3   Qualities of Job
Applicants

	Applicants		
Qualities	*M*	*N*	*P*
Diligence (q_d)	8	2	9
Experience (q_e)	1	7	6
Intelligence (q_i)	8	9	5
Personality (q_p)	4	4	8

Before formulating the objective function enabled single-scale valuation of candidates as in equation 10.13, the personnel department reported to the programming supervisor all qualities of all applicants. The supervisor then had to weigh in his mind all qualities against one another—trying, for example, to judge whether M's greater diligence offset N's advantages in experience and intelligence. With vectors of qualities reduced by the objective function to single numbers, the supervisor's decisions on hiring are greatly facilitated. This and the possible greater consistency of decisions as a result are the main arguments for collapsing the vectors of qualities.

10.8 ARGUMENTS AGAINST
COLLAPSING VECTORS OF ATTRIBUTES

The case against collapsing the vector of applicant qualities is based on the variability of suitable forward adjustments: Different forward adjustments are needed for different positions, and for specific positions they might vary over time. The same set of applicants, for instance, might also be interested in other jobs for which their individual qualities would be valued differently. In hiring sales personnel, it is likely that diligence, experience, and personality would carry greater weight and intelligence less weight than in hiring programmers. Applicant P, the third choice for computer programmer, might well be the best choice for a sales position.

The desirable qualities in a programmer may change over time or may be set differently by different supervisors. If interpersonal frictions simmer, an agreeable personality becomes more prized. One supervisor may dislike having to provide instruction and may therefore value experience more highly.

Whether the analyst should make the forward adjustments is a variant of the question faced in Sections 5.10 and 5.11: whether to reduce the many categories of gain and loss to a two-term ratio. If future context and the values associated with it are known, the analyst aids decisionmakers by forward-adjusting. This reduces the vector of qualities to a single number to be passed on to decisionmakers. When future context is variable (a person might be made a programmer or a salesman) or when the values attached to it are subject to change or to judgment, the analyst should leave valuation to the decision-maker. In this case, the analyst would transmit all pertinent information (all of Table 10.3) to the decisionmaker.

10.9 COMPLEMENTARITY

Example: Valuing Road Links

R and U are towns in a desert separated by uninhabited territory. S and T are points on a line between them. What is the value of a road connecting S and T?

Example: Research

V, W, and X are research tasks essential to finding a cure for a given disease. If any of the three tasks remains unfulfilled, the disease will go unchecked. What is the value of accomplishing task W?

Example: Assigning Blame

Mr. Jones was killed in an automobile accident. If the intersection had been better marked, or if his brakes had been sound, or if he had worn his seat belt, he would still be alive. How much should Mrs. Jones collect in suing the manufactuer of the faulty brakes?

These examples have the common element of *complementarity:* The valuation of the various components depends on how they are complemented with other components. A road between S and T cannot be valued until one knows the state of roads between R and S and T and U. If R and S and T and U are connected with roads, a road between S and T can be valuable; if R and S and T and U will not be connected, road ST will be worthless. This suggests that the policy question should be whether to build a road between R and U and that the question is only confused by breaking it into parts and asking about the values of segments RS, ST, and TU. The proper unit of analysis must be focused on.

10.10 USING PROBABILITIES TO HANDLE COMPLEMENTARITY

In the second example, the individual research tasks may be the units of decision. One can argue that the three tasks V, W, and X, should simultaneously be considered as the appropriate unit of analysis, but study sections may in fact have to consider limited research proposals—such as one for W—in isolation. How should the study sections value a given proposal to decide whether it merits its proposed budget?

With no control over tasks V and X (which go to other study sections), their fulfillment can be regarded as a random event. The decision can then be displayed as a tree, as in Figure 10.1. The probability of success with task W if the research is funded is labeled p_1. This is larger than p_2, the probability that W would be accomplished (perhaps by other researchers) if the proposal is not funded. In either case, a cure for the disease is achieved only if tasks V and X are also successful. This happens with probability p_3. (This framework could be refined to have the outcome values depend on the waiting time until a cure is perfected.) The gain realized in funding the proposal is an increased probability of realizing the cure. The rise in probability is

$$(p_1)(p_3) - (p_2)(p_3) = (p_1 - p_2)(p_3). \qquad [10.16]$$

This gain is weighed against cost in deciding whether to fund the proposal.

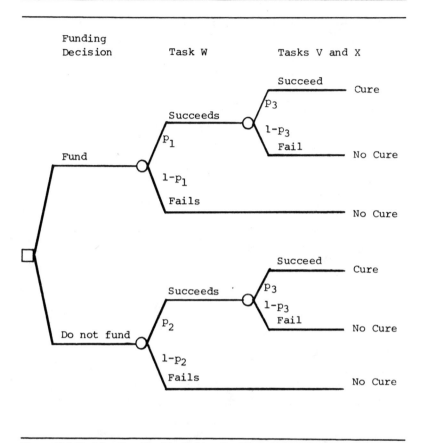

Figure 10.1 Decision Tree Used in Judging the Likely Value of a Research Proposal

10.11 RESPONSIBILITY AND INCENTIVES

Determining the appropriate award for Mrs. Jones may be approached by assigning responsibility for the harm done by the implicated factors: the poor marking of the intersection, the failure to fasten the seat belt, and the faulty brakes. Each factor, in a certain sense, uniquely caused the accident: Had it been altered, the accident would not have occurred. Thus, the value of better marking or of wearing the seat belt or of better brakes is the entire gain in averting the accident. A society could decide to penalize each factor in the accident for the marginal harm it created: make the intersection markers and the brake manufacturers each wholly liable for the loss realized in the accident and yet not have these awards go to Mrs. Jones inasmuch as her husband's carelessness was also to blame. Alternatively, a society could decide which of the three implicated factors in such accidents it makes most sense (is most cost-effective) to remedy. Those responsible for that factor could then be made wholly liable for the harm in the accident and the other factors held legally blameless. This indicates that, while analysis may identify and value the consequences of each factor, awards and redress may depend on socially established incentive systems.

10.12 BROADENING THE PERSPECTIVE

Example: Saccharin

Saccharin increases the statistical risk of cancer. Should it therefore be banned?

Example: A Conference

A scientific conference organized at considerable expense witnesses no valuable exchange of information. Is it a mistake?

Example: Ecology

An insect pest is eliminated from an area. Is this good?

Example: Housing Subsidies

A housing subsidy program helps those with incomes between $6,000 and $8,000 more than those with incomes between $4,000 and $6,000. Is this unjust?

A common point in these examples is that valuation processes must be broad-minded. They must encompass (1) the full range of consequences, (2) the effects of other related programs, and (3) all social values pertinent to an action. In the first example, saccharin may reap gains in reducing obesity that outweigh its harm in contributing to cancer. The wisdom of a saccharin ban will also depend on the efficacy of cancer therapy. Scientific conferences and management meetings whose substantive quality was abysmal have served valuable purposes in publicizing the concerns of their organizers. Eradicating insect species often upsets the ecological balance and in particular increases the numbers of its natural prey. These effects should be weighed along with the direct harm caused by the species in deciding whether to eliminate it. While the housing subsidy program may be regressive in helping the richer of the poor, it may be complemented by other redistributional programs benefiting the very poor. All the programs, including the housing program, taken together may constitute a fair redistribution scheme channeling greater support to greater need. The focus of analytic valuation must be as broad as the extended body of consequences about which decisionmakers care.

10.13 THIS CHAPTER AND OTHER WRITINGS

All fundamental concepts in this chapter have been covered elsewhere—albeit with somewhat different emphasis than our stress here on how assigned values depend on contextual considerations. Backward and forward adjustments are familiar procedures, if new terms. Boruch and Rindskopf (1977) consider backward adjustments to be "fitting" and "adjusting." An important work on backward adjustments through fitting structural equations is Goldberger and Duncan (1973). A common means of adjusting is the covariance adjustment as seen in Overall and Woodward (1977).

Forward adjustments seem to be made more frequently to reflect value differences than contextual differences. One example is the methodology of Edwards and Guttentag (1975). Keeney and Raiffa (1976) discuss the problems of collapsing vectors of attributes and the various mathematical properties this may involve.

Appendix:

Problems for *Benefit-Cost Analysis for Program Evaluation*

1.1 DAMMING EFFECTS

A dam is planned for a river. The dam is expected to (1) cost money; (2) displace people; (3) save lives through improved flood control; (4) save property through improved flood control; (5) reduce the beauty of the natural environment; (6) enable swimming; (7) cost workman lives during construction; (8) provide agricultural irrigation; (9) enable water skiing; (10) endanger plant and animal species; (11) enable lake fishing; (12) take away stream fishing; (13) lead to more drowning deaths; (14) decrease the cost of electricity; and (15) inundate good areas for hiking and camping.

Which of these effects would you consider commensurable and collapse into smaller numbers of effects? In what units would you measure the effects? For which effects is it most difficult to specify units of measure?

In what format and terms should a prospective evaluator of the dam present his findings to decisionmakers?

1.2 DAM VALUATION

Another region choosing among alternative dam plans is much more simplistic. It cares only about (1) x, the difference between the savings in electricity generation and construction costs; and (2) y, the capacity of the dam. Measuring x in millions of dollars and y in tens of millions of gallons, the objective function for the region is

$$OF = x + \sqrt{y}.$$

Plot some indifference curves consistent with this objective function.

2.1 INSULATION

Suppose that you own a house and expect to sell it three years from today. You may install insulation at a cost of $1,000—the best time for which is six months from today. Insulation will save you an average of $100 per year in heating costs which you may assume to fall due nine months from today and every year thereafter. You assume that insulation will increase the resale value of your home by some increment. All your money is in a bank account paying six percent interest compounded quarterly. The incremental value in resale contributed by the insulation must be at least how much, in order to make insulation a wise decision by you?

2.2 HOUSE OR APARTMENT

A young couple wonders whether to buy or to rent. For $50,000, they could buy a house that would give them a residence equivalent to what they could rent for $220 per month. They would, if they bought the house, take out a 20-year mortgage at nine percent on $35,000. The other $15,000 of the purchase price they would have to put up themselves. The bank calculates that the annual payment required on a $35,000 20-year mortgage is $3,834, of which $3,150 (nine percent of $35,000) in the first year is interest. The interest payment can be itemized as an income tax deduction (the couple can deduct the interest from their income before calculating their tax). The couple is in the 20 percent marginal income tax bracket. Real estate values on this kind of house are expected to continue appreciating at four percent per year. If the couple did not buy a house, they could invest their $15,000 of savings at six percent.

The couple decides to base its decision on the first-year effects of renting and buying.

(a) What is the first-year income tax saving due to the deduction of interest?

(b) What is the first-year gain in terms of house appreciation?

(c) Given that capital gains (e.g., house appreciation) are taxed at half the rate of regular income, what tax increase is associated with the gain in (b)?

(d) What interest income is forgone by putting up the $15,000 down payment on the house?

(e) Should the couple buy or rent? What if no itemized deduction were allowed for interest payments?

2.3 CARBURETOR EVALUATION

Your mechanic recommends that you install a new, more gas-efficient carburetor. It would cost $200 and would reduce your gasoline consumption by 10 percent. You spend $500 per year for gasoline. While you ponder, your mechanic says, "Look. With this carburetor, you can immediately sell your car for $140 more, plus you'll be saving $50 per year in gas. You'll keep your car for at least two more years, so it clearly pays to get the new carburetor."

(a) Your mechanic does not know about discounting. Your discount rate is 10 percent. Suppose that you do not discount your first-year gas savings, that you discount your second-year savings over one year, and so on. What (assuming no inflation in gas prices) is the present value of two years of gas savings? Does this change the conclusion of your mechanic's argument?

(b) What has your mechanic overlooked? His reasoning is an example of what?

(c) When pressed, your mechanic admits that immediate installation of the carburetor will increase the resale price of your car according to the following schedule:

Time of Sale	Increase in Resale Value
Now	$140
In 1 year	$110
In 2 years	$ 90
In 3 years	$ 75
In 4 years	$ 65

In order for it to pay you to install the carburetor, you must keep the car for at least how many years? (Give an integer answer.)

3.1 COMPENSATING AND EQUIVALENT VARIATIONS

(a) The town is thinking about building a new library. The Jones family would use it frequently. They would be indifferent between (1) having the library built (at no cost to them) and (2) getting a gift of $200. They would also be indifferent between (1) their present status without the library and (2) getting the library but having to pay $190 in taxes for it. What are the CV and the EV of the Jones family for the library?

(b) The town might have a subway extended through it. Mr. Smith would not ride the subway and would not like the construction disruption or the influx of subway riders. He would be indifferent between (1) not having the subway built and (2) having it built and getting $600. He would also be indifferent between (1) having the subway built and (2) having $500 taken away from him. What are his CV and his EV for the subway?

3.2 EVALUATING SOCIAL INSURANCE PROGRAMS

An average person in a riverside town earns $10,000 in a year. He never borrows or saves and therefore consumes each year what he earns. In any year, the river has a .1 chance of overflowing and of causing the average citizen damages which he must pay $3,600 to repair. Private insurance against flooding does not exist, but the state government is thinking of reimbursing citizens for their repairs. What is the fair actuarial value of this insurance? The average person has an annual utility function, u, which is the square root of his annual consumption c: $u = \sqrt{c}$. What is the CV of the average person for the state's reimbursement policy? What is his EV (more difficult to calculate) to the nearest dollar?

4.1 AMORTIZATION

The World Health Organization (1976: 67-68) computes the total annual cost of a gamma camera. The capital cost is $131,700 and the lifetime is 10 years. An interest rate of six percent is assumed. WHO computes the annual interest costs to be $7,902 and the annual depreciation to be $13,170. This leads to total annual costs of $21,072 for the lifetime of the instrument. Why is this wrong? What are the true total annual costs?

5.1 LITTER REMOVAL

As evaluative assistant to the regional director, you are to help him decide whether or not to implement a manpower training program in

1981. The program would train 1,000 persons to pick up litter. Those persons would otherwise be unemployed and would receive $5,000 annually in welfare payments from the government. For their training and one year of employment (after that, there will be no litter to pick up), they would receive $7,000 each from the government and would pay no taxes. The persons are willing workers and would be indifferent between drawing their welfare payments and working if the pay were reduced to $5,500 per year. Cost of the training program is $800,000. Each of one million people in the region would be willing to pay four dollars for the aesthetic benefit derived from unlittered highways.

(a) What are the gain-loss, the partially consolidated, and the public-private benefit-cost ratios you would compute for this program? What three ratios would be computed by the regional director if he did not (he actually does) care about the welfare gains of the workers?

(b) Suppose that the council to which the regional director is responsible has not made up its mind what a mile of unlittered highway is worth. What kind of analysis would you then perform? In what units would the final results of that analysis be expressed?

(c) The staff of the training program are yam farmer helpers. If they did not staff the program, they would earn $600,000 on the farms (loving the land, they are indifferent between yam farming at its lower wage and working in the training program—which is why they did not have to be reflected in part a). With their help, the yam farmers would raise 5.8 million bushels of yams in 1977; without their help, only 4.8 million bushels. Assume that the higher production level does not increase the cost of materials and overhead. The worldwide price of yams is $1.20 per bushel. What is the opportunity cost of the workers?

(d) With this further information, what are the gain-loss and public-private benefit-cost ratios now?

5.2 SUPPORTED WORK

A small city decides to put its unemployed to work in supported establishments. One such establishment is a laundry. Previously the going rate for shirt cleaning in the city was $0.50. The supported laundry cleans shirts for $0.35 apiece.

(a) Joe, an average customer, used to average three shirt cleanings in a week. With the new price, he changes shirts daily and averages six shirt cleanings a week. The price at which he switches from three to six shirts a week is $0.40 (he is indifferent between three and six shirts per week at that price). How much additional consumer surplus does Joe reap weekly with the new laundry?

(b) Tom is employed by the laundry. Previously he had been unemployed and received unemployment checks of $90 weekly. He earns $120 each week at the laundry. Frankly, he is indifferent between this job and the alternative of collecting $80 a week in unemployment compensation. But this alternative is purely hypothetical since the city now refuses unemployment compensation to the able-bodied: It is the laundry or nothing. How much does Tom gain or lose with the implementation of the program?

(c) Sam had been earning $150 per week at another (private) laundry. The lower price offered by the supported laundry causes him to be laid off. He gets a new, less pleasant job making photocopies at $130 a week. The unpleasantness can be gauged by the fact that Sam would be indifferent between the copying job and his old job with the pay cut to $125 per week. How much does Sam lose?

(d) The supported laundry is staffed by 15 Toms. Ten Sams at private laundries become copiers. The clientele consists of 2,000 Joes. Two Bobs suffer declines in profits of $125 apiece per week on private laundries they own. To maintain the supported laundry, the program (administrative overhead plus operating deficit) costs the city $1,600 per week. The city is saved the unemployment compensation to the Toms but loses $100 a week in taxes (because the Sams and Bobs have lower incomes). Based on this information, what are the gain-loss, the partially consolidated, and the public-private benefit-cost ratios for the program?

5.3 WHEN THE BENEFIT-COST RATIOS ARE THE SAME

When is the gain-loss ratio the same as the partially consolidated ratio? What other two ratios will be the same in this case? When is the partially consolidated ratio the same as the public-private ratio? When are all four ratios shown in Table 2.15 the same?

5.4 DAY CARE CENTERS

The government contemplates establishing a day care center. Mothers think this is a great idea—they could get a consumer surplus of $6.2 million from it. The center would cost the government $8 million. Many of the mothers would be enabled by the center to work. This work would enable the government to collect $1 million more in taxes. The various companies employing the mothers would increase their profits by $3.3 million. The main losers are psychiatrists who are paid far fewer visits by distraught mothers. Their loss is put at $0.5 million (this figure, like all others given in this problem, is a CV).

(a) What are the gain-loss, the partially consolidated, the public-private, and the budgetary benefit-cost ratios for this program?

(b) There is some uncertainty about the gain in company profits that is to be expected: it could vary from $2.5 to $4 million. As a rudimentary sensitivity analysis, show the range within which the budgetary benefit-cost ratio would vary as the result of the uncertainty about effects on profits.

(c) Suppose now that there is uncertainty regarding the additional taxes raised due to the program. The decisionmakers, however, have made up their minds that the program is worth funding if its public-private benefit-cost ratio is at least 1.20. As a rudimentary threshold analysis, indicate within what range the additional taxes could vary and not affect the decision on the program. (Alternatively put, the taxes gained would have to amount to at least how much to assure that decisionmakers would be in favor of the program?)

5.5 INDIVISIBILITIES

The general rule in choosing projects to use up a budget is to pick them in the order of the benefit-cost ratios. Sometimes, however, this does not quite work. Because the projects are indivisible and because the budget limit is inflexible, one has to try out different combinations of projects to see which is best.

An administrator has a budget of $100,000 for the next fiscal year. Four alternative projects may be funded with this money, as indicated in the table.

Project	B÷C	Costs
A	1.9	$70,000
B	1.8	$55,000
C	1.7	$40,000
D	1.2	any

The first three of the projects have set costs; the fourth, D can then be implemented to use up the remainder of the budget. The administrator seeks to maximize the total benefits over all funded projects. Which should he fund? Should A, the project with the highest net benefits and the best benefit-cost ratio be funded? Why or why not?

5.6 CHOOSING PROJECTS

Three projects, A, B, and C, have benefits as indicated by the table below.

Project	Benefits	Costs
A	$204,000	100,000
B	$240,000	120,000
C	$264,000	140,000

(a) Which project would you implement if you were a Kaldor-Hicks person (that is, you acted to obtain any possible potential Pareto improvement) and could not fund more than one of these? Why?

(b) Suppose now that you have to choose from a long list of projects similar to these (same general sizes and benefit-cost ratios), enough projects to use up (or approximately do so) a $10 million budget. Which project of the three above would be first chosen as one of the projects to be funded from this budget? Which would be second? Why?

(c) Suppose now that the three projects are mutually exclusive and that any monies not spent on them can go toward other projects with benefit-cost ratios of 1.5. Which of the three should you choose? Why?

(d) Suppose that a government is planning to spend $360,000 to fund all three projects when suddenly someone formulates a project D costing $260,000. It is decided to forgo Projects B and C in order to obtain the $260,000 needed to fund D. What is the opportunity cost of this money (that an analyst doing a benefit-cost analysis of D should figure in)?

5.7 BUDGET CHOICE

You have a budget of $100,000 and six possible projects to spend it on:

Project	Benefits	Costs
A	$115,000	$60,000
B	$133,000	$70,000
C	$147,000	$80,000

D	$ 32,000	$20,000
E	$ 48,000	$30,000
F	$ 64,000	$40,000

(a) What are the net benefits and the B/C ratios for the six projects?

(b) You wish to maximize net benefits. Which two projects should be chosen (any combination of two costing no more than $100,000 together is a feasible choice)? Explain your reasoning (a variety of explanations is possible).

5.8 HEALTH BUDGET ALLOCATION

You are a decisionmaker in the department of health in a city government and must decide what programs to fund in the area of health education, prevention, and screening. The city council has an overall budget limit of $167,000 for these programs. You are asked to decide which set of programs should be funded in order to maximize net benefits. The possible funding levels of the various possible programs are shown in the Table A.1. PUG is zero for all programs. The programs of alcoholism treatment and health education require the same staff and, hence, cannot both be funded.

Use the methodology of Section 5.20 to determine which projects at which funding levels should be funded.

6.1 OPPORTUNITY COSTS

A paper-products firm is thinking of producing cardboard boxes out of recycled newspapers. One thousand tons of newspapers would be used in the process. The firm has exactly 1,000 tons of newsprint which it purchased for $20,000.

(a) What is the opportunity cost of the newspapers if they would otherwise be processed at a cost of $50,000 into 2 million egg cartons that would sell for five cents apiece? Why should the firm focus on this opportunity cost in calculating the value of the newspapers?

(b) What is the opportunity cost of the newspapers if they would otherwise be (costlessly) burnt up?

(c) What is the opportunity cost of the newspapers if they cannot be burnt and must be hauled away to the dump at a cost of $5,000?

(d) What is the red herring in this problem?

TABLE A.1   Funding Possibilities for a Budget for Health Education,
             Prevention, and Screening

Possible Program			Funding Level (PUL)	Net Private Benefits (PRG-PRL)
Alcoholism treatment			50	132
Anti-smoking program			15	27
Exercise classes	a.	poorly done	11	9
	b.	well done	22	34
Health education			40	108
Neonatal screening	a.	minimal	15	42
	b.	standard	20	60
	c.	more intensive	30	78
	d.	most intensive	35	90
	e.	all tests repeated	60	125
Pamphlets			34	29
School health	a.	grades 3 and 4	32	80
	b.	grades 2, 3, and 4	42	106
	c.	grades 2 through 5	61	136
	d.	grades 2 through 6	70	152
	e.	grades 2 through 7	83	185

6.2 INVISIBLE INTEREST

A project would cost a city $1 million which would be covered by debt financing. This borrowing would change the city's bond rating from AA to A and would thus increase the rate of interest to be paid by the city from 6.5 to 6.8 percent. The higher rate would have to be paid on $10 million of borrowing (including $9 million on other projects). What is the total annual interest cost of the project itself? What are the invisible interest costs?

6.3 IMPACT ON INTEREST RATES

A project has PUL of $10 million, PUG and PRL of zero, and PRG of $13 million (all present-valued). The gain-loss benefit-cost ratio is accordingly calculated as 1.3. This calculation failed, though, to take into account that the financing of the project by borrowing would raise the interest rate on car loans and home mortgages by one percent. This means that car and home purchases would have to pay a (present-valued) total of $3 million more in interest to the lenders. What is the gain-loss benefit-cost ratio with this effect taken into account?

6.4 EXCESS BURDEN

A state decides to raise money by placing a $10 excise tax on digital watches. These watches are manufactured outside the state at a fixed price—a price that does not depend on the number bought in the state. The state figured that this would raise $100,000 annually since 10,000 digital watches were bought each year without the tax. With the tax, only 8,000 digital watches are bought annually—raising only $80,000 in taxes. What is a reasonable estimate of the excess burden occasioned by the tax? Why is this estimate not exact?

6.5 EXCESS BURDEN AND EXCESS UNBURDEN

A factory produces machines. Its supply curve is given by

$$q = 10p - 5,000, \text{ for } p \geqslant \$500,$$

where q is the number of machines produced monthly and p is the price of the machines in dollars. Without a tax, the factory gets $1,000 per machine. A tax is imposed that has the effect of reducing the sale price of the machine for the factory to $900. What is the excess burden deriving from the reduced producer surplus of the factory?

In producing the machines, the factory releases one pound of pollutants into the air for each machine made. The total monthly disbenefit, d, these pollutants cause to people living near the factory (measured as negative CVs) is given by

$$d = .01 \, q^2,$$

where d is in dollars per month. What is the excess unburden resulting as the tax leads the factory to reduce its production and its pollutants?

6.6 PRIVATE CONSUMER SURPLUS

A real estate speculator acquired 100 acres of land which he intended to divide into one-acre plots. The demand curve for the land is given by

$$q = \frac{20,000 - p}{100},$$

where p is the price in dollars and q the number of plots sold at that price. The speculator would maximize the money he would get from the land by setting a price of $10,000 per plot—a price at which he could sell all the land. This would bring him $1 million.

A local government decides to acquire the land for a dump. It pays the speculator $1 million for the land. What are the losses in terms of forgone private consumer surplus due to this action?

6.7 GLOBAL EFFECTS

An airport plan must be approved or rejected by a city. The new airport would cost $60 million. Citizens of the city would get $50 million dollars in benefits in terms of increased travel convenience. Nearby residents would suffer noise disbenefits of $15 million. Throughout the city, both travelers and nontravelers would take pride in having a beautiful new airport—to the extent that they would be willing to pay $40 million to have such an airport in their city. What are the gain-loss and the public-private benefit-cost ratios for the airport?

6.8 ESTIMATING EXTERNALITY EFFECTS

Suppose that analysts of housing prices discover a relationship between the cost of new houses and the value of nearby houses. It is that for every $10,000 in the cost of a new house: Next-door houses gain $800 in value; houses directly across the street gain $600; houses diagonally across an intersection gain $400; houses successively further away gain $200 less in value than the next closer houses.

A government is deciding between constructing $30,000 houses or $40,000 houses on lots that it owns. The houses would then be sold at a subsidized price to deserving families. What is the externality gain to other homeowners if the government decides to build a $40,000 house instead of a $30,000 house on a lot in the middle of a long block (more than four houses away from an intersection)? If budgetary constraints require that some houses be constructed at both prices, should the $40,000 houses tend to be placed on corner lots or in mid-block? Why?

6.9 PRICE EFFECTS

Suppose that the national demand for corn is inelastic at 100 million bushels per year. The supply curve is

$$q = 20,000,000 \, p - 60,000,000,$$

where q is the number of bushels produced annually at a price of p dollars. What is the market equilibrium price?

An irrigation project enables farmers in the irrigated region to grow one million bushels of corn at an average cost of $5 per bushel. The supply curve above then applies only to all other corn farmers in the nation. What will be the effect of the irrigation project on the national price of corn? By how much will the consumer surplus on corn grow due to the project? How will producer surplus be affected? The average farm producing corn at a cost of about $8.00 per bushel is large enough to produce 50,000 bushels per year. The average cost for these farmers to switch from corn to other crops or to abandon farming altogether is $15,000. This is amortized as a loss of $1,500 per year. How should this be reflected in the benefit-cost analysis? What are the net benefits or net costs of the project for the corn consumers and the corn farmers (including those who abandon corn farming)?

6.10 DISPLACEMENT AND OPPORTUNITY DISBENEFITS

Park A is 10 years old. The fee for using it is $15.00. Campers and hikers have an average annual consumer surplus of $20 in using the park. Their average consumer surplus would, however, double if the number of park users were halved.

Park B is built and lures away one-half of the former users of Park A. What are the benefits associated with the displacement of campers and hikers? What are the opportunity disbenefits?

6.11 TRICKLE-DOWN

A tuition assistance program is proposed for a nation divided into the three sectors of farming (F), industry (I), and professional services (PS). Whenever either of these sectors receives a monetary benefit, it is passed along according to Table A.2.

(a) Suppose that the program grants $1 million to F, $2 million to I, and $3 million to PS. Taking the first round of the trickle-down effects into account, what is the distribution of the benefits?

(b) What is the ultimate distribution of benefits?

7.1 ESTIMATING CONSUMER SURPLUS

The elasticity of demand is defined as

$$\frac{\Delta q}{\Delta p} \div \frac{q}{p},$$

TABLE A.2

Sector Receiving a Monetary Benefit	Fraction of Benefit Passed Along		
	to F	to I	to PS
F	.01	.05	.04
I	.02	.07	.04
PS	.02	.06	.03

where q is the quantity demanded; p, the price; and Δq and Δp, the changes in each (Δq resulting from Δp). A government-run service for assisting the calculation of income taxes costs $8 per hour. At this price, 1.5 million hours of service are demanded. How might the demand elasticity be measured?

Suppose that demand elasticity is measured as 1.2. What is the slope of the demand curve at the current levels of price and demand? Assuming that this slope remains constant, what is the total consumer surplus associated with the service? Draw alternative demand curves showing why this method of estimating consumer surplus might result in too high or too low a figure. What would be the estimated increase in consumer surplus if the price of the service were reduced to $7.50 per hour? Would you expect this estimate to be more or less accurate (in terms of proportional error) than the estimate of total consumer surplus? Why?

7.2 ECONOMETRIC VALUATION

Suppose that econometricians have estimated the following relationship for home value in a metropolitan area:

$$HV = CC + (10,000)(L) - (1000)(A)$$
$$+ (2,000)(N) + (500)(C)$$
$$- (100)(T) + E;$$

where

CC is the current estimated construction cost to build a comparable house;

L   is the number of acres in the lot;

A   is the age of the house in years;

N   is an index of neighborhood attractiveness;

C   is an index of convenience to shopping, playgrounds, schools, etc.;

T   is the travel time in minutes to the downtown area; and

E   is the residual, random error of the estimation.

A radial highway decreases travel time from one suburb to the downtown area by five minutes. Assuming that the highway does not affect N or C, what is the increase in house value that homeowners should expect to realize when the road is constructed? Suppose that one family in the suburb rarely travels downtown. What must this family do to realize the potential gain made possible by the road? What is the positive CV to this family if it will move in six years and if the nominal discount rate is 13 percent and the real discount rate is six percent?

7.3 OBSERVING POLITICAL CHOICES

A city council wants to maximize net benefits in its choice of a park plan. It values converted parkland acres and jobs created. It values each completed acre equally (the thirtieth acre is just as valuable as the tenth—a finding that does not depend on the location of either). It also values each job created equally.

The council considers the four alternative park sites: A, B, C, and D.

Park Site	Acres	Jobs Created	Cost
A	20	120	$500,000
B	40	50	$430,000
C	40	100	$600,000
D	50	110	$750,000

After due deliberation, the council chooses to develop Park Site C. What does this decision reveal about the values the council attaches to creating jobs and to developing acres of parkland? (The problem is most easily worked by graphing L, the value of a developed acre of land, against J, the value of a created job. That C was preferred to A, B, and D restricts the values that L and J may take on.)

7.4 VALUING SUBSIDIZED PRODUCTS

A regional government wonders whether to construct an irrigation project. A firm from outside the region would construct and maintain the project for an annual cost of $550,000 (which includes the amortized construction costs). The water it would provide farmers would enable them to increase annual output by 100,000 bushels of wheat without any additional input (of labor, land, seeds, fertilizer, or equipment) from them. Wheat sells for $5 per bushel outside the region. Within the region, however, the regional government, as a means of subsidizing its farmers, has been buying wheat from them at a price of $6 per bushel—in effect, a price support payment of $1 per bushel. The farmers pay 15 percent of their marginal income to the region as taxes. Would the project constitute a net gain or loss to the region? What would be its effect on public funds of the region?

7.5 CHOOSING DISCOUNT RATES

An analyst is comparing two projects, A and B, whose costs and benefits are spread out over five years (see Table A.3).

(a) The analyst's client decides that, for political reasons, he wants Project A to be implemented. Find a discount rate at which Project A has greater present-valued net benefits than Project B.

(b) The client changes his mind and wants B to be implemented. Find a discount rate at which Project B has greater present-valued net benefits than Project A.

(c) This decision was determined by the choice of discount rates, but this is not always the case. Describe a Project C that always would be preferred to A and B regardless of the discount rate.

7.6 PRIVATE AND PUBLIC DISCOUNTING

A family in a society without inflation contemplates buying a new car. It will either (1) buy a model now for $3,000 for which it would be willing to pay up to $3,400 (if there were no other car purchase possibilities) or (2) save the $3,000 in a five percent interest account for five years, then use the money to buy a car for $3,750. It would then be willing to pay $4,200 for that car.

The family acts to maximize the present-valued consumer surplus from its car purchase. It discounts at five percent. The government observes that the pretax rate of return on investment is 10 percent and accordingly discounts at that rate total compensating variations present-valued at 10 percent.

(a) What should the family do in accordance with its own taste and values?

(b) What does the government prefer that the family do?

TABLE A.3

| | | Benefits in Years | | | |
Project	Costs in Year One	2	3	4	5
A	$45,000	$15,000	$15,000	$15,000	$15,000
B	$65,000	$20,000	$20,000	$20,000	$25,000

(c) What types of policies might the government adopt to induce families to make investment decisions that are in the best interest of the society as a whole?

7.7 PLANNING FOR FUTURE EXPENSES

A foundation has expressed interest in funding a special program for you for five years. It wishes to give you one grant for the whole period and will do so if your competence in discounting convinces it that you are worthy of the grant. You must plan for expenditures on personnel, consumable items, and nonconsumables. You can invest your money at 11 percent, which is your nominal discount rate. Inflation is running at seven percent. For simplicity assume that all payments for personnel and consumables are made on the first day of the year.

(a) What is the real discount rate?

(b) The first-year personnel costs come to $200,000. What is the present value of five years of personnel costs assuming (1) that they rise at the inflation rate? (2) that the personnel sign and will stick to an agreement providing them with exactly $200,000 each year?

(c) Consumables cost $25,000 in the first year and are subject to inflation. What is their present value over five years?

(d) Nonconsumables are contracted for in a five-year lease which would commit you to paying $40,000 on the first day of each year for five years for them. What is the present value of this?

7.8 A SOCIAL VALUE FUNCTION

A city values programs by (1) determining the compensating variations for all households affected, (2) multiplying the CVs by a factor of

$$\frac{10,000}{1_h + 3000},$$

where I_h is the annual income of the household in dollars, (3) multiplying all negative CVs by 1.2, and (4) summing the resultant values. The city plans to tax condominia in order to construct subsidized housing for poor families. With the construction, wages would rise for construction workers throughout the city. The effects of the program are shown in Table A.4. Is the housing program a potential Pareto improvement? Explain. Should the city, given its values, enact the program? Why or why not?

8.1 VALUING LIVES THREATENED BY STROKE

A government wants to know whether it should devote massive resources to discovering new methods of stroke prevention. An important factor in this decision is the estimated value of the lives extended due to stroke prevention. Typical of the various lives that might be extended are:

(1) a 40-year-old man whose life would be extended from 40 to 55 by stroke prevention and

(2) a 70-year-old woman whose life would be extended from 70 to 75.

(a) The nominal discount rate is 15 percent and the real discount rate is seven percent. What is the rate of inflation?

(b) The man earns $20,000 this year and consumes $17,000. Each year these figures rise at the same rate as inflation. Which discount rate is it most convenient to use in calculating the CLV, the ELV, and the SPLV for this person?

(c) What are the CLV, the ELV, and the SPLV for the man's life extension? Assume that the first year's consumption is discounted over one half year, and so on.

(d) The woman has a pension of $10,000 annually and savings of $8,000. She has no earnings. The pension payments remain constant in nominal dollar terms. The woman invests her money in a bank account paying six percent annually. She wishes to consume the same nominal amount this year and each of the following four years. Assuming that consumption has to be paid for at the middle of each year, how much of her savings should the woman consume each year (to exhaust it exactly after five years)?

(e) Which discount rate should be used in calculating the CLV, the ELV, and the SPLV for the woman?

(f) What are the CLV, the ELV, and the SPLV for the woman's life extension?

TABLE A.4

Affected Group	Number Affected	Annual Household Income	CV per Household
Poor families	1,000	$5,000	$2,000
Construction workers	2,000	17,000	800
Condominia dwellers	10,000	27,000	−400
Condominia owners	100	197,000	−15,000

(g) The man has savings of $12,000 and would be willing to reduce his consumption to $9,000 per year in order to prevent his getting a stroke. What is his OLV under these circumstances?

(h) Under what assumptions is this OLV also the man's WTPLV?

(i) The government decides to use the ELV as its best estimate of life values. Why do you think this choice may have been made? What are some arguments against using the ELV to value the lives of this man and woman?

8.2 VALUING FIVE LIFE YEARS

A man needs expensive treatment for a disease recently developed. He is 60 and would live to 65 with the treatment (the age he would have lived to had the disease not developed). If treated at government expense, he would have the same earnings and consumption behavior as he would have had had the disease not developed: He would earn $14,000 each year and would consume $17,000. If he had to pay for his own treatment, he could pay off the bill by reducing consumption to $11,000 per year—a level he regards as his minimum. His savings amount to $12,000. The discount rate in this economy is 10 percent, and there is no inflation. Consumption and earnings in each year are assumed to occur on average in the middle of the year. That is, first-year earnings and consumption should be discounted over a half-year, those of the second year over one and a half years, and so on.

(a) Verify that the man's savings are sufficient to sustain him for five years of earning $3,000 less annually than he consumes.

(b) What is his OLV? his SPLV? his CLV? his ELV?

8.3 CONGESTION EFFECTS

A 45-year-old will die this year unless he receives expensive therapy that could, however, extend his life for 10 years. During these 10 years, the person would commute an average of 200 days per year. The time of commuting for the average individual is given by the equation

$$TC = 8m^2 \times 10^{-9},$$

where

TC   is the average individual time of commuting in minutes, and

m   is the number of persons commuting on a given day.

On average, 60,000 persons commute daily. These people value their time at 14¢ per minute: they would pay that much for each minute of reduction in commuting time. The societal discount rate is seven percent.

(a) What is the indirect effect (IE) associated with this aspect of the life extension?

(b) Is it inhumane even to calculate this? Why or why not?

9.1 QUALITY OF LIFE

When a 60-year-old patient is stricken with sudden debilitating disease (SDD) his expected future life is immediately reduced to one year (a cruel hypothesis except in sparing you, the analyst, the chronic inconvenience of discounting). If nothing is done for SDD, the amount of suffering is indicated by the following table:

Life Quality of 60-Year-Old with SDD but without Treatment	Proportion of Patients
.8	.3
.6	.5
.4	.1
.2	.1

At a cost of $300 per patient, alleviating treatment is possible. Treatment A, if immediately administered, brings all patients who survive it to a life quality level of .75. Five percent do not survive the treatment. Unfortunately, beforehand you know neither which patients are more likely to survive treatment nor which would have had a life quality of .8.

(a) What is the cost-effectiveness ratio for Treatment A?

(b) If a fully healthy life year is valued at $4,500, what is the benefit-cost ratio for Treatment A?

(c) Treatment B, which costs $500 per patient, has a survival rate of 90 percent. All survivors have a life quality of .85. What is the cost-effectiveness ratio for Treatment B?

(d) What is the benefit-cost ratio for Treatment B?

(e) Which treatment should be implemented?

(f) At what valuation of a fully health life year is the decisionmaker indifferent between providing Treatment A and providing Treatment B?

9.2 EVALUATING TESTS AND TREATMENTS

You are analytic assistant to an HMO that contemplates instituting a screening test for deficiency of an enzyme that breaks down cholesterol. The screening test costs $100 per person and has a specificity of .90 and a sensitivity of .90. Treatment for test positives costs $2,000 per person and occurs immediately upon test confirmation. Ten percent of the 50-year-old population has the enzyme deficiency.

(a) Use a tree of chance nodes to determine the relative numbers of true positives, true negatives, false positives, and false negatives that would result from screening 50-year-olds. What is the likelihood that a 50-year-old with a positive test result has the enzyme deficiency?

(b) What is the cost (on average) of screening 100 50-year-olds and treating the test positives?

(c) Among 50-year-olds who have the enzyme deficiency and are not treated, 20 percent live on average until age 55, 40 percent live to 65, 30 percent live to 75, and 10 percent live to 85. Among treated 50-year-olds with the deficiency, 10 percent live to 55, 30 percent live to 65, 50 percent live to 75, and 10 percent to 85. Everything in the HMO is discounted at 10 percent. What is the cost-effectiveness ratio for a program that would screen and treat 50-year-olds?

(d) *(Optional)* You could wait until age 55 for screening. The test at that age has a specificity and a sensitivity of .95. By age 55, 20 percent of the enzyme-deficient 50-year-olds will have died off, as will 10 percent of the non-enzyme-deficient 50-year-olds. Treatment at age 55 costs $3,000. Among 55-year-olds treated for the deficiency, three-eighths live on average 10 more years, one-half live 20 more years, and one-eighth live 30 more years. What is the cost-effectiveness ratio for a program of screening and treatment at age 55? What cost-effectiveness ratio should you use in deciding between screening at 50 and at 55? What is the value of this ratio? For various values of discounted life years, what screening policy should the HMO adopt?

9.3 COST-EFFECTIVENESS OF SCREENING FOR HYPOTHYROIDISM

A profit-maximizing hospital in a developing country contemplates implementing a one-year program of screening for hypothyroidism among the population aged five and over. The government has recently encouraged such programs by offering to subsidize hospitals for one-half the labor cost incurred by hypothyroidism-screening programs. In addition, it will pay the hospital a bonus of $80 for each confirmed case discovered. Therapy consists of T_4 tablets which the government provides free of charge to the hypothyroids. The hospital would fund the program from monies currently in a bank account yielding eight percent interest. This rate is also the government's official discount rate. Program staff would be hired from outside the hospital and would receive total one-year wages of $80,000 for the basic program. The program would be housed in a building on which the hospital holds a long-term lease at a rent of $5,000 per year. If not used for the thyroid-screening program, the hospital would sublet the building to a day care program and would receive $10,000 per year in rent. Materials and equipment costs for the basic program are $50,000 for the 100,000 individuals expected to be screened during the year. Hypothyroidism has a prevalence in the screened population of five percent. The basic program of testing has perfect specificity, but only 80 percent sensitivity.

(a) What, from the hospital's perspective, is the opportunity cost of the space for the program?

(b) What benefit-cost ratio should the hospital compute for the basic program? Is it better to have the basic screening program or no program?

(c) The basic program tests are radioimmunoassays for T_4 and TBG. An alternative program—the refined program—would also test for TSH. The refined program would raise the total wage bill to $100,000 and the charges for materials and equipment to $70,000. The refined test is also perfectly specific and has a sensitivity of 90 percent. What is the benefit-cost ratio for the refined program? Of the three options—no program, basic program, and refined program—which should be chosen by the hospital? Why?

(d) What are the net benefits of the refined program?

(e) A government analyst is asked to perform a benefit-cost analysis of the basic program only (ignoring the possibility of the refined program). The idea is to see whether the forms of governmental encouragement make sense from its viewpoint. The analyst focuses his study on the potential program at the specific hospital. His initial task is to value the cost of the T_4 tablets per patient on the assumption that the typical case of discovered hypothyroidism will live 30 more years. The tablets cost $3 per year per patient. The yearly dose is presumed to be purchased at the beginning of the year by the government. What is the present value of the cost of a lifetime of T_4 therapy per average patient? (One may simply describe how the answer would be calculated and not work out the exact numerical answer.)

(f) The answer in (e) is rounded off to $35 per patient. Other governmental costs are for the bonuses and labor subsidies. Private gains amount to $300 of positive compensating variation per discovered case. The monetary gains of the hospitals are simply excluded from the government's consideration. The government gains a total present value of $50 per case discovered in additional tax revenues. Unfortunately, slipshod sterilization procedures in similar programs in the past indicate that one percent of all screenees will contract hepatitis as a consequence of being tested for hypothyroidism. Hepatitis is associated with a negative compensating variation of $350 per case. What are the gain-loss, partially consolidated, public-private, and budgetary benefit-cost ratios from the governmental viewpoint?

(g) Which benefit-cost ratio do you feel it most appropriate for the government to focus on? Why?

(h) The government decides that it is philosophically impossible to value getting hepatitis or curing hypothyroidism as compensating variations in money terms. It therefore wants to compute a cost-effectiveness ratio involving quality-adjusted remaining lives (a remaining life being 30 years on average). Hepatitis kills within a month six percent of the screeness who contract it. Longevity is otherwise not affected by the hypothyroidism-screening program. The general population has an average life quality of .95, which is lowered to .82 for the remaining life (.82 being an average of a very low life value during the disease and .90 afterward) of the hepatitis survivor. The typical hypothyroid has average life quality of .75, which is raised to .90 under T_4 therapy. What is the cost-effectiveness ratio for the program? (You should assume for analytic convenience that, by chance, none of the hypothyroids would contract hepatitis.)

9.4 CHOOSING A TEST

In a developing country, two alternative methods are available for testing for a chronic hormonal disease. The accuracy and costs of the tests are estimated to be:

Method	Cost Per 10,000 Population	Number of Cases Identified Per 10,000	Cost Per Case Found
1	$5,000	570	$8.77
2	$7,500	600	$12.50

The country is in the process of deciding what the value of a case-finding is. At what value of a case-finding should the country (1) use neither method, (2) use Method 1, or (3) use Method 2?

9.5 HYPERTHYROID TREATMENT

Society cares for its 60-year-old thyrotoxic patients with radioiodine therapy at a cost of $400 per treatment. Ten percent of the patients require retreatment after one year, and one-tenth of these patients must be retreated again one year later. Retreatment costs are also $400. The discount rate is taken to be eight percent because that is the rate at which individuals can lend or borrow.

(a) Write down—but do not solve for the precise numerical value—the formulation for the expected present value of care for the 60-year-old with thyrotoxicosis.

(b) Because the average life quality following radioiodine therapy is .75, it is proposed to substitute surgery for radioiodine treatment. Surgical mortality is one percent, and another five percent of the surgery patients develop vocal cord paralysis, hypoparathyroidism, and other complications. For survivors with complications (assumed to occur immediately), life quality is .5. For other survivors, average life quality is .9. The cost of surgery is $1,000. A perfectly healthy life year (quality of 1.0) is valued at $10,000. Taking only the first year following treatment into account (i.e., ignore radioiodine retreatment) what is the benefit-cost ratio for surgery compared with the status quo ante or radiotherapy?

(c) If unable to settle on the value of a perfectly healthy life year, how would you couch your answer to (b)?

(d) How does your answer to (b) change if the price of surgery covers an all-expenses-paid week of recuperation at a mountain resort for which the surgical survivors would willingly have paid some amount of money?

(e) Give a hypothetical illustration of the way in which your answer to (b) might change if the opportunity costs of the resources required for the surgery are taken into account.

(f) How would you amortize the cost of surgery over the 10-year remaining life of the average survivor? Explain, but do not calculate.

(g) It is argued that you may have used the wrong discount rate. Why might this be the case? What should you do about it?

9.6 DETERMINING LEVELS OF STROKE PREVENTION PROGRAMS

Stroke prevention programs extended many lives—as shown in the following table.

Program	Lives Saved	Cost (000,000)
Minimum	1,000	$200
Average	1,200	$266
Maximum	1,300	$307

(a) At what value of a life saving would one be indifferent between the Minimum and the Average programs? Between the Average and the Maximum programs?

(b) Some of the lives saved are extensions from age 58 to 68. Consider one such person whose life might be extended. Until age 65 he will work as a bank president earning $35,000 every year. He presently spends $20,000 per year for consumption—a figure that will rise at the inflation rate of nine percent annually. The nominal discount rate is 17 percent. What is his earnings life value for this life extention? His consumption life value? His simplified Pareto life value? (It is sufficient to write down the expressions indicating how these would be calculated; exact numerical answers are not necessary.)

(c) What is the real discount rate?

10.1 VALUING DRUG CONTROL IN CONTEXT

Two firms specializing in social service have applied to the government for funds to set up hard drug control programs in their respective cities: A and B. Each firm has pilot-tested its program in its own city with the findings shown in Table A.5.

The cost figures cover both screening and treatment. The screening tests are perfectly specific (they never falsely identify a nonuser as a user). The cure values are compensating variations for all other members of society. (To take into account the value of the cure to the users is conceptually difficult since before the cure they prefer not to be cured and after the cure they prefer to be cured—which is what the cure is all about.)

The government can afford to fund only one of the programs and in doing so seeks to maximize the cure values less costs. The City A firm is rather confident about the whole thing. Its program, after all, is better on all counts: it is cheaper, more accurate in screening, has more users to find, and has more effective therapy. Which firm should be funded by the government? Why? What types of factors might underlie the discrepancies in the cure values?

10.2 EVALUATING HITTERS

A baseball team, the Doves, is shopping for designated hitters in the annual free agent market. The two most promising players available are Slugger and Chipper, whose past records have been:

	Batting Average	Average Number of Home Runs Per Year
Slugger	.260	30
Chipper	.300	12

They are of equal age and roughly comparable in other respects.

The Doves have more distant fences than Slugger's previous home ballpark and a softer infield. Other players traded from Slugger's old team to the Doves have averaged 10 percent fewer homers and a 10-point-lower batting average with the Doves. Chipper's home ballpark is roughly equivalent to that of the Doves.

(a) What backward adjustment should be made?

(b) The Doves have many home run hitters and have calculated that the expected annual run production (EARP) for a player may be estimated as

$$500 \ BA + 1.4 \ HR$$

TABLE A.5

	City A	City B
Cost of full program	$150,000	$200,000
Fraction of all hard drug users identified by screening segment of program	.8	.7
Number of hard drug users in city	700	600
Effectiveness of therapy (cures ÷ users identified)	.75	.625
Value of cure	$5,000	$16,000

where BA is the batting average over the season and HR the annual number of home runs. Which player would have a higher EARP with the Doves?

(c) The Pigeons, who have a home ballpark like that of the Doves, are also interested in the two players. They have many more singles hitters than the Doves. There is consequently more of a premium on home runs (more people are likely to be on base) and less on batting average (a batter who singles is less likely to be batted in). The Pigeons figure EARP as

$$390 \text{ BA} + 1.9 \text{ HR}.$$

Which player would have higher EARP with the Pigeons?

SOLUTIONS TO
SELECTED PROBLEMS

2.1 $837.

2.2 (a) (.20) ($3,150) = $630.
   (b) (.04) ($50,000) = $2,000.
   (c) (.10) ($2,000) = $200.
   (d) (.06) ($15,000) = $900.
   (e) Yearly rental = (12) (220) = $2,640.

   First year effects of buying = $3,834 + $900 + $200 - $2,000 - $630 = $2,304.

   The couple should buy.

   Without the interest deduction, buying costs $630 more = $2,934; the couple should rent.

3.1 (a) CV = $190; EV = $200.
   (b) CV = -$600; EV = -$500.

3.2 Fair actuarial value = EMV = (.1) ($3,600) = $360 per person.

   EU (without reimbursement) = $(.1) \sqrt{6400} + (.9) (\sqrt{10,000})$

   $$= 8 + 90 = 98;$$

   u (with reimbursement) $= \sqrt{10,000} = 100.$

Consuming \$9,604 per year would give u of 98, implying that a person with the program could pay \$396 and be as well off as without the program.

CV = \$396.

EV is that amount of money given to a person without the program such that his expected utility rises to 100:

$$100 = (.1)(\sqrt{6400 + EV}) + (.9)\sqrt{10,000 + EV}.$$

Trial and error yields
EV = \$394.31.

5.1 (a) $\text{G-L B/C} = \dfrac{1.5 + 5 + 4}{7 + 0.8} = 1.35;$

$\text{PC B/C} = \dfrac{1.5 + 4}{7 + 0.8 - 5} = 1.96;$

The P-P B/C is the same in this case as the PC B/C (because there are no private disbenefits).

(b)   Cost-effectiveness analysis—couching the answer as dollars spent per unlittered mile achieved.

(c)   Using the workers on the yam farms would have increased yam revenue by \$1.2 million: the opportunity cost.

(d)   We now have a PRL of \$0.6 million: the loss to yam farmers. This leads to:

$\text{G-L B/C} = \dfrac{1.5 + 5 + 4}{7 + 0.8 + 0.6} = 1.25;$

P-P B/C = 1.75.

5.2 (a)   Joe gains an additional 3(\$0.15) + 3(\$0.05) = \$0.60 of consumer surplus (CS) each week. The first term is his savings on the three shirts he would have cleaned anyway; the second term, the CS associated with the three additional shirts he wears each week when the price drops below \$0.40.

(b)   Tom loses \$10.

(c)   Sam loses \$25.

(d)   PRG = \$1,200; PRL = \$150 + \$250 + \$250 = \$650; PUG = \$1,350; PUL = \$1,600 + \$100 = \$1,700.

$$G\text{-}L \ B/C \ = 1.09;$$
$$PC \ BC \ = 1.2;$$
$$P\text{-}P \ B/C \ = 1.57.$$

5.3 G-L B/C = PC B/C when PUG = 0.
In this case, we will also have P-P B/C = B B/C.
If PRG = PRL = 0, the four are the same.

5.5 If A is not funded, both B and C can be.

Benefits (A + $30,000 of D) = $133,000 + $36,000 = $169,000;
Benefits (B + C + $5,000 of D) = $99,000 + $68,000 + $6,000 = 173,000.

Best choice to fund B, C, and D at $5,000.
A is not funded because it falls too far short of the budget limit with the difference having to be made up with projects (D) with a low B/C ratio.

5.8 Steps 1 through 6 conclude with alcoholism treatment, anti-smoking, the most intensive program of mental screening, and school health for grades 2 through 5. Adjustments in Step 7 find a better list to include alcoholism treatment, the more intensive version of neonatal screening, school health for grades 2 through 7.

6.2 $68,000. $27,000.

6.3 1.23

6.4 Excess burden ≅ $10,000.

6.5 Excess burden = $50,000 per month.
Excess unburden = $90,000 per month.

6.6 $495,000.

6.7 G-L B/C = 1.2;
P-P B/C = 1.25.

6.8 $5,800.
The $40,000 houses should be built on corner lots—to gain $8,400 in externality benefits per house.

7.1   Slight variations in charges should enable reasonable estimations of elasticity.
Slope = 225,000 more hours demanded per $1 reduction in price.
Total consumer surplus = $5 million.
Increase in consumer surplus from price reduction to $7.5 per hour = $778,125 (which should be a more accurate estimate).

7.2 $500; sell the house; $352.

7.4   Net loss of $50,000: the farmers gaining $510,000 and public funds losing $560,000.

7.7   (a)   3.7 percent.
      (b)   (1) $930,478. (2) $820,489.
      (c) $116,310.
      (d) $164,098.

7.8   Not a pPi since there are net costs of $1.9 million. The city should enact the program since its value function finds it to achieve a net gain of $1.61 million.

8.2   (b)   OLV = $23,927;
           SPLV = - $11,927;
           CLV = $67,589;
           ELV = $55,661.

8.3   (a) $12,121.

9.1   (a) $2,667 per QALY.
      (b)   1.69.
      (c) $3,030 per QALY.
      (d)   1.485.
      (e)   B.
      (f) $3,810.

9.2   (a)   0.5.
      (b) $46,000.
      (c) $6,876 per QALY.

9.3   (a) $10,000.
      (b)   3.2. The basic program is better than no program.

(c) 2.77. The hospital should choose the refined program.

(d) $230,000.

(e) $36.48.

(f) PRG = $1.2 million; PRL = $350,000;
PUG = $200,000; PUL = $500,000.
G-L B/C = 1.65;
PC B/C = 1.85;
P-P B/C = 2.83;
B B/C = 2.1.

(h) $300,000 ÷ 420.8 QARLs = $713 per QARL.

9.4 (1) Less than $8.77.

(2) Between $8.77 and $83.33.

(3) Over $83.33.

9.6 (a) $330,000; $410,000.

(b)
$$ELV = \frac{\$35,000}{1.17^{\frac{1}{2}}} + \frac{\$35,000}{1.17^{3/2}} + \ldots + \frac{\$35,000}{1.17^{13/2}} = \$\,148,495.$$

$$CLV = \frac{\$20,000}{(1+rd)^{\frac{1}{2}}} + \frac{\$20,000}{(1+rd)^{3/2}} + \ldots + \frac{\$20,000}{(1+rd)^{19/2}} = \$143,279.$$

SPLV = ELV - CLV = $5,216.

(c) $rd = \frac{1.17}{1.09} - 1 = .0734.$

10.2 (a) Estimate that Slugger would have averaged .250 with 27 home runs per year if he had played in Chipper's— or the Doves'—circumstances.

(b) Chipper (with EARP of 166.8).

(c) Slugger (with EARP of 148.8).

References

Abt, C. C.
1977   "The issue of social costs in cost benefit analysis of surgery." Pp. 40-55 in J. P. Bunker, B. A. Barnes, and F. Mosteller (eds.), Costs, Risks and Benefits of Surgery. New York: Oxford University Press.

Acton, J.P.
1973a   Demand for Health Care When Time Prices Vary More than Money Prices. Rand Corporation Report, R1189-OEO/NYC. New York: Rand Corporation.

Acton, J. P.
1973b   Evaluating Public Programs to Save Lives: The Case of Heart Attacks. Report R950 RC. Santa Monica: Rand Corporation.

Acton, J. P.
1976   "Measuring monetary value of life-saving programs." Law and Contemporary Problems 40(4):46-72.

Allingham, M. G. and G. C. Archibald
1975   "Second best and decentralization." Journal of Economic Theory 10:157-173.

Anderson, D. R., D. J. Sweeney, and T. J. Williams
1976   An Introduction to Management Science: Quantitative Approaches to Decision Making. St. Paul: West Publishing.

Barsby, S. L.
1972   Cost-Benefit Analysis and Manpower Programs. Lexington, MA: D.C. Heath.

Baumol, W. J.
1968   "On the social rate of discount." American Economic Review 58:788-802.

Beesley, M. E.
1965   "The value of time spent travelling: some new evidence." Economica 32:174-185.

Bergson, A.
1938   "A reformulation of certain aspects of welfare economics." Quarterly Journal of Economics 52:310-334.

Berry, R. E., Jr. and J. P. Boland
1977   The Economic Cost of Alcohol Abuse. New York: Free Press.

Bierman, H., Jr. and S. Smidt
1975   The Capital Budgeting Decision. New York: Macmillan.

296

Boadway, R. W.
1974   "The welfare foundations of cost-benefit analysis." Economic Journal 84:926-939.

Boruch, R. F. and D. Rindskopf
1977   "On randomized experiments, approximation to experiments, and data analysis." Pp. 143-176 in L. Rutman (ed.), Evaluation Research Methods: A Basic Guide. Beverly Hills: Sage.

Bush, J. W., M. Chen, and D. L. Patrick
1973   "Cost-effectiveness using a health status index: analysis of the New York State PKU Screening Program." Pp. 172-208 in Berg, R. (ed.), Health Status Indexes. Chicago: Hospital Research and Educational Trust.

Chase, S. B. (ed.)
1968   Problems in Public Expenditure Analysis. Washington, DC: Brookings Institution.

Cochrane, J. L. and M. Zeleny (eds.)
1973   Multiple Criteria Decision Making. Columbia: University of South Carolina Press.

Cohn, E.
1972   Public Expenditure Analysis, with Special Reference to Human Resources. Lexington, MA: D.C. Heath.

Conley, R. and A. Milunsky
1975   "The economics of prenatal genetic diagnosis." In A. Milunsky (ed.), The Prevention of Genetic Disease and Mental Retardation. Philadelphia: W.B. Saunders.

Cooper, B. S. and D. P. Rice
1976   "The economic cost of illness revisited." Social Security Bulletin 39(2):21-36.

Diamond, P.
1968   "The opportunity costs of public investment: comment." Quarterly Journal of Economics 2:682-688.

Dorfman, R.
1965   Measuring the Benefits of Government Investments. Washington, DC: Brookings.

Edwards, W. and M. Guttentag
1975   "Experiments and evaluation: a reexamination." In C. A. Bennett and A. A. Lumsdaine (eds.), Evaluation and Experiment: Some Critical Issues in Assessing Social Programs. New York: Academic Press.

Edwards, W., M. Guttentag, and K. Snapper
1975   "A decision theoretic approach to evaluation research." In E. L. Struening and M. Guttentag (eds.), Handbook of Evaluation Research, Volume 1. Beverly Hills, CA: Sage.

Fein, R.
1958   Economics of Mental Illness. New York: Basic Books.

Fein, R.
1971   "On measuring economic benefits of health programs." In G. McLachlan and T. McKeown (eds.), Medical History and Medical Care. London: Oxford University Press.

Feldstein, M. S.
1964   "The social time preference discount rate in cost-benefit analysis." Economic Journal 74:360-379.

Feldstein, M. S.

1972   "The inadequacy of weighted discount rates." Pp. 311-332 in R. Layard
        (ed.), Cost-Benefit Analysis. Harmondsworth, England: Penguin.
Feldstein M. S., B. Friedman, and H. Luft
1972   "Distributional aspects of national health insurance benefits and finance."
        National Tax Journal 25(4):497-510.
Fischer, G. W. and J. M. Vaupel
1976   "A lifespan utility model: assessing preferences for consumption and longe-
        vity." Working paper for the Center for Policy Analysis, Duke University.
Fischhoff, B.
1977   "Cost benefit analysis and the art of motorcycle maintenance." Policy
        Sciences 8:177-202.
Friedlaender, A. F.
1965   Interstate Highway System. Amsterdam: North-Holland.
Freidman, L. S.
1977   "An interim evaluation of the supported work experiment." Policy Anal-
        ysis 3: 147-170.
Friedman, M. and L. J. Savage
1948   "The utility analysis of choices involving risk." Journal of Political Economy
        56:279-304.
Goldberger, A. S. and O. E. Duncan (eds.)
1973   Structural Equation Models in the Social Sciences. New York: Seminar Press.
Good, D. A.
1971   "Cost-benefit and cost-effectiveness analysis: their application to urban
        public services and facilities." RSRI Discussion Paper Series, No. 47., pp.
        11-12. Philadelphia PA: Regional Science Research Institute.
Grosse, R. N.
1967   "Preface." In T. A. Goldman (ed.), Cost-Effectiveness Analysis: New
        Approaches in Decision Making. New York: Washington Operations
        Research Council/Praeger.
Hammond, J. S. III
1967   "Better decisions with preference theory." Harvard Business Review
        45(6):123-141.
Hanke, S. H. and R. A. Walker
1974   "Benefit-cost analysis reconsidered: an evaluation of the mid-state project."
        Water Resources Research 10(5):898-908.
Hanke, S. H., P. H. Carver, and P. Bugg
1975   "Project evaluation during inflation." Pp. 325-334 in R. Zeckhauser et al.
        (ed.), Benefit-Cost and Policy Analysis, 1974. Chicago: AVC.
Harberger, A. C.
1969   "The opportunity costs of public investment financed by borrowing." Pp.
        81-88 in G. G. Somers and W. D. Wood (eds.), Cost-Benefit Analysis of
        Manpower Policies, Proceedings of a Conference. Kingston, Ontario, Canada:
        Industrial Relations Centre, Queens University.
Harberger, A. C.
1971   "3 basic postulates for applied welfare economics: an interpretive essay."
        Journal of Economic Literature 9:785-797.
Harberger, A. C.
1972   Project Evaluation: Collected Papers. Chicago: Markham.
Harrison, D., Jr. and D. L. Rubinfeld
1978   "The distribution of benefits from improvements in urban air quality."
        Journal of Environmental Economics and Management 5:313-332.

Haveman, R. H. and J. V. Krutilla
1968   Unemployment, Idle Capacity, and the Evaluation of Public Expenditures. Baltimore: Johns Hopkins University Press.
Haveman, R. H. and J. Margolis (eds.)
1970   Public Expenditures and Policy Analysis. Chicago: Markham.
Haveman, R. H. and J. Margolis (eds.)
1977   Public Expenditure and Policy Analysis (second edition). Chicago: Rand McNally.
Haveman, R. H. and B. A. Weisbrod
1977   "Defining benefits of public programs: some guidance for policy analysts." Pp. 135-160 in R. H. Haveman and J. Margolis (eds.), Public Expenditure and Policy Analysis (second edition). Chicago: Rand McNally.
Hicks, J. R.
1943   "The 4 consumer surpluses." Review of Economic Studies 9:31-41.
Holtmann, A. G. and R. Ridker
1965   "Burial costs and premature death." Journal of Political Economy 73:284-286.
Jackle, M. J.
1974   "Life satisfaction and kidney dialysis." Nursing Forum 13(4):360-369.
Joint Economic Committee, U.S. Congress
1968   Economic Analysis of Public Investment Decisions: Interest Rate Policy and Discounting Analysis. Washington, DC: U.S. Government Printing Office.
Jones-Lee, M.
1969   "Valuation of reduction in probability of death by road accident." Journal of Transport Economics and Policy 3:37-47.
Kahneman, D. and A. Tversky
1979   "Prospect theory: an analysis of decision under risk." Econometrica 47(2):263-291.
Kain, J. F.
1964   "A contribution to the urban transportation debate: an econometric model of urban residential and travel behavior." Review of Economics and Statistics 46:55-64.
Kaplan, R. M., J. W. Bush, and C. C. Berry
1976   "Health status: types of validity and the index of well-being." Health Services Research 11:478-507.
Kaplan, R. M., J. W. Bush, and C. C. Berry
1978   "The reliability, stability, and generalizability of a health status index." Pp. 704-709 in Proceedings of the American Statistical Association, Social Statistics Section.
Keeney, R. L. and H. Raiffa
1976   Decisions with Multiple Objectives: Preferences and Value Trade-offs. New York: John Wiley.
Kendall, M. G. (ed.)
1971   Cost-Benefit Analysis. New York: American Elsevier.
Klarman, H. E.
1965   "Syphilis control programs." Pp. 367-414 in R. Dorfman (ed.), Measuring the Benefits of Government Investments. Washington, DC: Brookings.
Klarman, H. E.
1973   "Application of cost-benefit analysis to health systems technology." In M. F. Collen (ed.), Technology and Health Care Systems in the 1980's. DHEW Publication No. (HSM) 73-3016. Washington DC: U.S. Government Printing Office.

Layard, R. (ed.)
1972   Cost-Benefit Analysis. Harmondsworth, England: Penguin.

Levin, H. M.
1975   "Cost-effectiveness analysis in evaluation research." Pp. 89-122 in E. Struen-
        ing and M. Guttentag (eds.), Handbook of Evaluation Research, Volume 2.
        Beverly Hills, CA: Sage.

Linnerooth, J.
1975   A Critique of Recent Modelling Efforts to Determine the Value of Human
        Life. Laxenburg, Austria: IIASA RM-75-67.

Lipsey, R. G. and K. Lancaster
1956   "A general theory of second best." Review of Economic Studies 24: 11-32.

Little, I.M.D.
1960   Critique of Welfare Economics. London: Oxford University Press.

Little, I.M.D. and J. A. Mirrlees
1974   Project Appraisal and Planning for Developing Countries. New York: Basic
        Books.

Maciariello, J. A.
1975   Dynamic Benefit-Cost Analysis. Lexington, MA: D.C. Heath.

McKean, R. N.
1968   "The use of shadow prices." In S. B. Chase (ed.), Problems in Public
        Expenditure Analysis. Washington, DC: Brookings.

McNeil, B. J., P. D. Varady, B. A. Burrows, and S. J. Adelstein
1975   "Measures of clinical efficacy: cost-effectiveness calculations in the treat-
        ment of hypertensive renovascular disease." New England Journal of Medi-
        cine 243(5):216-221.

Mansfield, E.
1975   Microeconomics. New York: W.W. Norton.

Marglin, S. A.
1963   "The opportunity costs of public investment." Quarterly Journal of Eco-
        nomics 77:274-289.

Mishan, E. J.
1970   "What is wrong with Roskill?" Journal of Transport Economics and Policy
        4(3):221-234.

Mishan, E. J.
1971a   "Evaluation of life and limb: a theoretical approach." Journal of Political
        Economy 79(4):687-705.

Mishan, E. J.
1971b   "The postwar literature on externalities: an interpretive essay." Journal of
        Economic Literature 9:1-28.

Mishan, E. J.
1976   Cost-Benefit Analysis. New York: Praeger.

Morrall, J. F. III
1979   "Reducing airport noise." Pp. 147-160 in J. C. Miller III and B. Yandle
        (eds.), Benefit-Cost Analyses of Social Regulation: Case Studies from the
        Council on Wage and Price Stability. Washington, DC: American Enterprise
        Institute.

Musgrave, R. A.
1959   The Theory of Public Finance. New York: McGraw-Hill.

Mushkin, S. J. and F. Collings
1959   "Economic costs of disease and injury." Public Health Reports
        74(9):795-809.

Nath, S.
1969   A Reappraisal of Welfare Economics. New York: Augustus M. Kelley.
Neuhauser, D. and A. M. Lewicki
1976   "National health insurance and the sixth stool guaiac." Policy Analysis
        2:175-196.
Overall, J. E. and J. A. Woodward
1977   "Nonrandom assignment and the analysis of covariance." Psychological
        Bulletin 84:588-594.
Patrick, D. L., J. W. Bush, and M. W. Chen
1973a   "Methods for measuring levels of well-being for a health status index."
        Health Services Research 8(3):228-245.
Patrick, D. L., J. W. Bush, and M. W. Chen
1973b   "Toward an operational definition of health." Journal of Health and Social
        Behavior 14(1):6-23.
Pauly, M. V.
1968   "The economics of moral hazard: comment." American Economic Review
        58:531.
Pliskin, N. and A. K. Taylor
1977   "General principles: cost-benefit and decision analysis." Pp. 5-27 in J. P.
        Bunker, B. A. Barnes and F. Mosteller (eds.), Costs, Risks, and Benefits of
        Surgery. New York: Oxford University Press.
Prest, A. R. and R. Turvey
1965   "Cost-benefit analysis: a survey." Economic Journal 75:685-705.
Quade, E. S.
1967   "Introduction and overview." Pp. 1-16 in T. A. Goldman (ed.), Cost-Effec-
        tiveness Analysis: New Approaches in Decisionmaking. New York: Washing-
        ton Operations Research Council/Praeger.
Quade, E. S.
1975   A Critique of Cost-Effectiveness. Santa Monica, CA: Rand Corporation.
Ramsey, D. D.
1969   "On the social rate of discount: comment." American Economic Review
        59:919-924.
Rice, D. P.
1966   Estimating the Costs of Illness. PHS Economic Series #6. Washington, DC:
        U.S. Government Printing Office.
Rice, D. P. and B. S. Cooper
1967   "The economic value of human life." American Journal of Public Health
        57:1954-1966.
Ridker, R. G.
1967   The Economic Costs of Air Pollution. New York: Praeger.
Roemer, M. and J. Stern
1975   The Appraisal of Development Projects: A Practical Guide to Project Analy-
        sis with Case Studies and Solutions. New York: Praeger.
Rossi, P. H., H. E. Freeman, and S. R. Wright
1979   Evaluation: A Systematic Approach. Beverly Hills, CA: Sage.
Rothenberg, J.
1975   "Cost-benefit analysis: a methodological exposition." Pp. 55-88 in E. Struen-
        ing and M. Guttentag (eds.), Handbook of Evaluation Research, Volume 2.
        Beverly Hills, CA: Sage.
Sackett, D. L. and G. W. Torrance
1978   "The utility of different health states as perceived by the general public."
        Journal of Chronic Diseases 31:697-704.

Samuelson, P.
1976   Economics. New York: McGraw-Hill.
Schelling, T. C.
1968   "The life you save may be your own." Pp. 127-176 in S. B. Chase (ed.),
        Problems in Public Expenditure Analysis. Washington, DC: Brookings.
Schoenbaum, S. C., B. J. McNeil, and J. Kavet
1976   "The Swine-influenza decision." New England Journal of Medicine
        295:759-765.
Scitovsky, T.
1971   Welfare and Competition. Chicago: Richard D. Irwin.
Smart, C. N. and C. R. Sanders
1976   The Costs of Motor Vehicle Related Spinal Cord Injuries. Washington, DC:
        Insurance Institute for Highway Safety.
Squire, L. and H. van der Tak
1975   Economic Analysis of Projects. Baltimore: Johns Hopkins University Press.
Staats, E. G.
1968   Survey of Use of Federal Agencies of the Discounting Technique in
        Evaluating Future Programs. Report to the Joint Economic Committee, U.S.
        Congress, January 29.
Starr, C.
1972   "Benefit-cost studies in sociotechnical systems." Pp. 17-42 in Committee on
        Public Engineering Policy, National Academy of Engineering, Perspectives
        or Benefit-Risk Decision Making. Washington, D.C.
Stokey, E. and R. Zeckhauser
1978   A Primer for Policy Analysis. New York: W. W. Norton.
Sugden, R. and A. Williams
1978   The Principles of Practical Benefit-Cost Analysis. London: Oxford University
        Press.
Swint, J. M. and W. B. Nelson
1977   "Prospective evaluation of alcoholism rehabilitation efforts: the role of
        cost-benefit and cost-effectiveness analyses." Journal of Studies on Alcohol
        38(7):1386-1404.
Thaler, R. and S. Rosen
1974   "The value of saving a life: evidence from the labor market." Discussion
        Paper 74-2. Department of Economics, University of Rochester.
Thompson, M.
1975   Evaluation for Decision in Social Programmes. Westmead, England: D.C.
        Heath.
Usher, D.
1969   "On the social rate of discount: comment." American Economic Review
        59:925-929.
United States Department of Housing and Urban Development
1974   Housing in the Seventies. Washington, DC: U.S. Government Printing Office.
United States Senate Committee on Public Works
1974   Air Quality and Automobile Emission Control, Volume 4. Washington, DC:
        U.S. Government Printing Office.
Wabe, J. S.
1971   "A study of house prices as a means of establishing the value of journey
        time, the rate of time preference and the valuation of some aspects of
        environment in the London metropolitan region." Applied Economics
        3:247-255.

Wagner, H. M.
1975   Principles of Operations Research. Englewood Cliffs, NJ: Prentice-Hall.
Ware, J. E., R. H. Brook, K. N. Williams, et al.
1979   Conceptualization and Measurement of Health for Adults in the Health Insurance Study. Rand Corporation Reports R-1987/1-HEW through R-1987/8-HEW. Santa Monica, CA: Rand Corporation.
Weinstein, M. C. and W. B. Stason
1977   "Foundations of cost-effectiveness analysis of health and medical practices." New England Journal of Medicine 296:716-721.
Weinstein, M. C. and W. B. Stason
1976   Hypertension: A Policy Perspective. Cambridge, MA: Harvard University Press.
Weinstein, M. C., D. S. Shepard, and J. S. Pliskin
1980   "The economic value of changing mortality probabilities: a decision theoretic approach." Quarterly Journal of Economics 94(2): 373-396.
Weisbrod, B. A.
1961   Economics of Public Health. Philadelphia: University of Pennsylvania Press.
Weisbrod, B. A.
1968   "Income redistribution affects and benefit-cost analysis." Pp. 177-222 in S. B. Chase (ed.), Problems in Public Expenditure Analysis. Washington, DC: Brookings.
Weisbrod, B. A.
1971   "Costs and benefits of medical research: a case study of poliomyelitis." Journal of Political Economy 79(3):527-544.
Wildavsky, A.
1975   Budgeting: A Comparative Theory of Budgetary Processes. Boston: Little, Brown.
Williams, A.
1973   "Cost-benefit analysis: bastard science? and/or insidious poison in the body politick?" In J. N. Wolfe (ed.), Cost Benefit and Cost Effectiveness: Studies and Analysis. London: George Allen & Unwin.
Willig, R. D.
1976   "Consumer surplus without apology." American Economic Review 66(4):589-598.
Winch, D.
1971   Analytical Welfare Economics. Harmondsworth, England: Penguin.
World Health Organization
1976   Nuclear Medicine: Report of a Joint IAEA/WHO Expert Committee on the Use of Ionizing Radiation and Radioisotopes for Medical Purposes, Geneva: World Health Organization.
Zeckhauser, R.
1975a   Benefit-Cost and Policy Analysis, 1974. Chicago: AVC.
Zeckhauser, R.
1975b   "Procedures for valuing lives." Public Policy 23:419-464.
Zeckhauser, R. and E. Schaefer
1968   "Public policy and normative economic theory." Pp. 27-102 in R. Bauer and K. Gergen (eds.), The Study of Policy Formation. New York: Free Press.
Zeckhauser, R. and D. Shepard
1976   "Where now for saving lives?" Law and Contemporary Problems 40(4):5-45.

Index

About the Author

MARK S. THOMPSON is Assistant Professor of Health Services and Research Associate in the Center for the Analysis of Health Practices at the Harvard School of Public Health. He was previously Assistant to the Director and Research Scholar at the International Institute for Applied Systems Analysis in Laxenburg, Austria. His research has focused on the application of decision-analytic, economic, and evaluative techniques to policy analysis. Previous works include *Evaluation for Decision in Social Programmes* and *Systems Aspects of Health Planning* (co-editor with Norman Bailey).